Praise for
SEND M

"*Send Me* is a gripping story that transcends the battlefield, illuminating the intricate balance between love, duty, family, and sacrifice within the secretive realm of special operations. Joe Kent and Marty Skovlund Jr. share the legacy of Shannon Kent's remarkable life and the impact she made, not just at the tip of the spear in our nation's most elite units but on all those who knew her in this emotional journey that will remain with you long after you turn the final page."

—Jack Carr, *New York Times* bestselling author
of the Terminal List series

"*Send Me* is a riveting story of service, sacrifice, and unyielding commitment by a true American hero. From her role as an elite operator and highly respected combat veteran to her journey as a wife and mother, Shannon Kent's story highlights a remarkable commitment to service and a drive for excellence. Shannon leaves behind a powerful legacy of courage, resilience, and selflessness that serves as an enduring example for all."

—Colonel Kim "KC" Campbell (USAF, Ret.), author
of *Flying in the Face of Fear*

"Shannon Kent was an incredible human being—a genius with languages, a highly gifted signals intelligence analyst, a sailor, a mother, an artist, a wife. *Send Me* is a touching and honest legacy of her work in this world, not just as a member of the armed forces hunting the world's deadliest terrorists but as an advocate off of the battlefield for those suffering from PTSD."

—Jason Kander, *New York Times* bestselling author
of *Invisible Storm*

SEND ME

SEND ME

*The True Story of
a Mother at War*

MARTY SKOVLUND JR.
AND JOE KENT

wm

WILLIAM MORROW
An Imprint of HarperCollinsPublishers

Grateful acknowledgment is made to the following for the use of the photographs that appear in the art insert: courtesy of Marty Skovlund Jr./ *Coffee or Die* magazine (page 1; page 3, bottom; page 5, top; page 7, top right, middle, and bottom; and page 8, top and middle left); courtesy of Claire Eskdale (page 2, top); courtesy of Cassandra Nolan (page 2, middle); courtesy of Mariah Smith (page 2, bottom, and page 8, middle right); and courtesy of Joe Kent (page 3, top left, top right, and middle; page 4; page 5, middle left, middle right, and bottom; page 6; page 7, top left; and page 8, bottom).

HarperCollins books may be purchased for educational, business, or sales promotional use. For information, please email the Special Markets Department at SPsales@harpercollins.com.

A hardcover edition of this book was published in 2024 by William Morrow, an imprint of HarperCollins Publishers.

FIRST WILLIAM MORROW PAPERBACK EDITION PUBLISHED 2025.

Designed by Michele Cameron

Title page art © Shutterstock/2085148693

Library of Congress Cataloging-in-Publication Data has been applied for.

ISBN 978-0-06-344600-7

25 26 27 28 29 LBC 5 4 3 2 1

To Josh and Colt.

*And to the unnamed warriors who fought
alongside Shannon, who remain in the shadows
to this day, still fighting.*

The best of Shannon lives on in you.

CONTENTS

CONTENTS

CONTENTS

A NOTE FROM JOE

This book is for our sons, Colt and Josh, who had their mother taken from them far too early. I want them to understand who Shannon was, what she stood for, and why she was killed fighting in far-flung Manbij, Syria. I want our sons to understand not just their mother's valor, but also her love for them, for our brothers and sisters in arms, and for our nation. Every day that passes as our boys get older, I see Shannon in everything they do, and I know she lives on in them and is with us every day, telling us to press forward.

Shannon came of age in a military that technically forbade women from serving in combat roles, so her deeds and the deeds of so many women warriors have gone unmentioned in those chaotic years. For guys like me who fought in our wars, we have a title that quickly asserts our place in history and conjures images of battlefield glory, but for women like Shannon, there is normally dismissal, disbelief, or outright omission. Shannon would want the world to know her story is not just about her; it's the story of a small but ever-growing group of women warriors who are in the fight alongside their brothers, fighting for our nation. In writing this book I hope to tell their story through Shannon.

To my sons, Colt and Josh:

As I write this now, I can feel the pain of knowing I'll never see or talk to my best friend. I can feel the anger that builds when I think about how you boys will never get to know your mother, or that Shannon, who lived for you boys, can't see you grow up. That anger ends with deep hopeless sorrow because there's no real solution. I can't fix it or plan for it. That's what our life is now.

Most days I'm okay. You boys are happy and healthy and surrounded by a loving family. I still have a hard time comprehending the finality of her death—never again is a long time for a mother not to see her boys, a long time for soul mates to not speak to each other. I can explain almost everything about how she died from the strategic to the nitty-gritty tactical reasons, but I can't wrap my head around its eternity. I had thought of my death in combat or training constantly; in a sick way, it never seemed like a bad way to go. I thought of it as a warrior's death, honorable and worthwhile.

Your mom was a warrior, as much as me or any man who has given his life for our nation. But there is something different about a woman, wife, mother, or daughter being killed. Women are the givers and nourishers of life; there's twisted cruelty in them being killed under any circumstance. I'm telling you her story so you know who your mom was and how much she loved you.

As confusing and hopeless as her death was, it brought some clarity to my life. I could not deploy anymore. Life is about you boys, not my desire to fight or avenge her death. I think about getting one more shot at ISIS every day, believe me.

Deploying again may or may not have been possible, but I knew

I could not risk it. Making my boys orphans is something I just can't do. Your mom would never forgive me if I did. I know my brothers and sisters still serving have the vengeance covered for us, but that part of the fight is no longer mine. My new mission is raising you, Colt and Josh, into the young men your mom would be proud of.

A NOTE FROM MARTY

Shannon Kent is one of the most inspiring people I've ever come to know, but I never had the honor of meeting her in person. Sure, it's possible we crossed paths at one point; we deployed under the same task force and she even had a photo of herself standing right outside of my room on Camp Lewis in Iraq. But after getting to know her family and friends during the course of research for this book, I feel like I know her. I just wish I *actually* had the privilege of knowing her today—she was truly the best among us, and our nation is a little less in her absence.

I hope you, dear reader, get to know her while reading this book too. That was our aim: tell her story, lest she ever be forgotten. Maybe even inspire a few people; I know that she is the role model I will point my young daughters to someday. But due to her work, there is so much that couldn't go into this story. Someday, after some of our nation's most sensitive secrets are declassified, maybe a fuller story can be told about Senior Chief Petty Officer Shannon Kent.

How did we come across the information used in this book? Simply put: carefully. Joe and I went to great lengths to preserve both operational and personnel security so as not to endanger any of Shannon's friends still working in the field. To ensure this, we submitted the manuscript for this book to both the Department of Defense and Central Intelligence Agency for prepublication review. You'll find most of their redactions can be identified by solid black bars throughout the book.

Additionally, many names throughout this book are redacted, pseudonyms were used, or only first names were mentioned. Many more people contributed to this book on deep background and remain uncredited due to the sensitive positions they still hold. In total, I talked to more than forty people who knew Shannon or were familiar with her work.

We also pored over documents. Her awards, Navy evaluation reports, notes that she took over the years, photos, text messages, emails, college papers she wrote—anything we could find. This reporting, along with Joe's knowledge of his wife, and our collective experience in the military, allowed us to craft this narrative. Every effort was made to make this book as factually accurate as possible, but you, the reader, should know that many aspects of Shannon's professional life needed to be omitted or altered due to the sensitive nature of her work.

You'll notice a flexible approach to quotes in this book, and many conversations are not meant to be perceived as a word-for-word transcript. Some quotes are directly from recordings of Shannon, or things she wrote in text messages or emails. Many of the quotes were relayed to us by people who had those conversations with her. And some situations in this book are re-created based on what she told Joe or other friends and teammates, and when we show her inner monologue, those are often things she told people she was thinking at the time, in that moment. In every case, we have vetted the dialogue used in this book with the people who knew Shannon best to make sure we authentically represented her.

Specifically, in chapters 1, 23, and 24, we re-created a type of mission she conducted based on details she told Joe on her calls home, Joe's knowledge of how these types of missions are planned and executed, and how these conversations usually go. We also talked to those who performed the same or similar work as Shannon in different parts of the Middle East. The driver in these chapters—call sign "Jake"—is an amalgamation of a few different people that Shannon and Scotty Wirtz regularly worked with, but whose names and description we didn't feel comfortable sharing as they are still actively working in sensitive positions. Our aim in crafting this narrative was to tell Shannon's truth, to tell her story, in the best way we could. Had we used only declassified transcripts and reports, this book would have fallen short in telling Shannon's truth.

"As to the speeches which were made either before or during the war, it was hard for me, and for others who reported them to me, to recollect the exact words," Thucydides once wrote of his work detailing the stories of early wars. "I have therefore put into the mouth of each speaker the sentiments proper to the occasion, expressed as I thought he would be likely to express them, while at the same time, I endeavored, as nearly as I could, to give the general purport of what was actually said. I have described nothing but what I saw myself, or learned from others of whom I made the most careful inquiry."

Joe and I took Thucydides's advice in telling Shannon's story, and we hope that it did her justice. To ensure all of these elements blended together seamlessly, and that we provided a true 360-degree view of Shannon's life, we opted to keep the voice in the third person.

I would be remiss to not thank a few people instrumental in this book coming to fruition: first and foremost, Joe Kent. He trusted me to help tell his hero wife's story, a sacred privilege that I take very seriously. Joe, I hope your boys know their mom just a little better when they're old enough to read this book someday, and that the whole world knows the legend of Shannon Kent.

Were it not for Larry Weissman, it's possible we may never have had the opportunity to tell Shannon's story on such a large platform. Were it not for our talented and very patient editors, Mauro DiPreta and Andrew Yackira, I'm certain the story wouldn't have been as good as Shannon deserves.

I personally owe a large debt of gratitude to my fellow storytellers, Matt Sanders, Michael R. Shea, and Dan Schilling, who helped and encouraged me along the way, and to Evan Hafer for connecting Joe and me so soon after Shannon's death. Dr. Matt Voll, Lieutenant Colonel (Ret.) Charlie Faint, and Paul O'Leary offered their expertise and allowed this book to be more in-depth on topics I was not personally familiar with enough to adequately incorporate into the story, and the story is better for it.

Last but not least, my wife, Lauren, has been there for me on long nights spent writing, rewriting, editing, and writing some more. She has been understanding and caring in a way that any author would be lucky to have, including being my go-to woman for explaining how to better write about a woman and her unique experiences (childbirth, for example).

Thank you, dear reader, for picking this book off the shelf to read and playing a small part in ensuring Shannon is never forgotten. Her life is an inspiration, and I have no doubt you'll feel the same as you flip through these pages.

CHAPTER 1

HUNTING HUMANS

SYRIA, 2018

Hunting humans, like most trades, is a craft mastered through repetition and experience. Many in the world of special operations spent the better part of the past two decades devoted to refining it, but very few transcend from craftsmen to true artisans. Like many great artists in the past, most of their names will not be known during their lifetimes.

A black Hyundai Elantra, covered in dust and sporting a few dents, cruised down a two-lane highway in the Syrian desert against the backdrop of a beautiful sunrise. *Red in the morning, sailors take warning,* Kay thought, sitting in the backseat. They didn't use real names on missions, but you still needed something easy to remember. "Kay" was easy enough.

The radio dial was stuck on Al-Madina FM, a manageable but annoying situation Kay and the other two operators dealt with on their ninety-minute morning drive. It was too early for nonstop Arabic music, but conversation died down about an hour ago, so *it is what it is.*

The mission was to meet a source at a small compound in the middle of nowhere. In post-ISIS Syria, allegiances changed rapidly, and "friendly" didn't mean much—especially when dealing with someone who made it clear the highest bidder could buy them. It was a potentially dangerous rendezvous. Air support would be nice, in case things went south, but you're in the wrong line of work if you expect that kind of safety net.

This meeting wasn't their first rodeo, and if anyone knew how to navigate it successfully, it was these three. They had a combined fifty years of military experience, almost all of it in special operations. They were all selected and trained for their ability to hunt humans off the grid, in ambiguous situations, with little to no support. They were entirely in their element.

They weren't wearing body armor or helmets—hell, they weren't even wearing uniforms—unless you count the faded New York Yankees ball cap Kay always had on. No machine guns or rocket launchers, just a Glock in the waistband and one spare magazine.

In their line of work, usual military grooming standards were not only disregarded but considered dangerous in the high-threat environments they routinely worked. Two of the three looked how most would picture a stereotypical operator on a low-visibility mission: tan skin, longish hair, and beards. Kay opted for a ponytail.

The driver was a native-born Iraqi who came to the United States after his parents fled Saddam Hussein–controlled Iraq during the 1990s. He sported Walmart knockoff Ray-Ban sunglasses and a

Timex Ironman watch, which complemented his old, beat-up flannel. His philosophy was to be frugal with money but liberal with a belt-fed. He went by the call sign "Jake," but only because "Jake from State Farm" was too long for a radio transmission during a firefight.

Scotty rode shotgun. An old frogman-turned-contractor, he wore a pair of Oakleys, a black Casio G-Shock watch wrapped around his tattoo-laden arm, and a well-worn Black House MMA T-shirt from Brazil. He was Kay's lookout during meets; if shit went south, he'd be first to draw. But if he had a choice, he'd rather be spearfishing off the coast of . . . well, just about anywhere there are fish.

Operator doesn't refer to everyone in special operations. The term is reserved for those few who weren't satisfied with their Special Forces tab, the color of their beret, or their Navy SEAL trident. Those, like Kay, who wanted to serve at the most elite level of special operations and volunteered to take "the long walk." Seventy thousand of the 1.3 million active-duty service members in the US military are assigned to the US Special Operations Command (USSOCOM).[1] Among them are the operators—the one percent of the one percent.

But few realize these same operators are the friendly neighbors and Little League coaches back home, tasked with balancing home and work like any other busy American. Well, almost like any other American.

Shit, I forgot to check in with Joe to see how Colt's doctor's appointment went today, Kay thought. Long drives like this allowed these hardened operators to get lost in their thoughts about the world back home. War or not, the kids needed to be taken care of, and marriages must be maintained. It's a delicate balancing act.

"We're about ten minutes out," Jake said, breaking the silence in the car. Kay sat up a little straighter and began mentally preparing for the looming prospect of violence that could occur if the source decided their loyalty to the coalition had a limit. Typically, it's all chai and smiles and empty promises—but bloodshed was always possible.

Hope for the best, prepare for the worst, Kay thought, while pulling the slide back just far enough to see a bit of brass in the chamber of her compact Glock 19, indicating a round ready to fire. Fluency in seven different languages, fifteen years of training, four previous combat deployments, and it all comes down to remembering that each mission is its own, and the enemy always has a vote.

"Let's do a first pass to check out the compound," Kay said. "I don't want to roll in there until we've had a chance to get eyes on."

"Sounds good," Jake replied before spitting tobacco juice into an empty energy drink can he had wedged between his legs. One dirty secret of the war on terror: it was fueled by chewing tobacco and energy drinks. Or, in Kay's case, Rothman cigarettes—but only because she couldn't find her preferred Marlboro Smooths while deployed.

The final ten minutes went by fast. The compound was in view, just off the main road. The Hyundai slowed and then turned right onto a gravel path that passed by the open front gate. Kay noted a few kids playing soccer and one military-aged male squatting nearby with an AK-47 slung over his shoulder as they drove by. The source was presumably inside.

After driving approximately one hundred meters past the compound, Jake performed a U-turn and headed back. He pulled over outside the gate, allowing Kay and Scotty to exit and walk into the compound's courtyard. He kept the car running.

The two approached the main building, and a man—a sheikh—emerged, dressed in traditional Arabic clothing with an orange kaffiyeh wrapped around his head.

"MarHaban, as-salaam'alaykum." Kay delivered the standard

Arabic greeting with a perfect accent for the region, immediately recognizing him as the source they were there to meet.

"Wa 'alaykum salaam," the man replied while placing his right hand on his chest. *So far, so good,* Chief Petty Officer Shannon Kent—"Kay"—thought. Scotty stood nearby, his eyes darting from the Sheikh to the young man with an AK-47, then back again.

Then, in perfect English, the Sheikh said, "I did not expect a woman."

⚓ ⚓ ⚓

Several miles away, thirty American commandos prepared for close combat in a large canvas tent—the "ready room"—filled with wooden cubbies that stored their tools of war. The operators had already double-checked the explosive charges they built for breaching gates and doors, carefully removed the safety from their grenades, and performed a functions check on everything from their heavy machine guns to sniper rifles to their medical gear. Their lives depended on it.

Outside their tent, specialized helicopters stood fueled on the tarmac, ready to whisk them away at a moment's notice. The pilots and crew chiefs were elite in their own right, specially selected for their talent and experience in special operations aviation.

Everyone was waiting on the green light to board those helicopters and a chance to kill or capture the enemy. To do that, they needed to know where the enemy was. In this case, the man in question was Abu Bakr al-Baghdadi, the leader of the Islamic State of Iraq and Syria, or ISIS. Al-Baghdadi was the most elusive and dangerous member of the militant extremist's cadre, responsible for an organized campaign of terror that swept across the Middle

East, resulting in tens of thousands dead, thousands enslaved, and providing inspiration for brutal terrorist attacks across the Western world.

He was still at large, with a proven capacity for continued attacks against the United States and her interests.

In an era of instantaneous global communication, he could launch a strike on the US homeland from a cell phone without warning. With someone like al-Baghdadi, every second counted. The commandos needed to take him out of the fight. But they were helpless until the information about his whereabouts came in, stuck on the airfield in a state of bored readiness.

Everything depended on Shannon.

Shannon replied to the Sheikh in Syrian Slang, "America ba'tat ashaukhos el wassqeen fee, em-Shan yalt'ie bil ashkass el wassqeen fee hoon." ("America sent the one they trust to meet the one they trust.")

Her response reminded him she represented the most powerful nation in the world while simultaneously flattering him by saying America trusted him. The latter part of her response was not true, but Shannon stuck with cultural norms by complimenting her host. Keeping up with local conversational norms by establishing rapport with a source often began with a compliment, and Arabs love exchanging pleasantries.

This mission wasn't the first time she had to respond to men surprised by a female operator. Her confidence and knowledge of local languages and customs helped her through countless situations over the previous fifteen years; her linguistic ability and guile were as much of a weapon as the Glock concealed beneath her shirt.

But every situation was different, and this one was either going to go really well or very poorly. The outcome depended on Shannon's ability to convince this man that doing the task force's bidding was in his best interest. Either way, she was ready. Focusing on projecting steady confidence while appearing personable was essential to getting sources to cooperate. She deserved an Oscar for the show she was putting on, considering how much was riding on this conversation.

Shannon's role as an operator was to find and fix terrorists like al-Baghdadi and his ilk in time and space. These are the first two steps in the Find, Fix, Finish, Exploit, Analyze, Disseminate (F3EAD) targeting methodology America's special operators use to dismantle enemy networks.

The cycle started with finding and fixing the target, meaning Shannon must determine precisely where the terrorist is and when he could be captured or killed. The next step was to finish the target, which could mean dropping a bomb in a "kinetic strike" or sending a special operations unit to conduct a raid. This methodology has been used with significant effect in both Iraq and Afghanistan, ultimately leading to the deaths of infamous terrorists like Abu Musab al-Zarqawi and Usama bin Laden. Shannon Kent was considered an expert at five of the six tenets of F3EAD and pretty damn competent in the remaining one.

On this day, the success of the task force rested on her ability to gain the Sheikh's trust and get him to tell her where al-Baghdadi was hiding.

Al-Baghdadi had been a ghost for the past six months, with reports of his location scarce and inconsistent—though the results of his work were not. He had been actively planning operations against the West ever since his reign of terror across the Middle East via an army of extremists came to an end. America was the prize target, but in the prior six months, ISIS lost its ability to control terrain and clandestinely fled into the same area where Shannon was standing—the area controlled by the Sheikh she was face-to-face with.

The magnitude of her mission was not lost on her. The pressure from the shooters to "paint the X on this motherfucker" was a heavy weight, and the information she needed to obtain would send her brothers toward violence. She was their eyes and ears, right up to the point they encountered the enemy in person.

A surprised smile spread across the Sheikh's face as he studied the woman in front of him. She looked American—like a woman out of an action movie—dressed in dark gray prAna pants, a black Arc'teryx jacket, and a purple Syrian kaffiyeh around her neck, yet she spoke with a native Syrian accent. America had sent her and just two men. *This is different,* he thought. This team must be powerful, and the woman seems to be in charge.

"Tafadil." The Sheikh welcomed her with an extended hand. They shook hands—Syrians are far from being strict Muslims who refuse to touch women they are not related to.

"Please, come inside!" he said warmly. Shannon was pleased to see his demeanor and tone improve after her initial introduction—her Syrian dialect was paying off, which meant the hours of watching Syrian soap operas to get the accent down was worth it.

The familiar sounds of a scampering toddler filled the courtyard of the Sheikh's house. "Ali Abdullah, come here!" his mother called after him.

Shannon was relieved to hear familiar sounds. *This guy is probably not going to risk killing us with his family here,* she thought while entering the living room. The living room was a modern take on the traditional Arab divan, but instead of having numerous overstuffed pillows on the floor, the Sheikh had couches along the perimeter of the room with an ornate gold desk at the head—a clear sign he was a tribal leader accustomed to holding court.

As the Sheikh entered the room, he slipped his feet out of his spotless leather loafers. *Damn,* Shannon thought as she followed suit and slipped out of her Salomon trail shoes. *Just once, I'd love to keep my damn shoes on.* Salomons are a favorite in the community. Most of the guys like these particular shoes for the support, and the grip, and blah blah blah. Shannon liked the quick-release shoelaces for source meets like this. *Bet the Salomon designers never thought about that during product development.*

Now that she was inside the Sheikh's house, she was much more at ease. Anything could happen, but sheikhs don't typically kill even their worst enemies in their own homes. The danger was getting to the meet and home again, as there were few ways in and out. That is why the team opted for the beat-up, old local car—can't kill what you can't find.

The Sheikh motioned to a seat on the couch to the right of his desk. As Shannon sat down, she glanced to her left and saw Scotty exactly where she knew he'd be, shadowing her and covering the door—her route out of the room if things went sideways. Scotty fought in the early days of the war on terror as a SEAL before switching over to the secretive world of the Defense Intelligence Agency. He and Shannon bonded over their shared Naval Special Warfare lineage as sailors who spoke the same language.

Shannon knew if she could see Scotty in the doorway, he could see Jake lingering in the courtyard. Jake covered the egress from the house to the car and acted as an early warning for trouble originating outside the home. He was also the most well armed, with a Heckler & Koch UMP 45 submachine gun concealed in a small duffle bag and several mini fragmentation grenades easily accessible.

With security confirmed, Shannon turned her attention to the reason they just risked a drive through the Euphrates Valley no-man's-land: the source. He was a key tribal Sheikh with a long history with ISIS, the Assad regime, the Kurds, and every other power broker in the region. He was the key to finding, fixing, and hopefully finishing al-Baghdadi.

The Sheikh's tribe controlled a large swath of territory in the area and was initially part of the anti-Assad Syrian revolution in 2011. He'd even worked with ISIS, as it suited his tribe's interest. The reality of the situation on the ground was nothing new; revolutions and even governments come and go, but the tribal system endures. The survival of governments requires buy-in from the tribes, but Assad forgot that and turned to brute force (like his father had) to crush the Sunni tribes.

To the Sheikh, ISIS was no different. He and his tribe worked with ISIS at one point but eventually chafed under ISIS's brutal rule and turned against them when the timing was right. Shannon needed to see where his allegiance was *right now,* if he and his tribe could help locate al-Baghdadi, and how much all that would cost the US taxpayer.

Shannon did her homework on him for weeks before the meeting, poring over intelligence reports about the tribe and the Sheikh himself. She was not surprised to see the classified information on him was lacking compared to what he put out on social media. *And to think, we used to have to steal this shit. Now everyone posts everything about their lives online, free for the taking,* she thought.

Shannon was a trained cryptologist, first and foremost. If it was an electronic communication, she could steal it. Despite her job title, or what the Navy called a *rate*, she was a natural human intelligence collector who thrived when working through people to obtain otherwise unobtainable information. In fact, Shannon's gift for striking up a friendship with anyone made her a sought-after asset in special operations.

First meetings were always rough, though. Not only did Shannon need to worry about obtaining specific information on al-Baghdadi, but she also needed to form a friendship with this man. She was asking him to take a good deal of risk, not just for him but for his family and the entire tribe. This level of commitment required at least a professional friendship and for the Sheikh to feel respected and to want to meet with Shannon again.

As advanced as intelligence collection has become, human intelligence still boils down to building genuine connections between you and your source. The softer side of relationship-building juxtaposed with the testosterone and adrenaline-fueled world of special operations requires a high degree of emotional intelligence. Human intelligence collectors in this world must seamlessly move from empathizing with a source to asking them to risk their life or even sell out family members. Few operators can balance these complexities while threading the needle of human nature.

"Thank you so much for meeting with me today and inviting me into your home," Shannon said. "My colleagues and I were sent here to thank you for your efforts against Daesh on behalf of the US government." Her initial assessment of the source started here, even if her opening line was seemingly benign.

She had referred to ISIS as Daesh, a derogatory word in Arabic for ISIS, which ISIS itself despises. The term takes ISIS's Arabic name and turns it into an American-style acronym (*al-Dawla al-Islamiya fi al-Iraq wa al-Sham*). They hate this term because it literally translates to "bigotry" and is also a feminine verb. Casually throwing the word *Daesh* into a compliment was a surefire way to gauge his feelings about ISIS.

Without warning, the telltale report of an AK-47 burst ripped through the air, echoing through the room from outside the building.

Shannon's hand instinctively moved to her pistol; the Sheikh was visibly confused. Scotty had already moved out, leaving Shannon alone. She had seconds to consider what to do.

Ultimately, she had a mission. People were depending on her.

Shannon channeled the pressure down a well-trained mental pathway: *focus on the task at hand, step by step, and let the other guys deal with whatever's going on outside.*

She diverted her attention back to the Sheikh. *First, he has to want to talk to you. Without that, we have nothing.*

CHAPTER 2

YES, I CAN

PLEASANT VALLEY, NEW YORK, 1985

Take a bath, then get the "footy" pajamas on. Then story time, maybe a short song or two, then bedtime. That was Steve and Mary Smith's routine in 1985 as they raised their young family in the small town of Pleasant Valley, New York. Sometimes Mom read, sometimes Dad. Tonight it was Dad's turn. The book of choice was *Close Your Eyes* by Jean Marzollo, a beautifully illustrated children's bedtime story.

"Shanni do! Shanni do!" Shannon demanded, grabbing the book away. Regardless of whether Mom or Dad was up to the plate, Shannon rarely let them read. Sure, she didn't yet know how to read herself—she was only two years old, after all—but she had memorized the line of poetry on each page and could recite the story from memory as she flipped through the book.

"Close your eyes, and you can be," Shannon said before turning the page. In her mind, this wasn't *her* bedtime story. She was reading a bedtime story to her dad. "Sound asleep, in an apple tree!"

She continued, Dad listening proudly. He was tired from a long day on patrol as a newly minted New York State trooper, and Mary, his wife, was pregnant with their second. There's something about a bright young daughter that can make all the day's stress disappear, if even for just the length of a children's book.

"For you're asleep in a cozy bed, with secret dreams in your lovely head. The end!" Shannon exclaimed. Then Mary came in for a good-night song, usually "You Are My Sunshine" or the old Irish lullaby "Tura Lura Lural":

Too-ra-loo-ra-loo-ral,
Too-ra-loo-ra-li,
Too-ra-loo-ra-loo-ral,
Hush now don't you cry!
Too-ra-loo-ra-loo-ral,
Too-ra-loo-ra-li,
Too-ra-loo-ra-loo-ral,
That's an Irish lullaby.

With that, the light went off, and Shannon drifted into her dreams.

It's those young bedtime moments a parent remembers most. They're pure and innocent, and your child's eyes are filled with all the optimistic hope in the world. It's in those moments you hope your child, whom you love more than you've ever loved anything or anyone, never endures hardship in their life. You know that won't be the case, that hard days are ahead. But at least you can cherish this bedtime ritual, this innocent time that seems to outlast all the memories of nasty diapers, restless babies, and sleepless nights all young parents inevitably endure.

PINE PLAINS, NEW YORK, 1988

Shannon Smith, five years old, watched as the other kids swung from rung to rung on the playground monkey bars. She had just started her tenure as a kindergartner at Seymour Smith Elementary School in Pine Plains, New York—about eighty miles north of New York City. The notorious horizontal ladder featured on both schoolyard playgrounds and military obstacle courses requires a bit of technique, grip, and upper-body strength to move from one end of the bars to the other—two things most five-year-old children are in short supply of.

"I bet you can't do it!" a young boy taunted Shannon.

"Yeah, huh! Yes, I can!" Shannon replied, not to be shouted down.

"No, you're too little!" The boy sneered.

Shannon confidently stomped over to the bars, determined to show this bully up. She didn't start the fight, but she'd finish it by gracefully swinging from bar to bar. Or so she thought.

Shannon grabbed the bars, her feet dangling below her. She missed as she tried to swing her hand to the next one, falling to the pea rock below. The boy laughed.

She got up, furious, and mounted the bars again. She swung again and failed again. It took everything in her to hold back the tears—she wouldn't give that boy the satisfaction of knowing she was upset.

"I told you you couldn't do it!" The boy pointed at her, laughing. It's the kind of taunting that haunts a child for years to come. The playground bully is a common scourge among children, but that doesn't make the experience less painful.

Shannon came home that day and told her mom all about it. She was upset specifically because it was a boy who told her she couldn't do it, and Mary could see Shannon wasn't defeated. If anything, she was more determined than ever.

The next day, Shannon snuck over to the monkey bars. She tried to make it across again but failed. She kept getting back up on the bars, over and over, gritting her teeth with fire in her eyes. *I'll show him*, she thought.

This went on for days, maybe weeks. The metal bars tore up Shannon's palms, bloodying them from her repeated attempts. Mary noticed one day after school.

"Okay, you need to take a break from the monkey bars," Mary told her. She applied Band-Aids and then called the school. The kindergarten teacher agreed and tried to negotiate with Shannon— maybe it was time to try playing with other things on the playground?

But Shannon was determined.

Despite her teacher and mother's request, Shannon kept sneaking over to the bars when the teacher wasn't looking. Her tiny five-year-old hands were newly bloodied with each attempt. There wasn't an ounce of quit in her. That's not something you can teach someone—you either have it, or you don't.

Slowly, day by day, she made it from one bar to the next. Then the next, and the next. Eventually, the momentum carried all the way through and she made it to the end. Landing back on her feet, triumphant, she earned the kind of confidence that kids get from conquering the seemingly unconquerable. It was the beginning of a lifelong trend; when somebody said, *No, you can't do this,* Shannon's response was always *Oh, yes, I can.*

Shannon's passion for language was evident from an early age, though not everyone saw it as clearly as Steve and Mary. Her first-grade teacher, a friend of Mary's, was convinced she would struggle academically.

"That's crazy. I don't believe that. I know how smart she is!" Mary told the teacher during a meeting about Shannon's performance in school. She couldn't figure out what the problem was either. How could her daughter, who was memorizing books at two years old, have issues in school?

One day Shannon had her nose in a book, as usual, but Mary noticed she was holding it farther away from her eyes than was natural. For children twelve and younger, 80 percent of learning is visual, but one in five students in America have undiagnosed vision issues.[1] This results in many students being misdiagnosed with a learning disability when all they needed was a pair of glasses.

Mary took Shannon to a local optometrist, who ran her through the usual battery of vision tests. The diagnosis: she was both near- and farsighted. After fitting her with an appropriate pair of glasses, the optometrist said, "Now watch her soar!"

And that's what she did. The first-grade teacher may have been both the first and last person to doubt Shannon's academic prowess. Within days, Mary noticed how much faster Shannon was reading. She was finishing books so quickly that Mary thought she might be fibbing. Mary recalls the plot of one of these books as described to her by Shannon: "The whole book was about whether this girl would get to go to a birthday party or not. It was really boring."

PINE PLAINS, NEW YORK, 1998

Back in fifth grade, Shannon moved to a different school for her last year of elementary school. That's where she met Cassandra Nolan and Claire Eskdale. The trio quickly became best friends, calling themselves "the Three Musketeers" and having fun by doing things like climbing grain silos in costumes on Halloween. Now in high school, they had graduated to more nefarious activities.

One night they were hanging out at Claire's house, sneaking sips of cheap beer—or was it wine coolers?—when Claire decided she wanted to do something edgy . . . some act of teenage rebellion that might drive her parents crazy. They settled on Claire piercing her nose.

The Three Musketeers surreptitiously gathered ice and a sewing needle without Claire's parents noticing, then, back in Claire's room, used the ice to numb her nose. Claire held the needle but became nervous. Now that the time had come, she was having second thoughts.

"Just do it, Claire! Just do it!" Shannon encouraged her, caught up in the moment. Normally, Shannon was the responsible friend— Cassandra and Claire were usually the ones trying to get her to break the rules, not the other way around.

"Seriously, don't think about it, just do it," Shannon said, not giving up. Cassandra was squeamish around blood and couldn't bring herself to watch. After a bit more liquid encouragement, Claire plunged the sewing needle into her ice-cold nose cartilage. The deed was done, and Shannon was elated.

"Oh my god, you did it!" Shannon laughed, barely able to believe her friend actually went through with it. Claire would have to confront her parents with a red, swollen nose the next day, but that night, they created a memory none of them would ever forget.

⚓ ⚓ ⚓

Mira que buen culito!" José said, taking notice of Shannon's backside while nodding at her. "Si! Si!" His fellow Argentinian groom also took notice as they worked on a horse, both chuckling.

Shannon was a bit farther down in the stable at the Mashomack Polo Club, performing chores on a different horse. She cared for five horses in total: Nave, Comanche, Julia, Pampa, and Copita. Shannon understood every word they were saying but kept her amusement to herself, knowing she had the upper hand. More time passed, and they moved to the next horse, a little bit closer to where Shannon was working.

This horse had just recently undergone surgery and required special care. *Perfect,* Shannon thought.

"Che José, tene cuidado con el tobillo del caballo que hace poco tuvo una cirugia!" Shannon warned in fluent Spanish, right as José was about to climb onto the still-recovering horse. Both José and his friend froze, shocked she spoke their language, and horrified at the realization that she probably understood their inappropriate compliment earlier that day. Before the tension could get any worse, the entire stable busted open in laughter, with the other grooms and stable hands poking fun at José's misfortune. He wouldn't live that one down for a long time.

Shannon smiled, satisfied with her small victory. She had a secret crush on José, and sure, she loved polo and working at the stable—but it didn't hurt that there was a cute boy to flirt with.

The well-established polo community in New York brings in some of the world's top polo coaches and their staff from Argentina each spring and summer to support demand for the sport. Shannon had been exposed to the world of equestrianism for nearly her entire life—her parents had owned a horse for about five years when she was younger, which allowed her to ride and train regularly. Horses always filled Shannon with passion and adventure, so during the summer of her freshman year in high school, she approached the owner of a local polo club and volunteered as a stable hand for whatever he could pay her.

Before long, Shannon found herself cleaning stables, grooming horses, learning to ride, which gave her opportunities to practice the Argentinian dialect of Spanish. Thanks to a foreign exchange student from France at her school, Shannon took an interest in learning French—and became nearly fluent over the course of one summer after borrowing a textbook from the French teacher. She'd also been taking Spanish classes in school, and the opportunity to be around native speakers at the stable quickly improved her ability with the language.

To the uninformed, working as a groom might seem like the bottom of the ladder in the polo world, but it's an essential role. Professional polo players credit their groom as a crucial element of the team, without whom victory would be impossible.

"Polo is ninety percent the horse and ten percent the player," Thomas Keesee told Shannon. He supervised her during her time as a groom at Mashomack. "Whether this is the correct ratio or not is open to debate, but no polo player will argue the ponies are not the key to the game. The key to having good ponies is to get them into top shape and keep them that way—and that is the job of the polo groom."

Polo is one of the most dangerous sports you can play, but that's likely what attracted Shannon to it. A polo player is expected to sit on top of an animal that weighs nearly a ton, runs at speeds up to thirty miles per hour, with their only means of control being a six-inch piece of metal in its mouth and the player's legs. But before the polo player ever mounts a horse, it's the groom who's responsible for mitigating the risk of serious injury by preparing the pony for both training and competition.

Despite the importance of a groom's work, the job is unglamorous and often without praise. It was not uncommon for Shannon to show up at the barns before the sun rose and leave after it had set behind the rolling New York hills. Although it's standard to have a day off every week, grooms were prepared to come in at a moment's notice.

To make life as a groom even more challenging, Shannon was just one of a few female grooms at the club. Polo was considered a man's sport at the time, with very few women competing and even fewer working as grooms. Despite the challenges, Shannon was an exemplary groom, and Keesee considered her among the best he'd seen in over twenty years of polo.

Shannon's role quickly expanded into translator once she noticed that none of the American polo club members spoke Spanish, and the Argentines spoke very little English. Communicating with people in their native tongue was her secret weapon, a skill few possessed because it was an artistic combination of listening and reading people's faces and body language.

Mariah Smith, Shannon's younger sister, followed her footsteps into equestrianism, with Shannon often training her and acting as her mentor. Shannon took every opportunity to go out riding with her sister, teaching her everything she could and passing on her passion for horses. That passion would be something the sisters would bond over for years to come.

Although the stable and its horses were where her heart was, Shannon also held a summer job at the local pharmacy, and was a scholar and athlete at school. She participated in year-round sports, excelling in volleyball, basketball, cross-country, and track and field. She sang in the chorus, played flute in the school band, and was involved with the school theater. Was there anything she couldn't do?

PINE PLAINS, NEW YORK, 2000

Stissing Mountain Junior/Senior High School was known for quality productions and attracted top talent from the nearby theater mecca of New York City to help coach and mentor their young theater students, which included most of the student body due to the school's modest size. Standards were high, but the experience level of the younger students was not. Nonetheless, Shannon always strived to be cast in a "mike" role, which was always a lead character.

In Shannon's junior year of high school she auditioned for the school play, *Crazy for You*. The romantic comedy debuted on Broadway in 1992, adapted from a George and Ira Gershwin musical from the 1930s about the complicated relationship between a young big-city banker and a small-town girl. Some of the roles required tap dancing, while others did not. Shannon had no idea how to tap-dance, so she hoped for a nontapping character.

The day finally came when students would find out who they were playing. As the cast list was posted, they all chanted "Mike! Mike! Mike!" over and over again, before rushing up to see who got what character. Shannon immediately saw her name on the list: she was cast in a mike role!

But it was as Tess, a young dance director pursued by a married man in the story—and it was the lead tap-dancing role. Shannon immediately felt overwhelmed. How could she pull this off? Fortunately, she had a friend who volunteered to teach her.

Every day during lunch, Shannon and a few other students snuck off together to go over basic tap-dance choreography. They donned their character's short-heel tap shoes and learned to do time steps, wings, and the traveling step "shuffle off to Buffalo," which hails from the nineteenth century and combines a leap, shuffle, and another leap. Shannon was dedicated and gave the lessons everything she had, to the point of developing blisters on her feet from all the practice. But, unfortunately, they didn't have much time to work with.

Opening night arrived, and ready or not, Shannon needed to perform. She was not only in the first scene but would deliver the first line of the show. The curtain rose, revealing Shannon and four other characters.

"Shoulders back! Heads high! One last time!" Shannon shouted over the music, kicking off the musical. Her character, Tess, instructed four "showgirls" on how to perform a routine. Just as they rehearsed, she then looked around nervously, then down at her watch. "Patsy, where's Bobby? He should have been here two hours ago!" Shannon said, standing confidently onstage. And so the play began.

Shannon's performance was remarkable. By the time she and her fellow follies took the stage again for the "Girls Enter Nevada" scene, it was clear she had put in enough work to pull the role off.

"When the moon at night lights, that's the best of bright lights!" The girls sang together and tap-danced as the cowboys waited to join in, before stopping for Shannon to go solo, shouting: "All right, girls, let's show 'em how we do it!"

No matter who you are, high school is filled with ups and downs. It's a time of growth, and although Shannon established herself as an overachiever academically, artistically, and athletically at every opportunity, she knew she was capable of more. Her natural ability to address problems with humor, humility, professionalism, and grit would be an asset in almost any facet of her life—she just needed to find a direction that would push her beyond her limits.

CHAPTER 3

WAR CHANGES EVERYTHING

PINE PLAINS, NEW YORK, 2000

The military recruiters always set up their folding tables in the lunchroom at Stissing Mountain Junior/Senior High School. Tablecloths draped over cafeteria folding tables were branded with whatever branch of service was there that day. Overworked and underappreciated midcareer noncommissioned officers (NCOs) forced into recruiting duty arranged key chains, water bottles, and an array of brochures the best they could manage.

The Army and Marine Corps pamphlets always looked the same to a layperson—usually an array of tanks firing or guys in camo running toward something. The Air Force put fighter jet pilots on the front, while the Navy always had SEALs coming out of the water, carbine rifles dripping, with streaks of green paint across their face.

The recruiters standing behind the table in their dress uniform rarely looked like the warriors pictured.

Shannon was not shy and was no stranger to the recruiters when they visited. "What about that?" Shannon said, pointing to one of the Navy pamphlets. *Now that,* she thought, *looks fun.* But she wasn't looking for fun. Her father, Steve—or "Smitty," as his friends call him—would eventually be the third-highest-ranked officer in the state police, and her uncle was a firefighter in New York City. Her brother served in the US Marine Corps. Shannon wanted to do her part too.

"How do I do that?"

"Well, those are Navy SEALs. They're the most elite, do the most dangerous missions, have the most training," the Navy petty officer replied. "But unfortunately, that job is closed to women."

"Why?" Shannon shot back.

"You seem like the kind of person who wants to make a difference," the recruiter said, sidestepping Shannon's land mine of a question. "What do you think about military intelligence? The Navy has some of the most sophisticated intelligence-gathering equipment in the world, and those SEALs wouldn't even know where to go if it weren't for the intel folks pointing them in the right direction."

Shannon ignored him ignoring her question—because the idea of military intelligence did sound interesting. She immediately recognized that her talent for languages must be an edge in the world of intelligence collection and analysis.

Shannon was raised in a family of high performers with high standards, and that had always been evident to her from a young age. The most important Smith family standard, the one that was so obvious that it went without saying, was selfless service—above and beyond a simple sense of duty to nation and community. Shannon wanted to exceed that standard of service.

"So what's the next step? How do I do this?" Shannon said.

"Well, assuming you haven't been in trouble with the law, don't have any major medical issues, and you're keeping up with school, the next step would be to sit down with your parents. How old are you?" the recruiter asked.

"Seventeen. Why?" Shannon replied.

"Well, if you aren't eighteen, we'll need your parents to sign a consent form for you to join."

⚓ ⚓ ⚓

Later that school year, Steve and Mary patiently listened to the Navy recruiter as he laid out his well-rehearsed pitch about service on the high seas. He had made an early evening appointment at the Smith household to talk about Shannon joining the Navy—a talk neither parent was thrilled to have. They were polite but not easily swayed.

"The Navy would be perfect for Shannon," the recruiter said confidently. "She's smart, athletic, and clearly passionate about serving her nation. I have no doubt she'd make a great chief someday, maybe even an officer!"

"How long has the Navy been around?" Mary asked.

"Well, over two hundred and twenty-five years at this point, I believe."

"Then it would be reasonable to think that it will still be there for Shannon to join once she finishes college?" Mary, an educator herself, firmly believed in the value of higher education and saw no possible upside to Shannon joining the military before at least giving college a try first. *And she's only seventeen!*

"And what about combat?" Steve asked.

"Look, Shannon is talking about joining the Navy here," the

recruiter said. "This isn't the Marines. She'll be underway on a ship translating intercepted communications from our nation's adversaries, not going to a landlocked country like Iraq. She'd never go to a place like that."

Well, that's a load of bullshit, Mary thought.

Steve broke the silence. "I think we'll need to sleep on this."

"That's understandable. I put a folder together with all the information we talked about tonight, as well as the paperwork you and Shannon will need to move forward." The recruiter stuck his business card into the inside flap and pushed it across the table.

The cover of the folder again featured Navy SEALs, serious-looking men with green faces creeping up a beach from the ocean, rifles raised, a full moon in the background.

After exchanging cordial goodbyes, the recruiter departed their driveway in his government-issued sedan. Steve and Mary sat back down to review the folder. It included brochures with generic lists of jobs in the Navy, a physical health questionnaire, and D.D. Form 1966, a five-page document. The fifth page, Section VIII, was titled "Parental/Guardian Consent for Enlistment" and included a signature block at the bottom of the page for Steve and Mary to sign. But before that, an ominous disclaimer:

I/we acknowledge/understand that he/she may be required upon order to serve in combat or other hazardous situations. I/we certify that no promises of any kind have been made to me/us concerning assignment to duty, training, or promotion during his/her enlistment as an inducement to me/us to sign this consent.

It was a sleepless night for Mary Smith. She wasn't comfortable with the idea of giving her daughter permission to join the military at such a young age. She wasn't comfortable with the idea of her daughter not going to college. Frankly, she was scared, as any parent would be at the prospect of their child being sent into combat. Regardless of anything the recruiter said, there was a possibility Shannon would find herself in harm's way.

The next morning, Mary tore up the paperwork.

"You know, you're only seventeen right now," Mary said. Shannon knew where this was going. "If you still want to do this when you're eighteen, then that's your decision to make. But I want you to go to college, at least give it a try."

The decision was final.

Shannon graduated from Stissing Mountain Junior/Senior High School in the spring of 2001. On the last day of school, Shannon and Cassandra let loose in the school parking lot, spinning donuts in a maroon Chrysler LeBaron and a black Nissan Stanza, respectively. Later, Cassandra read what Shannon had written in her yearbook: "I love you, man. If you want to come visit me, well, I probably won't be in the US . . ."

Acquiescing to her mother's request, Shannon enrolled as a freshman at the State University of New York at Plattsburgh the following fall to study communications and mass media. There was no war at the time, but Mary knew that could all change in an instant. And it did.

Not even a year after the recruiter visited the Smith home, on September 11, 2001, Shannon's father, Steve, and her uncle responded to the worst attack on American soil since Pearl Harbor, just down the Hudson River in New York City. That infamous day, which also included an attack on the Pentagon and the downing of United Airlines Flight 93 in western Pennsylvania, resulted in thousands of Americans dead at the hands of terrorists and millions more fighting a campaign against international terror organizations for more than two decades.

Shannon's younger brother joined the Marines shortly after the terror attacks, and to no one's surprise, Shannon's stint in college didn't last long. America was now at war. That changed everything. During her sophomore year of college, she talked to a Navy recruiter about how she could best leverage her talent for language in the service. Emerging from the ocean at midnight with a green face on a top-secret mission, like Shannon had seen on the brochures, was still out of reach due to a bar on women in combat positions. But they did have a job that seemed like a perfect fit: Cryptologic Technician—Interpretive.

By the time Shannon left for recruit training in late 2003, the US had lost lives in Afghanistan and Iraq, but both wars were still in their infancy. Rear Admiral John Paul Jones, famously known as the father of the US Navy, once said, "I wish to have no connection with any ship that does not sail fast; for I intend to go in harm's way."

Shannon Smith wanted to go in harm's way.

NAVAL STATION GREAT LAKES, ILLINOIS, 2003

Shannon arrived at the US Navy's only boot camp, located just north of Chicago, on a foggy, overcast evening, December 10, 2003. The bus she rode from the airport, full of new recruits, whispered rumors of what boot camp would be like, how hard it was according to someone's uncle, or how easy it was according to someone's friend from back home.

As they passed the welcome gate into Naval Station Great Lakes, someone cracked a joke about it being called "Great Mistakes." After some nervous laughter the entire bus fell silent. The gravity of each new recruit's decision to join the military during a time of war seemed to amplify in that moment. They'd just crossed the threshold from civilian to military life.

Shannon didn't blink. She was ready for whatever waited for her on the other side.

The bus rolled to a stop and the doors opened; the cold wind sent a chill through the aisle. A man dressed in khaki stepped onto the bus.

"Get off the bus," he said, without expression but leaving no room for misinterpretation. The first few recruits to get off the bus moved too slowly.

"Move! Move faster! Move with a sense of purpose, Seamen!" the cadre yelled. Shannon was off the bus and standing at attention in no time. She was now Seaman Smith, and this was the first day of her career in the Navy.

During in-processing, Shannon was identified as a candidate for the performing arts division, otherwise known as the "900 Division." Although these sailors must go through the same training and pass the same curriculum as those in the regular divisions, they had the added responsibility of practicing multiple times a week and being pulled from training to perform at retirement ceremonies and other functions on base.

Her audition went well. She was selected for the "Triple Threat" division, which consisted of musicians, singers, and the drill team. Within her first few days in the Navy, Shannon had already passed her first selection; it would not be her last.

Shannon was separated from the rest of the trainees she arrived with and sent to group up with the other 900 Division recruits. From there they entered a room and were given water to drink. Every recruit must take a urinalysis, but no one could go to the bathroom until everyone was ready to go. Until that time, Shannon and her fellow recruits were told to walk in circles and continue drinking water. No one was allowed to talk.

As Shannon walked in a circle impatiently waiting for the rest of the recruits to catch up to her full bladder, she made eye contact with another female sailor who looked equally annoyed. They passed each other a few times, and although they couldn't talk, Shannon sensed an immediate connection to this person. Her name was Molly Geraci, and she'd felt the same way.

Finally, every recruit was ready to give a urine sample. Shannon was among the first to burst through the bathroom doors, and despite the strict orders to not talk, yelled, "Ahhh, finally!" Molly burst out laughing. Shannon laughed too.

From that point forward, Shannon and Molly were best friends. They were assigned bunks next to each other in the barracks and identified early on for their leadership ability. The division selected Shannon as the assistant recruit chief petty officer, and Molly as a section leader.

Naval ships are expected to project power and be ready to fight and win anywhere in the world, often hundreds of miles away from land. These ships are isolated floating cities that need to be self-sufficient and capable of self-rescuing. Because there is nothing more dangerous than a fire on board while underway, every recruit is trained in the basics of firefighting during week five of the eight-week Navy boot camp. The training doubles as a stress test—can the young sailors keep their cool when the ship is on fire?

"There is no place to run on a naval ship on fire at sea," the damage control instructor said to the class full of recruits. "And there's no one to call, no one to come and save you. You need to know how to put out a fire, no matter how big or small. Every sailor is a firefighter!"

The recruits were formed up in lines, decked out in a red helmet, blue jumpsuit, full face mask, white gloves, a yellow tank on their back, and a hose at their feet. Molly was chosen as the lead hose operator, with Shannon right behind her for a demonstration.

The training was intense, with real alarms and real flames. The entire division shouted, "Relieve the nozzleman!" and "Door is cool!" over and over again. Like most military instruction, they trained the basics relentlessly.

Of course, they understood how serious the training was, that it could make the difference between mission success or failure, or life and death in future real-life situations. But in the military, boredom via repetition is inevitable, and boredom leads to jokes—regardless of the stakes at play.

"Help me hold the hose closer to our bodies!" Molly yelled through her breathing apparatus as sirens blared. The entire division watched, fixated on their every move—including the damage control instructor, a petty officer.

"Just grab it!" Shannon yelled back.

"Oh, you a gangsta, huh?" the petty officer, dressed head to toe in red to distinguish him from the basic trainees, said sarcastically.

"I'm gangsta!" Shannon said, not missing a beat.

The petty officer turned his attention to Molly.

"You a gangsta?"

"What! Am I what?" Molly yelled back, facing flames head-on and trying to communicate through the thick plastic mask. She turned around to face Shannon, "What did he say?"

"Are you gangsta!" Shannon yelled at the top of her lungs.

Having received the message but still very engaged as the lead hose operator, Molly replied, "Oh. Yeah. I'm totally gangster!"

The entire division went quiet. The petty officer didn't say a word. It was as if the world quit turning, and the flames themselves quit flickering.

Shannon leaned into Molly.

"Aaaa," Shannon said, enunciating the preferred end of the word while simultaneously wrinkling her nose and bursting into hysterical laughter. "You're a gangs*tah*. Never *-er*."

A few weeks later, Shannon and Molly graduated from recruit training and became sailors in the greatest naval force the world has ever known. Their initial training was far from over, though. It would take almost two years before they rated as fully qualified Navy cryptologists. Shannon and Molly were headed down a less-traveled path after graduation: the Defense Language Institute in Monterey, California.

While Shannon was busy working her way through the cryptological technician pipeline, the war in Iraq was escalating into a bloody insurgency. It would be a few more years before it was her turn to join the fight. All she could do was imagine her place in the war, while training for when the opportunity would inevitably arrive.

CHAPTER 4

BIRTH OF A TERRORIST MASTERMIND

BAGHDAD, IRAQ, 2004

W hen most Americans think of what a deployment to Iraq must have been like in 2004, they probably picture tan General Purpose–Medium tents, troops in sweat-soaked brown T-shirts and desert camouflage trousers, or maybe even the occasional Black Hawk helicopter flying overhead, kicking up dust onto everyone and everything below.

A marble swimming pool with bearded operators grilling out nearby in nothing more than a pair of ranger panties and a healthy dose of sunscreen is likely not in the mental picture conjured up. That's precisely how First Platoon, Charlie Company, Third Ranger Battalion and another secretive special operations unit lived during their deployment to Baghdad in early 2004. Days were spent sleeping in blacked-out rooms and lounging by the pool while they dedicated their nights to a surgical pursuit of the enemy.

It was their second pump in Iraq for most of the strike force, returning shortly after their first go during the invasion. Their mission set would define what most ████* deployments would look like for years to come: finding, fixing, and then finishing—aka killing or capturing—high-value targets (HVTs). Rinse and repeat, night after night.

Their focus was on the remnants of the infamous "Deck of Cards," which was an actual deck of cards issued to troops featuring the faces and names of the coalition's top high-value targets—mostly former Baathists up to and including the Ace of Spades: Saddam Hussein, who was captured in December 2003. But as the deployment wore on, emerging leaders of insurgent terrorists redirected their attention toward the growing insurgency in Iraq. In particular, a violent Jordanian known as Abu Musab al-Zarqawi, or simply "AMZ," was at the top of the list.

On a late January evening about halfway through their deployment, the sun fell below the Iraqi horizon. Rangers and operators alike filed into a large room on the second floor of an old Baathist mansion, one of ten next to the al-Sijood Palace, in which they lived and worked—collectively known as the Baghdad Mission Support Site, or simply the "MSS." They were gathering to receive the night's mission briefing. At a pace of two to three missions per night, these briefings were quick and largely informal—most targets were time-sensitive.

The ground force commander told the strike force they were going after what he considered a local troublemaker—a nobody by their

---

* Specific unit redacted at request of DoD.

standards—but maybe someone who could give them information on insurgent leaders higher up the food chain. This is how network-centric warfare works in the twenty-first century, after all. The target's name was al-Badri, and they believed he might be colocated with other militants responsible for attacks on US troops. A local religious nut, he said, but nothing the Glory Boys couldn't handle.

They had narrowed down al-Badri's location to a single building somewhere in Fallujah. Accurate intelligence like this was usually thanks to fearless intel collectors who either used advanced technical equipment to lock down someone's location in time and space or put their own skin on the line to meet with sources and verify information in person. Some of the most skilled intelligence professionals could wield both crafts, simultaneously leveraging technology and human interaction to ensure operators had the most accurate intel possible and the highest chance of success on target.

The senior enlisted soldier on the mission then stood up and identified which elements would be primary and secondary assault and who would be responsible for perimeter security. Finally, the lead vehicle commander, or "VC," briefed the route and order of movement. A quick call for questions, and then everyone was out the door to kit up and roll out—no time to waste.

Small talk filled the hallways of the mansion, which doubled as a "ready room" for the troops, while AC/DC's "Highway to Hell" blasted through a dusty stereo in the background. Nick Green, a Ranger who would be manning the turret machine gun on one of the Ground Mobility Vehicles (GMVs) for this mission, lifted a Kevlar plate carrier covered in various woodland camo pouches over his head and onto his shoulders, then a MICH helmet onto his head. He fastened the chinstrap, then lowered the PVS-14 night-vision tube to his eye, with one click to the right to turn them on and ensure they were operating correctly.

Satisfied that all his equipment was functioning properly, Green grabbed his shotgun—a Remington M870 loaded with double-aught buckshot. His shotgun was simply a backup in the event his M2 .50-caliber heavy-barrel machine gun went down during a firefight. He racked a shotshell into the chamber and made his way out to the vehicle staging area. In modern warfare, the sound of pea rocks crunching under combat boots and the smell of diesel in the cool evening air are often the omens of violence to come.

The drivers had already started the GMVs and put them through their own pre-mission checks. At this point in the war, most units didn't have up-armored vehicles fit to take on the emerging threat of improvised explosive devices (IEDs), so making sure you were ready for anything was of utmost importance. All that was left to do was check the radio.

"Gun Two, this is Gun One, radio check, over," Green said calmly into the headset for his radio. "Gun One, this is Gun Two, read you Lima-Charlie." Lima Charlie was military phonetics for "loud and clear"—his Ranger buddy responded with equal calm, despite the looming prospect of combat.

Before long, a column of GMVs and six-wheeled Pandur combat vehicles were rolling past the metal gate enclosing the secretive MSS, the cool night air filling their nostrils as the hunt began. It would take about an hour to get to the vehicle drop-off (VDO) point, but such was the hurry-up-and-wait nature of any military operation.

⚓ ⚓ ⚓

Ibrahim Awad al-Badri was a quiet man who was defined more by his pursuit of Islamic study than anything else in his early life. The son of a Sunni imam, al-Badri grew up in a lower-middle-class neighborhood in Samarra,[1] halfway between Baghdad and Tikrit—notable for the religiously significant al-Iskari Shrine and an ancient spiral minaret that punches into the sky from the desert floor.

Unlike his hometown, al-Badri was not notable in his early years. According to a *Newsweek* interview with Tareeq Hameed,[2] a former neighbor, he eschewed jeans and a T-shirt for a prayer cap and white dishdasha. He frequently showed disdain for any social activities that could be perceived as outside a strict interpretation of Islamic law. "For being so quiet, you could hardly hear his voice," Hameed said. "He was peaceful. He didn't like to chat a lot."

He did enjoy soccer, though, and by some accounts was a "decent athlete."[3] As a member of the al-Bu Badri tribe, he could claim to be a direct descendant of the Muslim prophet Muhammad (as could many others who lived in his neighborhood) and earned a bachelor's degree in Islamic law and theology while living in Baghdad in 1999. By the time the United States invaded Iraq in 2003, al-Badri was on track to earn his doctorate.[4]

Unlike Zarqawi, al-Badri did not show an early propensity for violence or crime. Unlike bin Laden, he did not come from a wealthy or powerful family. If it were not for the invasion, it is entirely plausible al-Badri would have lived out his days as a university professor or local religious scholar. With the exception of a possible stint in the Iraqi Army that nearly all able-bodied Iraqi males were drafted into during the Iran-Iraq War, al-Badri was not known as a fighter or warrior.

The one thing that is certain about al-Badri's motivations is that he was a student of Islamic law and texts and lived his life accordingly. In verse 2:190 of the Quran, it says to "[f]ight in the way of Allah against those who fight you and do not transgress. Verily, Allah does not like the transgressors." As the coalition kicked off the "Shock and Awe" bombing campaign and invaded neighborhoods and cities al-Badri called home, he likely felt compelled to follow the verses he had studied so carefully.

At some point, he started going by a new name: Abu Bakr al-Baghdadi.

Al-Baghdadi joined a local resistance group that was responsible for attacks on US forces and is also believed to have helped start the Ansar al-Islam offshoot Jamaat Jaysh Ahl al-Sunnah wa-l-Jamaah—a loose affiliate of guerrillas who had a somewhat tenuous relationship with Abu Musab al-Zarqawi. That affiliation with Zarqawi, however loose it may have been, is how he ended up on the target deck of US special operations forces.

"VDO, VDO, VDO," a voice crackled over the radio. The Rangers and operators quickly unloaded from their vehicles and moved down the block toward the target building. Local dogs barking in the distance, and the light slap of boots against the ground, were the only audible noises.

As the lead man on primary assault approached, his rifle's infrared laser moved up and down on the breach point, signaling the rest of his element to stack there and wait. A small explosive charge was attached to the door, and then a quick countdown over the radio commenced. These raids were well rehearsed and fluid for the special operators conducting them, one step moved quickly and seamlessly into the next.

"Breaching in three . . . two . . . one . . ." A push, twist, and pull on the M-81 igniter sent a near-instant signal through the non-electric shock tube and into the blasting caps embedded in the door charge, causing a violent chemical reaction and corresponding boom, cutting through the door and giving the assault force access to, hopefully, al-Baghdadi and his cohorts inside.

Al-Baghdadi was probably sleeping when the explosion happened. The Rangers and operators who entered and cleared the building he was in don't remember, as the mission to capture him was not particularly memorable. Like the other approximately one hundred raids the strike force conducted that deployment, he was probably yanked out of bed, and quickly zip-tied and searched before even having a chance to clear the fog of unconsciousness.

"Say again, one-three, over." The voice of the ground force commander crackled through the radio, direct yet monotone.

"Jackpot. We have Jackpot." The squad leader said, repeating his earlier transmission. *Jackpot* was the not-so-surprising term used to confirm the intended HVT was captured or killed during a raid. Al-Baghdadi wasn't the biggest catch—that was Zarqawi—but capturing one of the bad guys was always better than not. After all, if you're going to miss "mid-rats" (midnight rations—which was essentially lunch for troops who primarily worked at night), it might as well be for a successful hit.

After a short sensitive site exploitation (SSE) of the target building for documents and weapons, the call was made to "exfil." The Rangers walked their freshly zip-tied detainees out to the waiting convoy, loading them face-down on the vehicle's floor. Green, the turret gunner, smirked at al-Baghdadi's grunt of discomfort. *Better to be an uncomfortable terrorist than a dead terrorist,* he thought.

Intelligence drives operations. After the strike force returned to the MSS, their detainees and any materials collected off the target during SSE were turned over to experts who specialized in collecting and analyzing intelligence. First, the materials—usually hard drives, journals, and cell phones—were exploited and analyzed. Near simultaneously, interrogations of the new detainees would begin.

"The most cooperative they're ever going to be is right after they are brought in because they have the shock of being captured, and probably saw a couple of their buddies get killed, immediately followed by segregation." Lieutenant Colonel (Ret.) Charles Faint said during an interview about the ███████████████ ███████* in-country task force process for exploiting, analyzing, and disseminating intelligence. Faint served as a military intelligence officer while ████████████████,† including two deployments in Iraq, where he helped coordinate the task force's human intelligence effort.

According to Faint, detainees at a task force temporary screening facility were ████████████████████ ████████████████████████████████ ████████████████████████████████ ████████████████‡ "Because of the strength of our process and strength of our interrogators, we were able to really get a lot out of them," Faint said. "Then the utility of their information dwindled over time. So we had to get them out of there."

Indeed, with the industrial volume of task force operations in Iraq at the time, prisoners were held from a few days to a few weeks depending on the individual, before they either had to be released or "kicked up to the big house in Camp Bucca."

And that's exactly what happened to al-Baghdadi. At some point, he was moved to Camp Bucca in southern Iraq, named for New York City fire marshal and 9/11 victim Ronald Bucca. At its peak, it held as many as twenty-six thousand prisoners, according to the *New York Times*.[5] The prison is largely credited with being a breeding ground

---

* Name of unit redacted at request of DoD.
† Name of unit Faint was assigned to is redacted at request of DoD.
‡ Treatment of detainees redacted at request of DoD.

of extremism, mixing hard-line terrorists with young teenagers who were petty criminals at best.[6]

"So they're crowded, they're pissed-off, they're hungry," Faint said of the conditions at Camp Bucca. "All of a sudden they find themselves in this huge prison, where everybody there is angry, and they're already organized. It's like prisons in America—you have to do what you have to do to survive. Al-Baghdadi probably went into Bucca with an associate's degree in petty crime and came out with a doctorate of jihadism."

Camp Bucca was not just where new extremists were made, but where existing terrorists connected and expanded their network into what eventually would become the Islamic State. "So they come in and they make these connections and they build a network," Faint said, "then get back on the street and go back to war. That's probably what happened with al-Baghdadi."

According to the terrorism research firm Soufan Group, nine senior members of the Islamic State were imprisoned at Camp Bucca at some point.[7] Al-Baghdadi himself spent up to five years there, but reports differ on the actual date he was released. "Whatever connections he made were good enough to where eventually he rose to the top of the hierarchy," Faint said. "Yeah, he did pretty well in prison."

CHAPTER 5

LINGUIST IN TRAINING
PRESIDIO OF MONTEREY, CALIFORNIA, 2004

After graduating from boot camp, Shannon traded the cold, rocky shores of Lake Michigan for the sandy beaches of central California to immerse herself in language training at the prestigious Defense Language Institute (DLI) in Monterey.

Formally called the Defense Language Institute Foreign Language Center, DLI is the Department of Defense's premier institution for gaining fluency in a foreign language. Shannon arrived at DLI with her friend from boot camp, Molly Geraci, to learn alongside service members from all branches of the military as well as personnel from the Department of State and other elements of the Department of Defense.

Fluency in a foreign language was a key foundational element to

Shannon's new career in cryptologic warfare, and her assigned language, Modern Standard Arabic, was not easy to learn. Regardless of her natural talent, learning Arabic required the full sixty-four weeks at DLI, most of which was spent in an academic setting. The expectation upon graduation was that she would be able to read, write, and speak Arabic at a high level.

Fresh from boot camp and with their first taste of freedom, or at least free time, Shannon and Molly decided their hair was growing too long and their split ends were out of control. They needed a trim. They managed to escape the usually terrible haircuts most new recruits expect when joining the military, but were now overdue. Life in the military is significantly more difficult for female service members when it comes to maintaining nice hair that is also within regulation. Men can shave their head and be done with it, whereas women weren't allowed to shave their heads at the time, so there wasn't an easy way to stay within regulation.

They were still in their first few weeks at DLI, and didn't have off-post privileges yet, so a normal civilian hairdresser was out of the question. Their only option was the salon at the Post Exchange (PX). They didn't take appointments, so Shannon and Molly showed up and waited patiently for their turn in the chair, hoping the rumors about PX haircuts weren't true. Molly was skeptical about the idea to begin with, but Shannon reasoned they didn't really have a choice.

"Smith. Geraci," one of the hairdressers called out. Using their last names was customary on base. Shannon and Molly went back and sat next to each other in their salon chairs. Regret was already starting to take hold.

"Just trim the ends to just above my collar," Shannon said.

"Same for me, thank you," Molly echoed, feeling confident they gave the hairdressers clear instructions. This wasn't a major makeover, after all. Unfortunately, and very predictably for anyone who's ever had the pleasure of a PX haircut, the hairdressers had their own idea of how Shannon's and Molly's hair should look.

Before they could object, the sides of their head were trimmed up past their ears, forming a style somewhere between a bowl cut and a mullet. All Shannon could do was stare in the mirror, clearly furious. Molly sobbed quietly. They didn't dare make eye contact with each other.

Afterward, they walked out of the salon in silence, refusing to acknowledge what just happened. As young initial entry sailors on a small base, there weren't many options for fixing a bad haircut. They ducked into the main PX shopping area, which resembled a Costco but with people in uniform as the clientele, and bought everything that had anything to do with hair, not knowing what it would take to look normal again.

Their only saving grace was the military regulation that dictated they wear their cover—what the military calls a hat—anytime a service member is outdoors. They walked back to their assigned barracks room at Building 629 as fast as possible without drawing attention.

Molly and Shannon locked themselves in their room, showered, then spent the rest of the day trying to fix their hair. Molly sat on the floor while Shannon was on the lower mattress of the bunk bed. Curling irons, bottles of hair gel, mousse, hairpins, and any other fix-my-hair-now item they could get their hands on were strewn across the floor. They worked tirelessly to curl, straighten, slick back, and even spike up their hair in a last-ditch effort to avoid the ridicule of their fellow language students. They were both frustrated, and the tension in the room was palpable.

"Wow, great idea, Shan," Molly said.

"Well, where else were we supposed to go?" Shannon shot back. She wasn't a stereotypical girly-girl, per se, but hated the idea of looking stupid. They continued bickering like an old married couple, not mad at each other but at the situation.

But somewhere along the way, their frustration turned into uncontrollable laughter. Their predicament was just too ridiculous to take seriously. They continued working, one pin at a time, but it was an impossible task. Their hair was just too bad.

The next day in class, Shannon sat at the edge of her seat, chewing gum and drawing Arabic letters around the sketch of an Iraqi woman's face she made based on the picture in her textbook. She was thrilled to be learning a language that would allow her to contribute to the war on terror in a meaningful way.

"We want you to be able to speak spontaneously, and to speak for as long as you can," her language instructor said, with a noticeable Arabic accent. Approximately 98 percent of classrooms at DLI are led by instructors who are native speakers of the language they teach. The rest are military language instructors from across the services who attended DLI earlier in their careers but returned to teach. "You will run out of things to say if you run out of vocabulary. To build your vocabulary, you need to master the foundations of Arabic."

There are three schoolhouses at DLI: the School of European Languages, the School of Romance Languages, and the School of Middle East Studies—which is what Shannon attended. Her course of instruction was broken down into four semesters. The first semester focused on foundations, with the first six weeks being what DLI calls sound and script, but some students mockingly called it "scream and scribble" because Arabic can look like scribbles to the layperson. Shannon spent the majority of her time memorizing and learning to pronounce the twenty-eight characters of the Arabic alphabet. With the alphabet down, she started learning the root system next.

Arabic is a root-based language, with three-letter roots. There are some instances that have four-letter roots, but those are the exception. Every word is based on the root system and then a conjugation off that root system. Shannon needed to understand the root system and the specific conjugations so she could tell what any given word actually meant, while taking into account that the same word could have multiple meanings.

For example, the root of *bird* is also the same root of *airplane*. She was expected to deduce what the meaning was based on the context, and then what conjugation was being used, with over twenty different conjugations to consider. Context is what makes the Arabic language so difficult. Fortunately, this was an area in which Shannon excelled. Once she knew which conjugation was being used, she could figure out the word. Once she started to build up her vocabulary, it in turn helped her figure out the root system.

From there, Shannon learned daily baseline conversations of identification. She started with simple statements like *I am a female. I have red hair. I have blue eyes. That's a wall* or *that's a window.* She accelerated quickly from there.

Life at DLI wasn't all work and no fun, though. As Shannon entered her second semester, DLI's first-ever Navy Ball approached. The ball happens every year wherever Navy sailors are stationed to celebrate the service's birthday. It's steeped in tradition, with toasts to the fallen, a cake-cutting ceremony, and keynote speeches from high-ranking officers or notable Navy veterans.

Shannon was excited to dress up for a night of dancing, eating, and a break from the rigorous curriculum, so she bucked tradition and wore a bright magenta evening gown with a black scarf instead of her uniform. She quickly discovered that her choice of dress tricked senior leaders at the ball into thinking she was someone's spouse instead of a service member. Her fellow classmates could barely contain themselves as she posed for pictures with colonels and sergeant majors before swiping the wine off their table to bring back to her friends, who were too young to drink.

Per tradition, every attendee received some sort of commemorative item. DLI's Navy leadership chose a clear glass beer mug for that year's event. As Shannon, Molly, and their friends prepared to leave, they collected all of their commemorative mugs on one table. That's when a petty officer whom they'd had run-ins with in the past walked up and took Molly's mug in a brazen act of pulling rank in the most inappropriate way.

Molly was speechless, not believing what she had just witnessed. Shannon looked at her and realized Molly wasn't going to try to get it back.

"Okay . . ." Shannon said sarcastically, before disappearing into the crowd. She trailed the petty officer, watching as she stole more mugs from other people. An opportunity to get Molly's mug back presented itself, so she moved in for the grab before quickly walking back to her waiting group of friends before anyone noticed.

"Here," Shannon said, handing the mug to Molly.

"What?" Molly said, surprised.

"It's yours, isn't it?" Shannon said.

"Yeah . . ."

"Okay, let's go."

⚓ ⚓ ⚓

By the second half of the second semester, Shannon's instructors started covering conversation. She learned how to make a food order at a restaurant and how to ask for directions to a specific location. These were considered rudimentary language skills and largely demand-based, but important nonetheless.

In addition to the intense class schedule, students are still in the military and must complete daily physical training. Shannon excelled not only in the classroom but also athletically, and was consistently a top performer on the required physical training tests despite her reputation among the student body for having a bad smoking habit.

At DLI, the Navy competed against the Army, Marines, and Air Force every month in a two-mile race with eight people per team. Each team carried their detachment or unit guide and could not be more than arm's distance apart while running in formation, so participation required an exceptional level of fitness. Whichever team completed the fastest two-miler won. Shannon was always on the team.

Shannon was a beautiful redhead excelling in her language in the classroom, running a sub-thirteen-minute two-mile during PT, and constantly in the smoke pit with a cigarette in hand. The Navy cohort at DLI while she was attending was approximately 250 people strong, so everyone knew each other. She didn't know it, and certainly didn't want the attention, but she was being noticed everywhere she went.

She openly talked about how she wanted to eventually work in a special operations capacity, but was attending DLI before many women had a chance to prove their doubters wrong in combat, and eleven years before the conversation of women serving in combat roles gained any steam in the public zeitgeist. The idea of a woman going into special operations was outrageous to most at the time, especially among the rank and file. Male students often talked down to Shannon when she expressed ambition, mocking her with comments like, *Oh, yeah, you're going to be a spy? You're going to be Special Forces?*

They didn't appreciate that Shannon was following in the footsteps of legends who had paved the way in a past generation as women working in the world of intelligence, cryptology, and special operations.

In the specific field of cryptology, Elizabeth Smith Friedman was a pioneer.[1] Although her husband is often credited for their work in cryptoanalysis, Elizabeth was actually the one who introduced him to the crypto world. At the time, there was no code she couldn't break, regardless of language or complexity. It's impossible to gauge how World War II would have turned out, or how many more lives would have been lost, without her talents and innovations as a code breaker. She was inducted into the National Security Agency (NSA) Cryptologic Hall of Honor in 1999.

Virginia Hall served in the British Special Operations Executive (SOE) and the US Office of Strategic Services (OSS), both before and during World War II, as well as the CIA for many years after.[2] Despite being an amputee, Virginia established resistance networks across Nazi-occupied France, often working deep-cover assignments that required her to change her physical appearance and assume aliases. President Harry Truman awarded her the Distinguished Service Cross, the most prestigious award for valor after the Medal of Honor. She was the only woman in World War II to receive such an award.

Shannon and Molly knew the course was only going to get harder, and that more and more of any free time they had would likely disappear. So, while they still could, they went out some nights. On others, they stayed in watching *NCIS* and *Law & Order,* back when bingeing meant burning through binders of DVDs.

And then there were nights that took a more adventurous turn.

When Shannon and Molly were in Navy boot camp together, everything that had anything to do with being a new recruit was called a *ricky.* For example, the notoriously short showers that recruits take were called a *ricky car wash*, while using a hand to expeditiously smooth out a uniform was called a *ricky iron*. One night at DLI, Shannon and Molly opted to become "ricky ninjas" and wreak havoc on the campus.

To look the part, they dressed in solid black, one-piece bathing suits, black utility socks, black utility boots, and black ski masks—all issued to them in basic training.

"We look like bank robbers ready to go for a swim!" Molly said as they got ready.

Shortly after midnight, they ran toward the male barracks across the street, silent and armed to the teeth with tampons and maxi pads. It wasn't long before they hit their release point, intent on leveling a lethal display of ricky shenanigans at their fellow language students.

Shannon and Molly could communicate without words at this point. Shannon went up one stairwell, Molly took the other. They busted into the barracks and unleashed feminine hygiene products in every direction. Pads clung to doors and walls, and tampons were tossed grenade-style under doors and at innocent bystanders. Grown men shrieked and retreated from the brutal assault.

The ricky raid prank was a success.

Shannon and Molly retreated toward their own barracks, laughing so hard they could barely stay upright. Once they were out of sight of the male barracks, they walked to the common area at the back of their own barracks building. Several of their friends were still there, drinking and hanging out. Shannon and Molly joined them shortly before someone called out that the watch was coming. In most military barracks environments, a few service members are always tasked with keeping watch twenty-four hours a day. If there's a problem in the barracks, they are the ones responsible for responding.

Shannon remained calm, unfazed by the looming prospect of getting caught and facing punishment. Molly froze in panic, certain they were in serious trouble for the ricky ninja raid.

"What's going on here?" the watch said. He was another student at DLI, but took his duty seriously.

"We're just having fun, not a big deal, no one got hurt," Molly stammered, trying to explain the situation and plead their case to the watch. But the watch was dead set on holding the ricky ninjas accountable.

"What are you going to do about it?" Shannon said, interrupting the conversation abruptly with a cigarette in hand.

"What?" the watch said. Molly was in disbelief at what was happening.

"What are you going to do about it?" Shannon said, slower, as if to insult his intelligence. It worked. The watch didn't expect to be challenged—he backed down and walked away.

It rained later that night, and the next morning as Shannon and Molly walked to class, they listened as other students were perplexed by the tampons floating in the gutters and the maxi pads stuck to the sidewalk. The evidence of their carnage from the previous night was everywhere.

Out of an abundance of caution, the ricky ninjas never struck again.

⚓ ⚓ ⚓

In Shannon's third semester, the academic rigor increased significantly, with instructors moving into opinion and other more nuanced language. Opinion is considered a level-three language ability due to how difficult it is for nonnative speakers. For example, a native English speaker learning opinion in Arabic is like someone who doesn't speak English learning to use sarcasm. Sarcasm is everywhere in the English-speaking world, but it's not a universal aspect of language. In fact, some languages don't have a sarcastic level to them. For example, *The Office* is a hit in the United States but would not be received very well in the Arab world.

This phase of learning is where DLI starts to separate the high performers from everyone else—some students don't make it. Students who struggled during foundations tend to fall behind in a way that is almost impossible to rebound from. On the opposite end of the spectrum, there is a trend at DLI that indicates the younger the student, the faster they tend to learn a foreign language. Some of these particularly talented students are called "sponges," a term used for people who seem to have a natural talent for picking up language. Shannon was recognized as a sponge early on.

Although the students were learning in a safe academic environment, the stakes were still high. There are second- and third-order effects from not understanding how language, specifically colloquial and regional language dialects, affects the way a word is being said or the way a word is understood. In the life-or-death circumstances many students eventually find themselves in, the outcome can be disastrous.

Fortunately, Shannon learned her foundations well and built on them during the opinion phase. This was a stressful period for her, not because she was at risk of failing but because she wanted to be the best.

By the fourth semester, Shannon was fully immersed in the most difficult subjects, like politics and government. In the second semester she learned to say simple phrases like *America is a republic,* or *Iran is a theocracy,* but by the time she moved into the fourth semester, they were discussing deeply complex issues:

> *Hardline Iranians were deeply concerned about the Purple Revolution.*

> *Why are they concerned about the Purple Revolution?*

or

> *What precipitated the Sunni/Shia schism, and how does that affect today's Arab world?*

Language was constantly pumped into the students at this stage. Shannon was in a six-person classroom with native-speaking instructors on a teaching team usually five or six deep, allowing them to switch out every hour, or every two hours. This continued from 7:50 a.m. to 3:30 p.m., all while Al Jazeera news played continuously in the background. At the end of the day, Shannon returned to the barracks with approximately two hours of homework a night, with another three to five hours of homework on weekends. This rigorous pace was very intentional and resulted in the rapid progression of the student's language ability.

The students who do best are those who embrace their language. Shannon learned about the culture, customs, religion, geography, and socioeconomic conditions of countries that speak Arabic, and took part in opportunities for immersion training. All students were expected to participate in staff-led overnight field trips that placed them in realistic situations similar to what they may face during "real world" operations, such as negotiations at hostile border crossings or haggling in an open market. Shannon listened to Arab music and watched Arab movies or American movies dubbed in Arabic in her off time. Arabic music and movies helped her advance in specific dialects, and she grew to love them for more than just their educational value.

Modern Standard Arabic was the only version of Arabic taught at DLI at the time, despite it being the equivalent of speaking seventeenth-century English in the present-day United States. The thought process stemmed from the idea that MSA is the base of the Arabic language and that DLI-trained linguists could learn specific dialects—which varied from Gulf, Iraqi, Egyptian, or even North African or Somali dialects of Arabic—as the mission or their unit dictated.

For many service members at the height of the war, taking time to learn new dialects wasn't an option before they deployed, despite needing to use the right version of a language in real-world situations. It resulted in many American service members trying to talk to young Iraqis in the Arabic equivalent of Shakespearean English. The results were not good. For Shannon, putting in the effort to master dialect early was how she set herself apart from her peers, and one of the many ways she would distinguish herself on the battlefield in the future.

Shannon was a phenomenal linguist, and everybody knew it. She picked up the nuances of opinion, and Modern Standard Arabic came to her rapidly. By the time she graduated from DLI, she attained a language rating of 3-3-2, which meant she was rated as superior in listening and reading, and advanced in speaking—rare for a brand-new linguist straight out of basic training. In addition to her language rating, she earned an associate of arts degree in Modern Standard Arabic, which was awarded in October 2005, a month after she finished DLI.

But there's more to cryptologic warfare than language. Shannon's chosen field would require her to master highly technical disciplines like signals intelligence (SIGINT), cyberspace operations, and electronic warfare (EW). For some sailors, those skills are a one-way ticket to a dark office sitting behind a desk, poring over classified documents.

Although Shannon was perfectly capable of performing that aspect of the job, she wanted to work her way into a more "hands-on" niche. Her younger brother was a Marine fighting in Iraq, and although she was worried about him and hoped he would make it home safely, she couldn't wait to get in on the war herself.

CHAPTER 6

BAPTIZED IN SPECIAL OPERATIONS

BAGHDAD, IRAQ, 2007

After completing almost two years of training to become qualified as a cryptologic technician, Shannon was assigned to a desk at Fort Gordon, Georgia, where she was tasked with tedious, entry-level cryptology work in a windowless room. Her Fort Gordon assignment is regarded as one of the least appealing, most boring assignments in the career field. Although this was where all Arabic linguists in the Navy went right after DLI, it was the exact opposite of what Shannon envisioned herself doing in the military—about as far as she could get from those recruiting brochures she saw years before. In short, she hated it.

An opportunity to volunteer as a Navy Individual Augmentee (IA) in Iraq became available. An IA was a slot service members could volunteer for after a worldwide request for support was posted on an internal Department of Defense system. The assignment was sparse on details, but Shannon didn't care—anything in Iraq had to be better than what she was doing at Fort Gordon.

After she was approved for the assignment, she found out she would be deploying alongside Navy SEALs, assigned to ███████████████*, a special operations task force working alongside the fledgling Iraqi Counter-Terrorism Force to capture or kill high-value targets (HVTs). Some might say she was lucky to get an assignment like this straight out of her initial entry training, but it was Shannon who took the initiative to apply. She made her own luck.

The Air Force C-17 cargo jet dropped rapidly from the sky to avoid any rockets or surface-to-air missiles in the area, before leveling out and landing at Baghdad International Airport (BIAP). Despite it being at night, the dry heat of Iraq hit Shannon as soon as she stepped through the door of the jet. As she walked down the steps and her boots hit the tarmac for the first time, she looked up and out at the flight line. It was dark, and lights were kept to a minimum. She could hear hovering helicopters in the distance. *So this is Iraq . . . this is war,* she thought.

A line of Mitsubishi buses waited for her and the SEALs nearby. After a quick head count, they loaded the buses and drove directly to their secretive compound on BIAP. This was Shannon's first taste of the perks associated with deploying while attached to a special operations unit. She was with a SEAL team, and they didn't have to deal with the laborious in-processing that happens when a conventional military unit comes in, which often lasts days if not weeks. When a

---

* Unit redacted at request of DoD.

SEAL Team deployed, they needed to be ready to hit targets as soon as the next night.

After dropping bags off at her new home away from home, she was brought to the Joint Operations Center, or JOC. This was Shannon's first deployment, and that was obvious to everyone at the task force when she arrived. In addition to being young and clearly inexperienced, she was also something of an anomaly as one of the only women assigned to a special operations task force consisting of Green Berets, SEALs, and Iraqi special operators. Fortunately, there was a friendly face waiting.

"Shannon, I know you!"

Shannon looked at the man talking to her wild-eyed and crazy, still a little hungover from the Ambien.

"Clint Rowe," he said, introducing himself. "You were in my sister class at DLI. I was with Sierra, Ben, and Twyla." He not only attended DLI at the same time as Shannon, but came back later in his career to take a leadership position at the school. He had already been in the country for a few months, and recognized Shannon as soon as she walked in—the same girl from DLI who was running two miles in thirteen minutes and smoking cigarettes right afterward.

"Oh my god. What are you doing here?" Shannon said, shocked.

"I'm the team sergeant for this team, I'm gonna be working with you," Rowe said. They would work together for the next three months as part of a task force composed of a SEAL platoon and a ██████████████████████████* troop from the Fifth Special Forces Group, with a sister organization of the same composition inside the Green Zone that acted as an Emergency Response Unit (ERU). Both

---

* Unit redacted at request of DoD.

worked side by side with the Iraqi Counter-Terrorism Force (ICTF), which was the Iraqi equivalent of a high-level special operations unit.

The first big contingent of ICTF operators was created outside of Iraq. They initially trained at the King Abdullah Special Operations Training complex in Jordan, running their own selection monitored by senior Navy SEALs and Army Green Berets. They eventually moved back into Iraq to start going on real-world missions as part of an actual assault force, with American advisors who integrated with the Iraqis on every mission. The initiative was wildly successful, with those early efforts paying dividends in battles a decade later.

To round out the task force, there was an intelligence contingent that consisted of intelligence analysts, contractors, and a small tactical holding facility. Shannon was assigned to the cryptologic support organization of the intelligence team, which was a mix of both collectors and analysts. Some on the team performed signal intelligence reconnaissance while out on operations, usually with the sniper element, or with one of the assault troops. Others were tasked with building target packages, which required them to focus on patterns of life, making sure what was being brought in from missions was matching what they were seeing on the ground.

After the assaulters returned from a target, they brought all of their captured sensitive site exploitation (SSE) materials back to be processed and disseminated to the cryptologic support elements, who analyzed and disseminated their findings back to the assault force, thus starting the cycle all over again. Talking to the ICTF operators was Shannon's opportunity to stand out during that process.

It was 2007, and very few special operations personnel were able to speak to Iraqis in their native tongue. So Shannon taught herself human intelligence techniques and, already fluent in the language, would glean more accurate information for the ICTF.

Although the Americans and Iraqis slept in separate buildings, with four buildings for the Americans on one side of the JOC, and another four on the other side for the Iraqi quarters, they didn't have a chow hall. Mobile hot meals, called *mermites,* were delivered daily in containers from the palace complex, making it so everyone gathered at similar times to eat, work, and sleep. Like a middle school dance, the Americans usually congregated with their friends, as did the Iraqis.

Not Shannon.

She took every opportunity to talk to the Iraqi commandos in their native tongue. She could walk up to any of them and confidently converse with such ease that it actually threw many of the Iraqi commandos off. They became enamored with her because it was so rare to see a beautiful white American woman, and even more rare to hear them speak perfect Iraqi dialect. Her excellence was obvious to anyone who was watching. She was the only one who could do this because the ICTF was a completely mixed unit, which created a unique language environment. There were Shia and Sunni operators, working side by side with Kurdish and Christians, resulting in a mix of dialects and accents being used in any given conversation.

The Green Berets and the SEALs were beside themselves the first few times they witnessed Shannon at work, as they are typically the ones trained and responsible for rapport building through learning a language. But language proficiency had taken a back seat for many in Special Operations Forces (SOF) as the war in Iraq escalated.

Ali Hassoon, a Baghdad native who worked with Iraqi special operations at the time, heard other Iraqis talk about an American woman with red hair. Every person he talked to from both the Iraqi and American sides asked if he had met *Shay-Ma*—which was her Iraqi nickname. A legend grew around Shannon. Word spread so far that she was eventually tapped to translate for Major General Fadhil Jamel al-Barwari, a founding commander of Iraqi Special Operations Forces, who was regarded with fabled reverence.

Yes, Shannon could translate, but she could also analyze, and had a natural intuition for building excellent target packages. The Find, Fix, Finish, Exploit, Analyze, Disseminate (F3EAD) targeting methodology the task force used worked so fast that Shannon could develop a target, taking more than six weeks in some cases, dive deep into an HVT's pattern of life, line up where she thought they would be and why, then brief her conclusions to the ground force commander (GFC), who then used that information to inform his decisions about the next mission. Despite being brand-new and on her first deployment, she was quickly recognized as a subject matter expert, and unlike her experience at Fort Gordon, Shannon saw the immediate results of her work every time the assaulters came back from a mission.

It got to the point where if Shannon said a particular HVT was in this building, in this room, at this time, commanders could immediately launch an assault force—putting lives on the line—confident that her intel was solid and worth the risk.

Although her deployment began behind a desk as an analyst, the Navy SEAL lieutenant commander that she reported to recognized she was capable of more, and wanted her to start going out on target. It may seem like people in the military, especially those deployed to a war zone, would just intuitively know how to be ready for a real-world combat mission, but that is rarely the case. They need to be shown how to arrange ammunition pouches on their plate carrier, where the "bleeder kit"—or medical pouch—goes so anyone responding to an injury knows where to find it, and even what knot to use to tie down sensitive items like lasers and optics on an assigned rifle. Shannon was no exception, and had not received any formal special operations combat training at that point.

Rowe had already gone on some sixty or seventy combat missions, which made him the perfect mentor. The task force's operational tempo was so high during that deployment, it was not uncommon to go on a mission, then immediately be sent on a follow-on mission, then another follow-on. Under Rowe's tutelage, Shannon learned to not only set up her kit properly, but also narrow down the time frame she needed to get ready when alerted for a time-sensitive target (TST).

Shannon and Rowe were tied at the hip, and often alternated as the intel asset on combat missions. Sometimes Rowe would go out on missions resulting from information Shannon analyzed, and other times Shannon would go out based on Rowe's analysis. It became obvious to everyone around her that she was never going back to Fort Gordon. The trajectory of her career had been permanently altered; she had been baptized into the world of special operations.

This was all happening before cultural support teams— commonly recognized as the first women in special operations— were implemented, or anyone was talking about opening up combat arms or special operations roles to women in general. Shannon was becoming more than just a pioneer for females in SOF; she was creating a space for female special operators who fit a very unique niche within the special operations enterprise.

Shannon grew up quickly and adjusted to the realities of war while keeping up a facade that she was up to the task, no matter what. It's something many young service members go through, and often their only outlet to talk about their life and what might be bothering them are emails and letters home to friends and family. For Shannon, her confidant was her cousin Sharron Kearney.

From: Shannon Smith
Sent: Thursday, July 12, 2007, 10:22 PM
To: Sharron
Subject: RE: Hi Shar!

Hi Shar,

I've had a very long couple of weeks. I was in Basra for a week (by the Iran/Iraq border) and we were getting mortared constantly, I mean where I am now we get mortared about 5x a day but in Basra the mortars actually HIT stuff, so I couldn't take the gear off the entire time I was there and I think I lost 5 lbs in sweating alone . . . right now I think I'm about 110–115 but don't tell mom, it's just so damn hot and we run out of veggies and fruits and cheese and stuff all the time so what is there usually isn't that appetizing.

But Basra was still pretty cool cuz it's more laid back there and I didn't have to work as many hours and it's all Brits down there so I got to eat Brit food which was yummy after months of the left-overs our chow hall (which is a tent) gets from the big chow hall farther away (too far for me to go to) and listen to that accent all the time instead of just some of the time. . . .

I got back and a few days later 3 of our guys were killed and two were injured, and one that was killed was my friend and they asked me to give his eulogy and it was the most fucked up unbelievable thing ever and I still can't believe he's gone.

I was friends with the two injured as well, one is an interpreter from Morocco that taught me a lot and helped me immensely, the other is a SEAL named Kyle who writes to me 5x a day from the hospital between surgeries cause he's so damn bored! But I got to visit him while he was in the hospital here before he went to Germany, and it was so great to see him alive and blabbing away like usual.

Originally, they told me he died too. So I was just staring at him and smiling, seeing him with new eyes, because I thought he was dead but there he was, giving the nurses hell and saying "Yeah so that EFP went right through the humvee door, ripped it open like a can-opener, but the shit STOPPED IN MY LEG! I'm tougher than goddamn STEEL! WOOHOO!" and now he writes a lot, and jokes saying "Hey Shan this just in, I'm still not dead!"

So it's been a hard few weeks. But other than that all's well, just hanging in and trying to keep up with demands at work. We really work our asses off. My brain is getting tired. Well, I'm off to the gym—physical activity always makes me feel better. This sounds like a whiny letter. Well, I'm venting I guess. Better out than in, I hope you don't mind. Well, that's all for now. I love you and hope you are doing well.

—Shan

The word that Shannon had a knack for finding bad guys spread fast, and halfway through her deployment, it was not uncommon for other operators to ask her, "Hey, can you do that for us? What's your training? Can you work with these guys? Can you talk to the Iraqis for us? Can we bring you out on target to deal with females?"

She was eventually pulled to another side of the special operations world in Iraq at that time. It's not clear who found her, or how high up they had to be to have enough power to pull Shannon from her position.

Like most of Shannon's career, much of her work with this group was and is classified—and likely won't see the light of day for at least another decade. The citation for the Joint Service Commendation Medal she received for that deployment is the only unclassified documentation of her contributions. It describes how her efforts led "directly to the capture of hundreds of enemy insurgents and severely degraded enemy combat capability."

CHAPTER 7

JOE, MEET SHANNON

BAGHDAD, IRAQ, 2007

The morning call to prayer echoed through the streets, bouncing off every wall in Baghdad—including the one Joe stacked up on alongside five Iraqi soldiers. He looked the part of a Special Forces operator: tall, athletic, with dark hair and the sort of skin complexion that let him blend in almost anywhere in the Middle East. That's an advantage when your job is to work seamlessly alongside Iraqi special operators at the height of a civil war. He flipped the night-vision device on his helmet up, but it was that awkward time of morning: still dark but too light to use night vision. The radio crackled in his ear, a voice on the other end notifying him that all elements of the assault force were set.

Let's do this, he thought.

Joe lowered his rifle, rotating it away, so it hung by the sling on his left side. He grabbed the handle of the matte black breaching shotgun attached to his right, keeping his tired eyes focused on the door. This wasn't his first target; in fact, he couldn't remember how many times he'd performed the exact same ballet of violence at that point.

Hinges on the right, single-bolt lock on the left.

He shoved the short barrel of the shotgun into the door jamb near the handle. He exhaled, squeezed the trigger once, and quickly racked another round into the chamber, then again, obliterating the wood around the locking mechanism, causing the door to break free.

Almost simultaneously, Joe stepped back as his Iraqi partners flowed into the building just as he'd trained them. He'd already transitioned back to his M4A1 rifle and moved through the breach right as the last man crossed the threshold.

Find work.*

J oe Kent grew up in Portland, Oregon, and joined the US Army straight out of high school. He was initially selected for the Second Ranger Battalion before trading his black beret for a green beret and an assignment to the Fifth Special Forces Group. He deployed to Iraq in 2007—his fourth combat rotation.

His deployments to Iraq were every Special Forces guy's dream come true. He lived and fought with a small group of elite Iraqis that

---

* "Find work" is a common phrase used when training to clear rooms and buildings, denoting that the service member should never be idle during the clearing process.

his team hand-picked and trained to become special operators. They called this group the scouts, or recce (pronounced "reck-ee," common SOF slang for reconnaissance). Eventually, they gained renown as "the Mohawks."

They were a one-stop shop for hunting the enemy thanks to the access the scouts gave them, which they leveraged to collect their own intelligence and act on it. Joe and his team were given the autonomy to use whatever tactics they needed to get the job done, so they often dressed in Iraqi uniforms on raids or wore civilian clothing specific to the region and drove local vehicles to conduct low-profile reconnaissance and raids all over Iraq.

Raid after raid, the enemy captured or killed over and over; Joe realized taking them off the battlefield was the easy part because Americans were better trained and had far better equipment and resources than their insurgent enemies. The hard part was locating them.

For Americans, Iraq might as well have been the moon. They controlled the country in a military sense but did not understand the streets, alleys, slums, and mansions in Iraq's mosaic of tribes, politics, and shifting allegiances. Iraq was—and continues to be—an ever-changing hall of mirrors. Joe made it his goal to understand.

He felt a focused determination to use his previous experiences in Iraq to help the US turn the tide of the war, a sentiment that may seem naive after all the years of endless strife in the region. But the rush to "fix" Iraq seemed possible at the time, with almost cultlike levels of faith during those hectic days of the surge, when the US committed twenty thousand more troops to the war, and violence peaked.

His scouts uncovered several key smuggling routes that the Iranians used to supply Iraqi Shia militias with explosively formed penetrators (EFPs), which were a specific variety of IEDs capable of punching a hole in US armored vehicles with a molten piece of copper. At the time, this was a colossal intelligence win because the

EFPs had been wreaking havoc, killing Americans and making troop movements next to impossible. Many in the US government accused Iran of this nefarious activity but lacked the proof to justify direct action against Iranians in Iraq and their proxies, many of whom were members of the Iraqi government. In typical American government fashion, a meeting was called to determine the best way forward.

That meeting led Joe into the fortified Green Zone at an out-of-the-way location called the "Vill"—short for the Villas. According to the locals, every nice house in Baghdad was rumored to have belonged to some former Saddam regime boogeyman. Regardless of who owned it before the war, its new inhabitants had a mystique of their own.

The Vill served as the ████████████████████* nerve center of the war. Several US intelligence agencies were present at the Vill, as well as analysts from across the military. Palm trees provided shade for manicured lawns, and it even boasted a clear swimming pool. Life looked more like a country club inside the Vill, at least compared to the other, more rugged US military facilities spread throughout the country.

The combination of highly skilled people working in a high-stress combat zone and the Vill's creature comforts made it seem surreal to Joe. It was as if everyone inside had such an important role that no one was actually important. Everyone was on a first-name basis, and even the most serious matters could be discussed in board shorts by the pool. This stood in stark but refreshing contrast to the rank-and-file culture of the military but was a good fit for the special operations and intelligence communities.

Joe liked the people who lived and worked there and he enjoyed

---

* Entity redacted at the request of CIA.

more than a few drinks at the Vill's bar over the years, but the culture was a bit too laid-back for his taste in 2007. He felt that America had been at this too long and with too little success to enjoy drinks by a pool. The mystique wore off, and he was annoyed by buddies who spent too many nights at the Vill chatting up the intel women.

Joe couldn't shake the feeling of never having enough time, and guilt weighed heavy on his shoulders, as did the loneliness of constant deployments. Guilt from not preventing the deaths of his brothers and sisters in arms mixed with the emptiness of not having anyone in his life to confide in. Constant deployments made relationships near impossible; the guilt of not deploying made deployments irresistible.

Every day, every week, was an exercise in swallowing burning rage, anxiety, and pain. Iraq was in flames on all fronts, and Americans were being ripped apart daily by the melted copper erupting from Iranian-made bombs. The enemy was elusive, and Joe couldn't help but dwell on finding ways to reach out and strike back, to eliminate the entire threat . . . but he almost always fell short.

Joe was annoyed with having to stop what he was doing to attend another "interagency" meeting. *We should be blowing in the door of every Iranian "diplomat" in Baghdad, not going to the Vill to chat over espressos,* he thought. But this was as much a part of the job as performing direct action raids.

Joe stood in the corner of the palace room used as a JOC. He clearly was not like the others: they wore lightly used and recently laundered "tactical" clothes, while Joe wore faded black running shorts and salt from dried sweat draped across his faded T-shirt like a garland on a Christmas tree. Most in the room were pale from the lack of sun, while Joe, well . . . was it a tan or just a thick coat of Iraqi dust?

Everyone took turns giving their take on how to best exploit what Joe's team uncovered. Predictably, the special operations guys wanted to strike, the intelligence officials wanted to continue to collect information, and the diplomats lobbied to confront members of the Iraqi government. The meeting was a microcosm of how the entire war effort was going. It wasn't going anywhere.

Some kid from Ohio probably just lost his legs on the other side of town while we're sitting here arguing over semantics, he thought. His disdain for bureaucracy burned, and he could only take so much of this. *These people will solve nothing and be back by the pool relaxing before the day ends.*

Everyone eventually broke off into sidebars, so Joe excused himself to find their signals intelligence (SIGINT) analysts and pass off some information for them to check out, maybe see if it matched what the scouts were reporting.

As Joe rounded the corner, he heard a woman's voice discussing locations for Abu Abass, the leader of a Shia terrorist cell he was trying to run down. His eyes quickly homed in on the woman the voice belonged to. She was a gorgeous, slender young redhead wearing a faded New York Yankees baseball hat, with piercing blue eyes and a welcoming face. Almost instantly, nothing else mattered.

Wow, Joe thought.

He guessed the Yankees ball cap was part of an effort to play down her natural beauty, but it wasn't working. Her reddish-blond ponytail protruding from the back of her ball cap was somehow both elegant and casual. She wore a light red and white flannel button-down shirt with her sleeves pushed up and a pair of blue jeans with leather work boots. The SIG Sauer 226 9mm pistol in a black Kydex holster on her right hip contrasted her beauty. It snapped Joe out of his reverie and reminded him where they were and how serious this business was.

She stood with a map of Baghdad behind her while her computer monitor displayed Arabic text and map coordinates, addressing a few analysts from Joe's unit. He exchanged head nods with them and then stood to the side to listen to what the beauty in the Yankees cap had to say.

"Based on his pattern of life, we assess he lives in the al-Shullah neighborhood, in this area," she said, pointing to the map of Baghdad. She glanced up.

She made eye contact with Joe, and he held it.

His heart skipped a beat as she smiled at him like they were old friends. Joe caught himself staring into her eyes for a little too long, grinning as if he was relieved to see her. Sure, there was a spark of instant attraction, but there was also something new and more profound. Her gaze gave him a feeling of instant peace.

She held eye contact with him for a moment longer before turning her head back to the group of analysts, her face all business again.

"But I don't think that we have a complete POL, and I don't think that's his real BDL," she said, using acronyms for "pattern of life" and "bed-down location."

As she continued with her businesslike tone and demeanor Joe realized that he wasn't just enchanted with her looks; she was discussing an elusive but critical Shia militant his team was trying to locate.

"Why not?" Joe asked, wondering what her Abu Abass theory was.

Abu Abass's POL was the key to figuring out when and where he would be the most vulnerable. ███████████████████

██

██

████████████████████████████████████ * Piecing this information together was the combat version of stalking your prey.

---

* Description of methods redacted at request of the DoD.

The scout's reporting didn't match the SIGINT POL or BDL, so she had Joe's attention. In intel circles, SIGINT was king. It was much more binary than wily humans, especially Iraqis.

"Because from what I have read from his—I'm sorry, who are you?" she said, interrupting herself but still holding a smile. It was a fair question; Joe fulfilled several bad Special Forces stereotypes by barging in on someone else's briefing, asking a blunt question, and flirting with the pretty girl.

"Oh, I'm sorry, I'm Joe, one of the SF guys working the scouts."

She squinted at Joe a little. He couldn't tell if she was flirting or smirking. The Green Zone was like high school, with SOF guys and military contractors trying to out-macho each other for the attention of the few women working intelligence and support. For all he knew, she was cringing because there had just been some other SOF-type standing right there trying to tell her how awesome he was moments earlier.

"Ah, gotcha. Well, SF Joe," she said playfully, "Abu Abass is a bit of a player. His POL and BDL are consistent with what he tells his wife and where he leaves his phone, but his conversations with his girlfriends tell me that if we hit his BDL, all we are going to find is a pissed-off wife who wants to find him before we do."

Damn, she is something else, Joe thought.

"I agree with his POL and BDL being incomplete, and the girl-friends theory is new to me, but it explains the discrepancies," Joe replied, trying not to look too excited. Luckily, the affiliative humor surrounding the topic of terrorist marital infidelity was an easy way to keep the conversation lighthearted.

"Oh, I'm Shannon, by the way," she said, extending her hand. Joe reached out to shake it, and their eyes locked yet again. They both let out a nervous laugh. As they touched, there was an energy both could feel. Shannon moved just a little closer and let out an equally quick exhale. Joe noticed.

I smell like coffee—or maybe it was that sweet Iraqi tea I drank earlier? And cheap Miami cigarettes, Joe thought, suddenly very conscious of how Shannon might be perceiving him. What Joe didn't realize was that his eyes told a story to anyone who looked at him, a story he himself didn't know yet. He looked—and smelled—like war incarnate to anyone around him.

"Can you tell me about the girlfriend theory?" Joe asked. Of course he was interested in tracking Abu Abass, but found himself equally interested in talking with Shannon for as long as he could get away with it.

"Sure, check it out." She sat in her chair and faced her computer monitor toward Joe. She motioned to an empty chair next to her, which he happily accepted.

"We know the location of his phone is in al-Shullah; the problem is he is talking about going to Sadr City almost every night, and he's talking to two different chicks in Sadr City." She referenced the Arabic intercepts of his text messages and conversations displayed on her monitor.

Time to wow her, Joe thought as he stared at the screen. He was okay-ish at Arabic, considering most Americans put minimal effort into the language. He was frequently described as an Arabic speaker, even though he was far from it.

Joe identified a few of the locations in Arabic.

"I see what you mean. He's talking about his love in sector 30," he said, trying to simultaneously show off his Arabic and knowledge of Sadr City. As he read out loud, Shannon's eyebrows raised a little, and she nodded in approval.

"Right. Nice job with the Arabic, by the way," she said. Their eyes met again briefly before returning to the screen. She kept smiling while clicking on a new file on her desktop.

"So he's texting these two, Layla and Hibba." She pointed at their phone numbers on the screen. "I just don't have fidelity on where they are in sector 30."

This was where Joe's scouts could make a difference. Where SIGINT ends, human intelligence (HUMINT) often begins.

"Let me get my scouts over to that area, see if we can spot him and see where he goes," Joe said, hoping he could make that happen. It would not only get a terrorist off the street but also create more opportunities to talk to Shannon. This girl knew her stuff, and she was gorgeous.

There was something more, though. Joe didn't have time to contemplate his feelings too deeply, he had a mission to do, and the war would not wait. He was impressed by her drive to run down terrorists, but there was something else he could feel. *This is hardly the time or place for a relationship,* he thought.

But what was the alternative? Go home, find a girl from his hometown, and talk about the mundane, easy life in America? How the hell could he do that when a gorgeous woman like Shannon was right in front of him, hunting the same terrorists he was?

Experiencing a love-at-first-sight moment amid the palpable tension, anger, and senseless bloodshed of Baghdad's chaos was the last thing Joe expected that day. His life was Iraq and the mission, and he found he had very little in common with most women back in the States. He didn't think planning a family, or a future for that matter, was the smartest thing to do when a war showed no signs of slowing down. This wasn't some macho death wish, but he couldn't ignore that he'd seen countless friends either lose their marriages or step away from deploying because of family responsibilities. Joe wanted to stay in the fight and focus on being the best Green Beret he could be.

"If your guys are heading out there, I think they should start over in this area," Shannon said, pointing to a large building on the overhead surveillance imagery. "It's an apartment complex or hotel. I doubt his Sadr City mistresses live in residences."

Damn, Shannon is a thinker—no, a hunter, Joe thought as he looked at where she pointed while struggling to maintain focus.

"That's a great point." Joe returned his gaze toward hers. Every time their eyes met, he felt a pang of happiness.

"Thanks, just a guess, but it's at least a place to start." She leaned back in her chair, amused.

Without the pistol on her hip, Joe might have forgotten where they were and asked her out. Maybe he should have—or at least asked for her email address—but he could tell she was there for all the right reasons and wanted to get after the enemy just like he did. He got the impression that she didn't want to come across as a silly girl who was there just to hook up with commandos.

I come back here all the time. I'll probably see her again in a few days, Joe reasoned with himself. *Play it cool.*

"Hey, Joe . . ." Joe's teammate said as he rounded the corner of Shannon's cubicle. "We gotta roll soon, man."

Joe checked his watch. James was right. *Damn.* They had a meeting with their scouts in an hour, and the war wasn't going to wait for Joe to think of a slick way to tell Shannon she was the one.

A few days later, Shannon's knowledge of the target that Joe's team was tracking earned her a spot much closer to the fight. She was reassigned to a strike force in Baghdad, where she would prove herself as a more valuable asset closer to the fight.

CHAPTER 8

TRAILBLAZER

LITTLE CREEK NAVAL AMPHIBIOUS BASE, VIRGINIA, 2008

I t was an overcast October day at Little Creek Naval Amphibi-
ous Base, perfect for weapons familiarization training. Shannon
was the only woman in this Naval Special Warfare Direct Support Course class, and the only woman on the range that day. But
that's not what she was thinking about; she just wanted to get to the
part where she was sending rounds and burning brass.

"Point the weapon in a safe direction. That means not at your
buddy, nerds!" The SEAL providing this block of instruction had
no shortage of sarcasm, or disdain for support personnel for that
matter.

"Verify that it's clear and safe, then return your Mk 48 to condition four. Then open the cover and feeding mechanism and place

your dummy rounds on the feed tray. Then pull the charging handle back using an overhand grip, not underhand."

The SEAL paused for dramatic effect before repeating himself, "OVERHAND, not UNDERHAND!"

Yup, got it bud, Shannon thought. She was excited to be here, excited to be earning her spot in the special warfare community, but could barely stifle her own sarcastic inner monologue. She had worked with enough SEALs to spot when one was taking himself too seriously or carrying too much ego in his ruck. She figured it was the latter with this guy.

"Place the safety on safe, squeeze the trigger, and verify that the bolt does not go forward," the SEAL continued with his well-rehearsed monologue. "Push the charging handle forward and verify . . ."

Shannon crashed onto the special operations scene headfirst and didn't slow down once getting in. After Shannon returned from her first deployment, she made a quick pit stop in Garmisch, Germany, for language training—and a little snowboarding in the Austrian Alps—before volunteering for the new Naval Special Warfare Direct Support Course, which would allow her to serve in combat alongside Navy SEALs. She was the first female to attend, but she wouldn't be the last.

The course was a month long and involved timed, graded ruck marches, runs, swims, marksmanship, advanced training in close-quarters combat, and other activities required to serve alongside Navy SEALs in combat. Women on the SEAL teams were a new concept at that point, but Shannon set the standard and high expectations for other women coming into the program, finishing third overall in her class.

She was permanently assigned to Naval Special Warfare Support Activity 2 in Norfolk, Virginia, where she worked side by side with East Coast–based Navy SEALs. The SEALs were initially hesitant, not because she was a female but because non-SEAL support, in general, was a new concept at that time.

Because she was the first female to go through the direct support course and make it, some didn't believe she belonged there; they'd never heard of that happening before. The comments ranged from snarky to pure disbelief at times.

She's been through direct support?

Oh, no, she hasn't. There's no way.

But Shannon had the paperwork to prove it, and her performance at work always validated that piece of paper. It took a long time to get the course entered into her official records because people didn't want to deal with the ramifications of her having that qualification.

Every day after work, Shannon stepped off in a faded New York Yankees hat, brown T-shirt, black shorts, and earbuds to go for a run. She stayed quiet and humble, knowing actions speak louder than words and that she needed to earn her spot in Naval Special Warfare every day.

Shannon had been running her whole life and regularly used it as a way to show her physical prowess. Although contemporary special operators do a much better job at balancing cardiovascular endurance with weight training, the training philosophy was still very run-oriented in the late aughts. Anyone in SOF, from operators to support, was judged on their ability to keep up; dropping out of a run was akin to quitting. If you couldn't be counted on to keep up, how could anyone trust you to make it to target without falling out and potentially jeopardizing the success of a mission?

A typical training day might start with the East Coast SEAL teams Shannon was assigned to running on a sandy beach in combat boots before swapping those out for fins to conduct a half-mile swim in the Atlantic Ocean. After returning, those same boots would be put back on (now soaked from the ocean) for the return leg of the trip. Everyone, SEAL or not, was expected to hang for what many called the "Friday Funny" or "Monster Mash"—or simply the run-swim-run. Another typical run route took them from the Hot Tuna, a Virginia Beach restaurant popular with Navy SEALs stationed in the area, to the beachfront.

But the First Landing State Park route was particularly difficult, where the strong were separated from the weak. The first time Shannon did this route, she rode standard military Blue Bird school buses out to the unofficial trailhead, which led into First Landing State Park. From there Shannon stepped off on hiking trails that criss-crossed throughout the park, taking runners up and down hills and stairs and crossing bridges over the marshes and through the forest.

Andrew was a fellow special warfare sailor who worked in ████████████████████████████████.* When Shannon first showed up to the unit, he expected she could keep up just enough not to embarrass herself, thinking she looked like the type that was more worried about breaking a nail, never mind a sweat. The First Landing State Park trails were where Andrew first saw her in action.

He ran alongside Shannon, trying to make conversation as they climbed the tree roots that formed the steps up the hills in the park.

"The weather's great today, isn't it?" Andrew said. "Nice to get out into nature, right?"

"Yeah, nice weather today for sure," Shannon said, polite but unenthused.

"How do you like SA-2 so far?" Andrew said, using the short-hand for their unit. He was breathing hard and a bit surprised that Shannon didn't seem particularly fazed by the difficult terrain. He

---

* Unit redacted at the request of DoD.

wasn't the fastest in the unit, but he typically finished unit runs in the top quarter.

"So far, so good," Shannon said. Her replies didn't leave much room for a conversation to bloom. They continued with the small talk for a while longer. Shannon was trying to be polite but grew anxious that she would be perceived as more interested in talking than running.

"I'm sorry," Shannon said. "But I'm going to go ahead and start running now because I'm trying to set a pace for the next time I run this trail."

Andrew was stunned. She wasn't even breathing hard. The next time he saw her, she had already finished her cool-down and was casually stretching as the other runners rolled in.

Slowly, Shannon gained the respect and trust of the SEALs in her new unit. She was a true professional who wasn't afraid to step into any challenge. Her type-A personality and knowledge of trade-craft got her noticed in a positive way. It was an uphill battle, but she was making progress. Eventually she was selected to attend a special operations training course in Louisiana with a few others from her new unit.

Their class coincided with Mardi Gras, but they weren't allowed to go into New Orleans until after the festivities had already wound down—which also happened to be a week before they were scheduled to graduate. At that point, they were ready to blow off steam and have a few drinks.

They each started off with two Long Island iced teas at about 11 a.m. They proceeded to barhop from one location to the next, hitting everything from seedy hole-in-the-wall joints to swanky gay bars, doing their best to cure themselves of sobriety in the process.

The bayou barhopping continued well into the evening, and they eventually ended up at Marie Laveau's House of Voodoo on

Bourbon Street, drunk as the sailors they were. Inside, there were shrines of every variety adorned with skulls, beads, and more than a few voodoo dolls. Signs of varying sizes were posted everywhere, stating the obvious "nothing on the voodoo altar is for sale" or the more threatening "do not touch the voodoo altar or cops will be called." It was very clear the establishment did not want visitors to touch the voodoo altar—especially the drunk ones.

But Shannon considered the signs more like a suggestion than a hard rule. She picked up a small figure sitting on the altar, and before she could ask how much it cost, the staff started hysterically yelling at her. Shannon was startled and knocked over the entire altar, breaking several of the delicate voodoo figurines.

"Oh shit," Shannon said.

"You will all be cursed for nine generations!" one furious museum staffer yelled.

"Last bar!" Shannon's friend Birddog yelled, giving the signal that it was time to get out of there before police were called. The small group of drunk special operations sailors immediately executed their E&E—"escape and evasion"—plan. They quickly melted into the New Orleans crowds, never to be seen again by the mystics who allegedly cursed them.

Shannon and her teammates laughed the whole way back to base and made it through their last week of training without incident.

"Wouldn't it be crazy if this plane goes *Final Destination*–style and crashes and we all die?" Birddog said on their flight back to Virginia Beach. In this way, Shannon's voodoo curse had followed her.

"If we start to crash, the last thing I'm going to do is punch you in the face," another said, looking at Shannon.

"Yeah, seems fair," Shannon replied, blushing ever so slightly.

Fortunately, they made it home safely.

With the training course in Louisiana behind her, Shannon and her unit were about to leave for their next deployment to Iraq. As was customary, she and a few friends from work went out to a local bar in Virginia Beach frequented by frogmen for a few last drinks. AJ was a SEAL team leader out with his wife, and they were sitting at a table near Shannon's. His wife is Latina, and she overheard another woman in the bar, who was clearly not Latina, speaking Spanish perfectly.

"Who is *that*?" his wife asked.

"That's Shannon. She's new," AJ said, clearly impressed that she had caught his wife's attention. Shannon had successfully assimilated into her new unit and made a positive impression, even among the SEALs. Now it was time to go back to war.

BAGHDAD, IRAQ, 2009

Hey, the fuckin' women know something. Get them to talk, 'cuz this dude ain't gonna give up much," the SEAL said, motioning Shannon to a lifeless corpse on the ground with a caved-in forehead from the impact of the frogman's well-placed bullets. He was frustrated, tired, and dirty; he and his team had taken fire upon breaching the compound wall, and then had to fight their way inside in fierce close-quarters battle. Now the success of the mission was in Shannon's hands.

Even after a short but intense firefight, Baghdad can be a lonely place at night. The curfew left the streets empty, but the occasional rat-tat-tat of machine-gun fire could sometimes be heard off in the distance. Near-motionless silhouettes dotted a few rooftops, the faint outline of a ballistic helmet with dual-tube night vision devices attached created a unique outline against the night sky. Sometimes you could see a few tracer rounds bounce into the moonless night above the sprawling, ancient, war-torn metropolis. Maybe the errant rounds were from a troops-in-contact (TIC) on the other side of town or just some locals having fun—both were possible.

Dressed in desert fatigues and a plate carrier, rifle draped across her front, Shannon walked into a room the women and children had been corralled into. She immediately identified the wife of the deceased, who was visibly shaken and had likely watched as her husband was shot to death. Unfortunately for the wife, Shannon didn't have a lot of empathy to spare after seeing her brothers in arms nearly gunned down. But she had a job to do and needed to make her subject comfortable enough to talk. Comfortable enough to give up information that would lead them to their next target.

Shannon was with AJ and his platoon, a small group of Navy SEALs and Iraqi special operators assigned to a strike force in Task Force 17, charged with hunting Iranian thugs in the back alleys of a Baghdad neighborhood. It was her second deployment to Iraq, so the hot summer air that smelled like trash and expired humans was familiar, as well as a not-so-gentle reminder of what their fate entailed should they fail on any given night. These raids were so regular that it would be easy to become complacent, but Shannon took her work too seriously to allow that to happen.

She was tasked with producing some of the most valuable intelligence in the war, usually at great risk. This mission was no different—especially for Shannon. She was the lone female on the manifest with nothing but her wits and language ability to see her through the night. No other Americans had her talent with the local dialect, and the Iraqi operators were impressed with the way she was able to draw information out of people on target.

Rumors flew around the SEAL platoon prior to Shannon embedding with them. They were aware that some group of badass chicks were brought together to start a splinter cell, but assumed the worst. Then Shannon showed up, and the Team Guys recognized she wasn't the typical enabler or augmentee who gets attached in special warfare.

In the special operations world, people are often referred to as either shooters/operators or enablers. The former refers to direct combat positions, in this case the actual Navy SEALs. The latter refers to all other attachments who "enable" the shooters or their mission, which can range from doctors to intelligence analysts to supply personnel. Enablers almost never go through the same selection and training process that the shooters/operators go through, which can often lead to a lack of confidence in them.

The SEALs were initially concerned about figuring out the new rules and how to use their new enablers, but Shannon made it easy. They thought she was cool, and appreciated that they could have a normal conversation with her. She spoke the language of SOF, understood the niche references, and could generally blend in with the operators in the TOC or the ready room. Most importantly, they knew she wasn't deadweight on target.

Shannon could walk into a room of SEALs and immediately command their respect when needed. There was no flirtation given or received, and everyone knew she was all business. She established the standard for what was expected of enablers moving forward: Can you walk into a room with thirty-five dudes and not have gender be a thing? Shannon could do it, so that's what AJ expected of everyone else.

AJ and his fellow SEALs were all young at that point, though, both in age and experience. As a team leader, he had a little more interaction with Shannon, because she would have to brief her plan to the strike force leadership when they were preparing for a mission. The younger SEALs in the platoon didn't see that side of Shannon's work, and just knew her as the female who did SIGINT out on target. They didn't know the *why* of what they were doing in general, much less why Shannon specifically was so instrumental to their mission. Over time, they realized that not only did she do signals intelligence, but she was a linguist, knew multiple languages, and could pull information out of sources and detainees alike.

Shannon was no longer a young, naive sailor on her first deployment; she was an intelligence professional trusted to conduct some of the most dangerous missions in Iraq. She hit her stride at this stage of her career and gained notoriety throughout the special operations community for her prowess with language and willingness to go anywhere and do anything to contribute to the mission.

Having a female on target for a high-level HVT raid was almost unheard-of at the time, but she played a pivotal role by conducting on-target interrogations that led to follow-on targets. It's not an understatement to say that the secretive Task Force 17 was more effective (and deadly) because of her efforts, and her performance directly led to initiatives that resulted in a broader implementation of females in SOF for years to come.

Although their deployment was off to a busy start with frequent night raids, the task force was stood down for ninety-seven consecutive days after a Ranger made a controversial kill on target. After waiting for over half their deployment to start working again, and after it became clear the Rangers were on indefinite hold, AJ's platoon knew a change was needed.

They had developed good targets, but with the stand-down, there was nothing they could do to action them. They decided to move to Camp Warhorse and pursue a new line of targets. They took Shannon with them, knowing they would need her to develop all the new targets. She immediately got to work and was the driving force behind almost every mission the SEAL strike force went out on after the move.

One night, Shannon and AJ had a long conversation about her future in special operations.

"I don't know, do I stay in? Do I reenlist?" Shannon said. "I really think about going to the Agency. Or maybe the NSA?" She had the language capability, the technical and tactical experience, and time in combat to be competitive wherever she decided to go.

"You are too fucking talented to be sitting here doing this shit right now," AJ said.

"There's something else . . . there's an organization I can screen for," Shannon said, ███████████████████████████████████
███████████████████████████████████.* AJ had just screened for a ███████████████████████† himself, and they had been working together long enough that he had a good feel for what she was capable of.

"Dude, that has to be the move, that's the next evolution for you. You can't keep doing what we're doing here forever," AJ said—he could sense that moving up to ███████████████████‡ was her true calling.

They continued to talk about everything from getting a free-fall school slot to going to dive school. She asked him about the process of screening for ████,§ what it meant to him, and what it could mean for her if she went down the same path. Shannon was at the first of what would be many crossroads in her career. Their conversation made AJ realize how much he had taken for granted, and the liberties he had to attend advanced schooling as a male.

---

* Details about specific units redacted at request of DoD.
† Specific descriptions of units redacted at request of DoD.
‡ Specific descriptions of units redacted at request of DoD.
§ Unit redacted at request of DoD.

"In my opinion, you are the gold standard for females entering special operations, like, *the* gold standard," AJ told her.

Indeed, on only her second combat deployment, Shannon was responsible for and credited with "executing human intelligence operations in a very complex environment in support of a joint task force," and "expertly led an indigenous network producing many information intelligence reports, which were of national significance," according to her postdeployment awards.

Shannon returned home from Iraq at the end of 2009, back to her role at Support Activity 2 (SA-2). More women were being assigned to the Teams at this point, and Shannon was not only expected to assume more leadership responsibilities as someone who had been there, done that, but also to be a mentor as it pertained to women serving in SOF.

Brittany Burris was one of the women who arrived at the unit while Shannon was deployed. The first time they met was in a locker room on base. At best, it was a lukewarm exchange. Her first impression of Shannon was that she didn't like her and didn't want to mess with her. But after they talked a few times, Brittany realized their personalities were very similar.

Shannon and Brittany became quick friends over the course of the next year before their next deployment, leaning on each other as one of the few females in the unit. But while they were training and preparing for the next trip overseas, major events were happening that would change the course of the war in Iraq.

CHAPTER 9

TRANSITION IN IRAQ

TIKRIT, IRAQ, 2010

The war in Iraq was starting to wind down as the collective attention of the US military shifted to Afghanistan. In fact, all eyes were on Afghanistan, which was experiencing the deadliest year yet for American forces. Iraq was an afterthought, with a Status of Forces Agreement (SOFA) in place and an aggressive plan to draw down American forces.

Martin Huggins and his fellow Rangers from First Platoon, B Company, Third Battalion, 75th Ranger Regiment sat around the empty, dust-covered Tikrit Joint Operations Center . . . or what was left of it anyway. The air felt humid and mildewed, like a box of linens left in a basement for years. Half of their company was in Iraq, the other half in Afghanistan. It was April 17, 2010, and they had just flown in from Baqubah. All they could do was wait to hear an update on the mission in a familiar game of hurry up and wait.

Staff Sergeant Jimmy Patton, a squad leader in First Platoon, waited nearby with a fat pinch of Copenhagen in the lower-right of his bottom lip. Despite his maturity and combat prowess, he still looked very young at only five foot seven and 135 pounds.

"Oh maaaannnn!" His kidlike voice echoed through the JOC, followed by his telltale giddy laugh as he joked with a fellow Ranger. He was the son of a command sergeant major in the 101st Airborne Division and considered a rising star in the regiment who often carried the entire platoon on his back.

They eventually received word the mission was a go, and that they'd be going after the few high-value targets left in Iraq: Abu Ayyub al-Masri (AAM) and Abu Umar al-Baghdadi (AUB)—not to be confused with the future leader of ISIS, who also went by al-Baghdadi. They were the leaders of the deadly Islamic State of Iraq (ISI). Their platoon would be the main effort, with another platoon from A company supporting their efforts with Stryker combat vehicles. The target building was a rural farmhouse in the middle of nowhere, surrounded by other farmhouses on acres of farmland.

What the fuck are we doing here? Huggins thought to himself. Nobody actually knew what was going on, except for the leadership. The one thing they did know is that they wouldn't have ■

████████████████████* flying them into the objective that night.

The Rangers were making do with a conventional Army aviation unit. Although the Army has many experienced and capable pilots, they have inexperienced pilots too, and sometimes the Rangers didn't

---

* Descriptions of specific units redacted at request of DoD.

know which variety they would get. When you're used to flying with the best helicopter pilots in the world on a nightly basis, any downgrade feels significant.

Around 8 or 9 p.m. local time, they finally received the green light and loaded buses that took them over to their helicopters on the flight line. The temperature started to drop. A slight drizzle turned into a steady rain, making conditions less than ideal for the looming mission.

Five UH-60 Black Hawks were waiting for them on the flight line. The birds started to spin up, the Rangers loaded on, and the crew chief shut the doors. With the weather souring and pilots they didn't have one hundred percent confidence in, it was already feeling like a mission ripe for something to go wrong.

Jimmy Patton was in charge of Third Squad at the time and responsible for the primary assault on the objective. He loaded into the lead bird with his squad, piloted by someone who allegedly didn't have very much nighttime flying experience. They wouldn't be "landing on the X" or doing any other complicated maneuvers that night, though. In fact, the helicopters were planning to drop them off at least six kilometers away from the target building in what is referred to as an "offset infil."

They lifted off, rotors beating against the night sky as they moved toward the target building. The cold, wet wind forced its way into the cracks of the closed doors. The rain steadily intensified, which reduced everyone's visibility. Their night-vision goggles were nearly useless, as they fogged up with the rapid changes in temperature.

Once they reached the helicopter landing zone (HLZ), Huggins noticed that it took the pilots longer than usual to land. None of the pilots could see the ground because of how foggy it was. All they could do was slowly lower the aircraft and wait for a sign they hit the ground. As the helicopter descended, Huggins heard a loud, crashing sound, and noted lights and sparks in the distance. He knew something wasn't right, but with visibility nearly nonexistent, he'd have to wait to find out what was going on.

Maybe the first bird was being shot at or something? Huggins thought. Huggins and his squad exited their helicopter as soon as it touched down, quickly moving about fifteen feet away to pull security while waiting for the helicopter to take back off. They dropped down into the prone position, their night vision still limited by weather, and listened to the rotors of their UH-60 Black Hawk accelerate as all the helicopters prepared to take off simultaneously. Seconds later, they were up and off, disappearing into the fog.

Finally, Huggins thought, as his uniform and gear absorbed the cold rain. Huggins could hear yells and screams in the distance. His platoon sergeant was yelling into the radio, but it kept going in and out. All he could catch was "burned down," or something like that. He couldn't make out the rest of the transmission between the radio cutting out and the screaming when it did come through.

After forty-five minutes of pulling security, they learned the lead bird had landed so hard that it bounced and the rotor caught the ground, causing it to violently rotate and crash-land.

Unknown to Huggins at the time, Staff Sergeant James R. "Jimmy" Patton was killed instantly after his safety line failed, throwing him under the crashing helicopter. He was an Army Ranger who died in pursuit of the number one terrorist in Iraq, five days before his twenty-fourth birthday. Back home, his young wife and their baby daughter waited for him.

The crash happened at 10 or 11 p.m. local time. The rest of his squad was injured, requiring immediate medical evacuation. The twelve-hour mission had just begun. About an hour later, everyone who needed medical attention was evacuated, and the Rangers prepared to continue their mission. The target was simply too big a catch to turn back on, even after such a catastrophic start.

Intelligence relayed that their target, AAM, knew something was up. Both terrorist leaders were smart people and knew exactly what they were doing after years of evading capture. At this point in the war, they knew that cell phones were trackable. This increased the difficulty in narrowing down their exact location. The Rangers were facing a myriad of rural farm properties that had anywhere from five to ten acres surrounding them.

The Ranger platoon moved from one house to the next, methodically clearing each building. At one house they started taking fire, so they returned fire, and threw a grenade that blew up a car. If the entire area didn't already know they were there, they did now. They spent an hour and a half fighting at the house, which ended up being a nobody. Just a local trying to protect his house, which was all but destroyed in the process.

The Rangers continued walking back and forth through freshly plowed fields of dirt that turned to mud in the rain, searching for the house that held Jackpot. They felt they were getting closer, but no luck yet as they trudged along. Their heavy combat equipment weighed them down, their uniforms drenched in sweat and rain. No choice but to suffer in silence—they kept going, covering mile after mile, often feeling like they were walking in circles.

Finally, they received a promising intel update about a house that very likely held Jackpot. For the Rangers, their renewed motivation was as much about getting the mission over with as it was capturing or killing one of the top terrorists in the world.

They assaulted and cleared the house, but it was empty. There was nothing inside the house that looked any different than any of the other houses they hit that night. The Rangers laughed it off, trying to keep spirits higher than the situation probably warranted.

It was approximately five o'clock in the morning by the time they left that house, and hours had gone by since the crash. The sun was starting to emerge, which meant locals would be starting their day soon—more people for the undermanned platoon to keep track of, and more people who could potentially alert insurgents to their location. The temperature rose with the sun, burning off the fog. The brutal Iraqi heat gives no quarter.

The never-ending patrol was due for something bad to happen again. Everyone was miserable. At some point, as they walked the Iraqi farm fields, word circulated around the platoon that Staff Sergeant Patton had died in the crash on infil. There wasn't a formal, definitive radio call to announce his death at that point in the mission—the news spread more like a game of telephone. Whoever was closest to the crash started talking, and the word spread. Still, the Rangers put one boot in front of the other and continued pushing toward the next objective.

At approximately seven or eight in the morning, the Rangers were directed back to a house they had already hit hours before. As they approached, machine guns erupted from the windows, sending a wall of lead toward the strike force and driving them to take cover in the mud. There was chaos over the radio, with different elements calling out distance and direction of the gunfire and directing their elements accordingly. It was immediately obvious this was no disgruntled farmer.

Their fellow Rangers from A Company started reinforcing their position, pulling Strykers closer and surrounding the building in a kind of half-moon, before letting loose with their own heavy machine guns in an onslaught that seemed unsurvivable.

The Rangers on the ground backed off, as their position was completely exposed in an open farm field with no cover. The combat was fierce. Machine-gun fire was traded back and forth between the rural compound just outside of Tikrit, Iraq, and the Army Rangers who surrounded it. The intense fight confirmed the Rangers' suspicions that this compound was the meeting site of one of the most important leaders left standing from the war in Iraq.

Thirteen hours later, after walking what seemed like twenty miles over freshly plowed farm fields and clearing multiple houses, they had found what they were looking for. The sun was up, the rain had stopped, and the exhausted Rangers were channeling their hate and frustration in the direction of the top two most-wanted terrorists in Iraq they were sent to capture or kill the night before. Judging by the volume of 5.56mm and 7.62mm ammunition and rockets impacting the home, it seemed like the latter was more likely.

All of a sudden, explosions from inside the target building pierced the afternoon air. Some Rangers initially thought someone called in an air strike, but that was never an option due to the possibility of noncombatants inside. The explosions came from suicide vests initiated by the terrorists inside; it didn't matter to them that they were with their families.

The Rangers waited for at least ten minutes before moving toward the now-destroyed house. Whenever IEDs are in play, including suicide vests, it's wise to hold off moving up too quickly as there may be secondary explosions.

Finally, multiple Strykers arrived at the target building, now half-collapsed. Two squads moved in and cleared the building. The Rangers saw where the explosion cut through the terrorists' bodies, leaving a gruesome scene behind. They found the heads of the number one and number two most wanted men in Iraq separated from their bodies, with a V-shaped chest and guts dangling under their necks.

In spite of the fact they had subjected themselves to the effects of a detonated suicide vest, their disfigured faces were still recognizable. The call for "Jackpot" was sent over the radio, confirming that al-Masri and al-Baghdadi were indeed the people killed during the attack. Although they were considered to be the most important high-value targets taken out since Zarqawi's death in 2006, it came at a great cost.

Shortly after the confirmation, even with the house caving in, the Rangers found a toilet in the bathroom that didn't look right. Once they pulled the toilet up, they saw a low-ceilinged crawlspace. They found the terrorist's wives and kids, six or seven people in total, hiding inside. They had been hiding there the entire time.

Huggins helped to secure one of the wives, who kept trying to fight. She wasn't crying—she looked cold and emotionless as she struggled. She tried to steal a Ranger's pistol, but fortunately, they prevented her from drawing it from the holster. The Rangers moved out to prepare for exfil back to their base after a marathon mission.

"It was April 18th, 2010, and the day was young," Huggins would later write in a diary entry. "Sitting around the empty and dusty, what used to be, Joint Operations Center waiting . . . waiting to load the American-flag-draped casket onto the C-17 bird to fly back home. Jimmy was going home. It was one of the worst, worst fucking days of my life."

"Their deaths are potentially devastating blows to al-Qaeda Iraq," US vice president Joe Biden said while speaking to reporters about the operation. He added that the successful operation "demonstrates the improved security strength and capacity of Iraqi security forces. . . . The Iraqis have taken the lead in securing Iraq and its citizens by taking out both of these individuals."

Little did anyone know that the deaths of ISI's leaders that day would accelerate the transition of one of the most violent men in human history, Abu Bakr al-Baghdadi, from obscurity to the leader of ISI—which would eventually become ISIS. It all happened while the American military was largely focused on Afghanistan.

Within weeks, al-Baghdadi was already exacting his violent

revenge with coordinated attacks on both police checkpoints and regular civilians across Baghdad. These bloody assaults were a harbinger of what was to come.

VIRGINIA BEACH, VIRGINIA, 2010

Kyushu Japanese was easy to miss if you weren't specifically looking for it. The small sushi restaurant was located across the street from a mobile home park, on the corner of a strip mall that included a tailor shop, hair studio, and multiple diners. Cassandra, one of Shannon's best friends growing up, was in town for work and had been tipped off that this restaurant was one of the best-kept secrets in Virginia Beach. So, she and Shannon made a plan to rendezvous for lunch.

The two kept in touch over the phone and email, but an in-person meetup only happened once every few years. Every time they got together, they had a lot to catch up on.

"Shan, I can't imagine what it's like to be you, to be just getting back from some far-off place I'll probably never see," Cassandra said. "It's just . . . it's the weight of everything right now. It's so hard."

Shannon was single with another deployment to Iraq coming up, and Cassandra was a mother of two going through a divorce. As they ate sushi rolls and talked, it seemed like they were in polar-opposite places in life.

"The grass is always greener on the other side, Cass. I know the divorce is hard, but I dream about what you already have," Shannon replied. "I haven't been able to settle down, I haven't found *the one*, and I don't know if . . . with this lifestyle . . . if I will ever get to be a mom and have kids like you."

"You're right about the grass seeming greener. It just feels like you have the freedom to go anywhere at any time, on your own schedule," Cassandra said. "I don't see that happening for me anytime soon."

"Well, I don't know if the Navy would agree with you about me going anywhere, any time! But yeah, I love my job, my career. But . . . I want to put roots down. I don't know if that will ever happen for me."

IRAQ, 2011

We have a high confidence grid verified by both SIGINT and HUMINT." Shannon delivered her findings to her peers, a platoon of Navy SEALs who were already jocked up and ready to roll prior to the concept of the operation, or CONOP, planning briefing.

Shannon was deployed to Iraq for the third time in 2011, during a period of transition, with US forces drawing down and leaving the country in the hands of American military contractors and the Iraqi government while the Islamic State, or ISIS, gained momentum. As an intelligence professional, Shannon was skeptical of the path the US had chosen in Iraq, and it was more than news on the television to her; she had friends across the country who would be impacted, many of them negatively.

But with the war in Iraq ending, where else could Shannon go to contribute to the fight against terrorism that now defined her in so many ways? Or were her fighting days over?

"Is this shithead actually worth our time, Shan?" The SEAL was no stranger to fruitless raids and missed opportunities. With the war winding down, he wanted to make the most of his time while the gettin' was still good. "I'd hate to be out lookin' for this dude and then have one of our bigger objectives pop."

"The thing about ███████████████████ is that he is closely associated with ██████████████████, and although we don't have anything but rumors for ████████████, we have two different sources that swear they meet on the first Thursday of every month. Guess what today is?"*

"Surf n' turf night at the chow hall?" One of the SEALs in the back of the room could always be counted on to provide levity, whether it was needed or not. The rest of the room laughed in that tired, I-need-another-Rip It energy drink sort of way that was normal for a 1600 daily meeting-turned-mission briefing. Shannon couldn't help but smile.

"Look, guys, worst-case scenario, we definitely take ███████████████ off the board, and that's a win any way you cut it. Best-case scenario, we get both ████████████████████████."†

That's when the strike force commander spoke up. "Let's go, boys, war ain't gonna be around forever. Might as well go give the taxpayers their money's worth."

The night's GRGs, or grid reference guides, had already been printed out. Everyone took one and slid it into their forearm quarterback pad for easy reference. Each sailor on the manifest checked their night-vision devices, completed radio checks, and slid a magazine into their rifle as they walked out the door toward the flight line. At this point, it was always assumed Shannon would accompany them on target—she was too valuable to leave behind.

Not much later, three Black Hawk helicopters lifted off with the strike force on board and raced toward the objective. Tonight would be fun. Tonight they were landing on the X.

---

* Names of objectives and high-value targets redacted at request of DoD.
† Names of specific targets redacted at request of DoD.

About twenty minutes later, the crew chief inside Shannon's bird shouted, "Thirty seconds!" over the roar of the rotors, while holding up his two fingers in a pinching motion, in case someone couldn't hear his warning.

Thirty seconds out. Find your safety line, make sure your NODs are adjusted, and get ready to rock.

Moments later, the helicopter flared and landed about fifty meters from the target building. The SEALs sprinted toward the objective; speed, surprise, and violence of action are the keys to success on these types of missions. Shannon ran behind them, keeping close.

Infrared lasers bounced on the front door.

A light flicked on inside the building. The occupants knew they had company.

The SEALs mechanically breached the door with a donker—a portable battering ram—and flowed in, moving through the target building with a fluidity that comes with hundreds of hours of practice as a team.

As one SEAL buttonhooked into the prayer room, a teammate right behind him ran into a military-age male. Without hesitation, he took him to the ground and put a knee in his back. The other Team Guy in the room was doing the same with another.

The radio call went out moments later: "Objective secure."

Shannon was already making her way through the breach point, anxious to see if her analysis was correct.

"Hey, Shan, back here in the prayer room. Pretty sure we got muthafuckin' Jackpots one and two!"

Shannon rounded the corner and saw two of her friends standing there with two zip-tied detainees. She didn't need to take more than a quick glance at both to know they got both of their targets. *Fuck yeah*, she thought.

It was a good night, but not as good as a few nights prior when they'd hit thirteen objectives in one night. That was going to be a hard night to top, she knew. Mostly because she was aware this might be her last deployment to Iraq.

"I can report that, as promised, the rest of our troops in Iraq will come home by the end of the year," President Barack Obama said in a briefing given at the White House on October 21, 2011. "After nearly nine years, America's war in Iraq will be over. . . . The last American soldier will cross the border out of Iraq with their heads held high, proud of their success and knowing that the American people stand united in our support for our troops."

For Shannon, it would be a good, last deployment to the country in which she had spent so much of her adult life living and fighting. It was the best troop she was ever a part of. She was recognized for her "understanding of insurgent networks coupled with her impressive leadership. . . . She deftly managed several networks and extensive sub-networks producing numerous high-level intelligence reports providing critical information to special operations commanders targeting militia groups. Her dedication resulted in several operations that captured high-value individuals and disrupted well-known insurgent networks."

This wouldn't be her last adventure, though. She had recently volunteered for an assessment and selection course, which she would attend later that year. If she was successful, she would join the ranks of a ▮▮▮▮▮▮▮▮▮▮▮▮▮▮▮▮▮▮▮▮▮▮▮* that was regarded as the pinnacle of clandestine intelligence operations in the special operations community.

This selection would not be easy. There are no published standards and no real way to prepare for it. Both males and females can

---

* Description of specific unit redacted at request of DoD.

attend, and there is only one standard—*the* standard—to pass and be selected for further training. Shannon had seen SEALs try out and come back empty-handed—this was a no-joke program. But she was confident that she would crush whatever they threw at her.

Shannon was also recognized as the Department of Defense's Linguist of the Year. It was a prestigious honor and a meaningful validation of her skill, proof that she was playing on a different level than most others in the intelligence community.

There are perks associated with being recognized as the Linguist of the Year. For starters, Shannon was able to pick somewhere to go for an intensive period of language immersion after she returned from Iraq. She chose both France and Spain. She had plenty of practice with Arabic at this point but thought her French could use a little work, and it had been a while since she'd had a good conversation in Spanish. Living abroad was the perfect break from the military, as well as a chance to practice what she loved. Shannon didn't just speak foreign languages because it was required for a job—she was genuinely interested in foreign cultures and relished any opportunity to travel abroad and talk to people in their native tongue.

In Spain, Shannon lived in an international house in Barcelona with roommates from all over the world. She took full advantage of her time in the country, visiting cultural sites and museums, eating tapas, and drinking Spanish wine with the friends she made. When she came home, she was fully fluent, energized, and ready for her next evolution: another deployment and a chance at moving up to the "varsity team."

CHAPTER 10

SELECTION

BAHRAIN, 2011

In an increasingly complex war on terror, on-the-ground tactical experience and mastery of multiple Arabic dialects were needed to unravel terrorist and extremist networks sprouting up all over the Horn of Africa, the Arabian Peninsula, and countries like Iraq, Afghanistan, Iran, and Pakistan. The stakes were high: ships were seized and held for ransom by Somali pirates, and hostages were taken in Afghanistan, to name just a few issues.

This is how Shannon found herself deployed once again, but this time to Bahrain. Although this was not a combat deployment, it was every bit as important to the overall mission of fighting the spread of terror groups. Shannon was performing at the strategic level, which meant more responsibility and a broader mission. On previous deployments she advised commanders at the company and battalion levels. On this deployment, it was common for her to brief everyone from the Fifth Fleet commander to the US ambassador for a variety of different nations in the region. This assignment was indicative of the increased trust in Shannon due to her extensive experience in the field, but she viewed it as nothing more than routine.

Typically, someone in the intelligence community will work solely on the "big picture" assignments, or they'll work exclusively on the ground at the tactical level. But Shannon was unique: she knew what the shooters needed and what their perspective was, but could swap out her fatigues for a suit and brief high-level policymakers.

This deployment was more than another trip overseas, though; Shannon was at a crossroads in her career. She was twenty-eight years old and approaching the end of her enlistment with nearly eight years in the Navy. She couldn't imagine how a job this demanding would work if she wanted to start a family someday.

While in Bahrain, she was exposed to a dramatically different job, one that would allow her to have a family while still serving her country: that of a Foreign Service Officer (FSO) in the US State Department. She saw that FSOs were able to work overseas but bring their families with them. It was a stable lifestyle and a career that checked all the right boxes.

According to the Department of ▇▇▇▇,* the mission of a US diplomat in the Foreign Service "is to promote peace, support prosperity, and protect American citizens while advancing the interests of the U.S. abroad."

On its face, it was an attractive option for Shannon.

As a Foreign Service Officer, Shannon would represent the

---

* Specific department redacted at request of CIA.

United States in a way she had never done before. She would be hanging up her uniform for a life that would provide more balance but still offer adventure and the chance to immerse herself in foreign cultures. Most Foreign Service Officers have the opportunity to be stationed at more than 270 diplomatic locations, usually embassies and consulates, around the world. Could she really hang up her Navy uniform for the last time though?

The most significant change for Shannon would be switching from the Department of Defense to the Department of State, from defending the nation with what oftentimes included violence, to helping "shape a freer, more secure, and more prosperous world through formulating and implementing the President's foreign policy, while supporting and protecting American interests abroad."

In her heart though, the desire to be a Foreign Service Officer was never more than a plan B. The allure of working at the highest levels of special operations remained. Immediately following her trip to Bahrain, she reported for the screening and selection course for ███.* It would take everything she had to get selected.

[CLASSIFIED], 2011

Once you reach the final point, drop your ruck and stand by for further instruction," said Kevin, one of the cadre running selection.

"How long do we have to reach the final point?" asked one of the course's hopefuls.

---

* Description of specific unit redacted at request of DoD.

"It will take you as long as it takes you, the ruck weighs what the ruck weighs, and if you don't make it, we'll wish you luck in wherever your military career takes you. Any questions?"

Kevin doesn't seem like he wants any questions, Shannon thought.

If there was anything Shannon learned during her time at the Naval Special Warfare Command, it was "all you could do was your best" and "never quit." Don't worry about the rest; it'll work itself out if you'd prepared properly. And so it did.

Shannon's friends knew she wasn't professionally satisfied with Support Activity 2 anymore, not after she'd discovered there was another rung on the monkey bars. She had charted out a clear path in her head on what the next challenge would be.

For Shannon, that next challenge was passing this selection course. But there would be no beret, no tab, not even a badge for making it into this outfit. When a Ranger, SEAL, or Green Beret makes it through this selection, they are rarely heard from again back at their old unit. These operators are the stuff of legend: rumors about what they do and who they are circulate the military in hushed tones, but unless you've served there, you're guessing.

It should go without saying that there are no male/female standards in this selection. According to Shannon's Navy Evaluation & Counseling Record for that time period, she was trained in "technical skills, advanced medical training, mission planning, tradecraft, and high-risk environment training." If that sounds vague, it is—you either have what it takes, or you don't. Nobody knows exactly what the unit is looking for before they attend.

This course is the longest selection of any special operations unit at that level and it assesses service members from all branches for a unit that very few know the current name of. Brawn alone wouldn't get Shannon through; she would need to rely on her intelligence, as well as withstand incredible pressure. Nobody is selected without being pushed past their preconceived mental, emotional, and physical limits.

Alongside Navy SEALs, Green Berets, and Army Rangers, Shannon needed to show that not only could she compete at the highest levels of special operations, but she could also outperform some of her male peers in some areas contrary to the stereotypes that surround women in the military.

Ali Hassoon, the Iraqi-born Special Forces interpreter who had heard rumors of Shannon on her first deployment, was no longer working in Baghdad. He had immigrated to the United States and joined the Army as a linguist. He found himself side by side in selection with the famed American redhead he had heard about all those years ago.

He witnessed her breaking hearts and outperforming men who came from very elite units and, in some cases, helping them through some of the events—which was a blow to many egos. In fact, Hassoon was challenged by some of the swimming tests, so Shannon took time to work with him and make sure he was prepared to pass.

Brandon was another friend in the course who'd followed a similar path in the Navy as Shannon, first meeting her at DLI in 2004. Back then, the first several weeks of their relationship consisted of her yelling at Brandon for not joining her on the Navy run team and Brandon changing the subject as quickly as possible. They were eventually placed in different languages at DLI and parted ways a few months later.

Shannon had decided that since they were friends before, they would be friends again during the difficult training—Brandon didn't have a vote in the matter. The training was among the hardest things he had done in his career up to that point, but one day in particular was tougher than the others: it was his daughter's third birthday, and the second in a row he had missed. He wasn't even able to call and wish her a happy birthday.

With Brandon feeling depressed and like a failed father, Shannon talked him through it after they finished that day's events. After a while, she walked away with a plan in mind; she was not the type to let a friend's day be ruined.

"Happy birthday to you, happy birthday to you," Shannon sang as she rounded the corner into the room. She was carrying a plate full of an impromptu Meal, Ready to Eat (MRE) birthday cake. She combined marble pound cake, strawberry shake drink powder, and three matches carefully jabbed into the center in place of candles. It didn't look particularly appetizing, but that wasn't the point.

Shannon finished singing "Happy Birthday" to Brandon's little girl, then told him, "For your daughter's birthday this year, I think you should give her the only thing a little girl needs: a father to be proud of."

Brandon was in awe that Shannon could fly through the difficult training events they endured that day while singing random *South Park* songs in her best Cartman voice, to seeing a friend in need and instantly turning into the most compassionate person in the world. It wasn't a switch; it's just who she was. It wasn't the only time, or last time, or the hardest time she helped Brandon through. But it was the moment he realized how amazing she was.

Her positivity, humility, and humor in the most difficult training events made her shine above the rest. The unit's former senior enlisted advisor, who oversaw the course and requested that his name not be used, said she was the only person he ever saw go through that selection and know without a doubt they were the right person for the job. To him, she performed like the course wasn't even a challenge for her.

She successfully completed the secretive selection process, and was selected on her first try. Typically, the next step would be to move on to the Operator Training Course, or OTC, which was the next phase of training she would need to complete to become fully operational in this new unit. But she found out her East Coast SEAL brothers just had another deployment come up. Although she could have gotten out of that deployment to attend OTC, she could not stand the thought of her teammates in Afghanistan without her. So, in a selfless act, she deferred OTC for a year and deployed with her team to Afghanistan.

What was one more, after all?

CHAPTER 11

LIFE AND DEATH IN AFGHANISTAN
ZABUL, AFGHANISTAN, 2012

Shannon deployed once more with Naval Special Warfare in 2012 for her first trip to Afghanistan. She was assigned to NSW Special Reconnaissance Team 2 and tasked with supporting an East Coast SEAL platoon at a Village Stability Operations (VSO) site.

VSOs were the Afghan application of counterinsurgency (COIN) doctrine. SOF troops, supported by conventional forces, embedded with Afghan tribal elements and Afghan security forces at the village level in an effort to deny the Taliban the ability to exploit locals. Much like the Iraq COIN surge, these operations brought the US into daily close contact with the local populace. The VSO portion of the Afghan COIN strategy sent US SOF out to live in small village outposts, living side by side with Afghans and training the village's security forces at the local level.

The VSO program in conjunction with the Afghan surge brought the subject of women in combat, and in particular, women in special operations, into the public eye. Afghan culture segregated women from men in a more drastic way than US forces had experienced in Iraq. It was culturally taboo for male service members fighting in Afghanistan to interact with local women, so the need for women in combat roles shifted from luxury to necessity.

Like most innovations in the war on terror, SOF identified this need several years before the conventional military with the launch of the Cultural Support Team (CST) program. The CST program was started by the US Army Special Operations Command (USASOC), which recruited and screened females before putting them through a selection and qualification course. Upon successful completion of that course, they were attached to a variety of SOF units in combat. They went out on missions and performed a function their male counterparts could not, talking to females on target who refused to speak to anyone else.

This happened years after Shannon's first deployment in 2007, when she was invited to attend a selection course for NSW and become the first woman to pass and be accepted into the highly competitive SEAL-led ranks for SRT (at the time, SRT was called Support Activity). Two more Iraq deployments to Baghdad followed, and each trip Shannon found herself conducting ████████████████████* operations and building on her ability to collect actionable information for SEAL teams and other SOF elements. By the time Shannon

---

* Description of specific types of operations redacted at request of DoD.

was on her fourth deployment at the SEAL-platoon level, the "first women in SOF" were arriving at VSO sites.

But Shannon's mission was not just interacting with local Afghan females. She had mastered the ability to blend her HUMINT and SIGINT knowledge to become a virtual one-stop shop for painting an X on the enemy. That was a huge advantage for Shannon. With all her experience, she was assigned to a VSO site in Zabul and tasked with collecting actionable HUMINT and accompanying SEALs on operations. The Team Guys understood how unique her skill set was. They needed her to do what she did best: hunt the enemy.

When Shannon and her team arrived in the country, their VSO site was located in a contested village and not fully built yet, meaning they would have to provide their own security while establishing their camp. Once the primitive camp was operational, Shannon and her teammates went to work, beginning the tedious process of cultivating local informants to map out Taliban networks.

This deployment was also the first time Shannon and her friend Brittany Burris deployed together, with Shannon conducting operations on the ground and Brittany flying surveillance platforms overhead. They had forged a close friendship since first meeting in a locker room in 2009 as members of a small cadre of women assigned to NSW.

Much of Shannon's work was conducted off base, or "outside the wire." Due to how dangerous the area was, she was required to have an ISR asset overhead anytime she conducted a source meet or mission. Shannon was like a sister to Brittany, so she wanted to personally make sure her friend was safe. Brittany didn't trust the other sensor operators to pay as close attention to her as she did. Anytime Shannon went outside the wire, Brittany asked to be the ISR operator so she could watch Shannon's back and relay comms as needed.

Even if it was nighttime, or wasn't her shift, she would volunteer if she knew Shannon was going out. And with the demand for women on target so high, Shannon was going out a lot.

At one point during the deployment, Shannon conducted a source meet right outside their base. Burris was watching Shannon via the surveillance drone above while she talked to the source. They were almost ready to bring the drone back down when the JOC called and asked how much fuel they had left.

"Well, we've only been flying for an hour, and the fuel life is six to eight hours at a time," Burris said, confirming they could stay in the air if need be. The JOC had just received a call from Shannon. She had elicited actionable intelligence from the source about IEDs being buried nearby. They needed Burris to move her drone to the suspected location and confirm.

The mission commander was sitting right beside her, so they took Shannon's grid coordinates down and flew to the suspected IED location, where they found six military-age males burying IEDs. To no one's surprise, Shannon was spot-on with her intel. They immediately worked up a fire mission to drop a Hellfire missile on the enemy fighters. Burris landed her drone and hopped in a four-by-four to drive back to the JOC, where she could watch the strike.

Shannon had already returned and was performing her famous squeak dance as Brittany parked.

"Come with me," Shannon said.

"All right," Burris replied.

A care package from her cousin Sharron had just arrived, and it was full of Shannon's favorite super fudge brownies. Shannon and Brittany celebrated their mission success with brownie treats in hand as they watched the Hellfire drop, scoring a direct hit on all six bomb makers.

Shannon was responsible for finding six IEDs, preventing their use against American forces, and finding other explosives buried nearby. The information she returned with resulted in another successful line of targets, all derived from a relatively simple meeting conducted within eyesight of their base. But the highs of war, like life back home, are often followed by lows.

The death of friends in combat is one thing, but losing one to suicide is another. Unfortunately, both defined Shannon's fourth deployment. She would never be the same after Afghanistan.

Shannon worked closely with Commander Job W. Price, a forty-two-year-old Navy SEAL from Pennsylvania and respected leader of SEAL Team 4. He had been dealing with a lot on that deployment;[1] their task force had just lost thirty-two-year-old Petty Officer 1st Class Kevin Ebbert a few weeks prior on November 24. He was a Navy SEAL corpsman assigned to SEAL Team 4, and was killed in action on his second combat deployment during a firefight in the Uruzgan Province. At the time of his death, he was preparing to leave the Navy to pursue his medical degree and become a physician.[2] Shortly after his death, the Taliban killed a young girl. She was around the same age as Price's daughter.

Many in the task force felt like they were essentially losing the war at that point but continued to work around the clock to the point of exhaustion. It was all they could do to feel like they were making a difference. Shannon and most of her SOF and conventional counterparts were multiple deployments into the seemingly endless, certainly doomed war on terror that was over a decade old with no end in sight. The loss of teammates and the daily grinding stress of being in danger while cycling through never-ending deployments was one more thing for everyone to deal with—to suffer in silence, as the mantra goes.

On December 22, 2012, all outside communication was suddenly shut down. No one knew why their comms had been cut, but typically that only happened when a family back home needed to be notified of a death.

Commander Price was found in his room with a pool of blood on the floor, still holding his assigned pistol.[3] A picture of his daughter was missing from his desk. His death came as a shock to everyone.

Shortly after, Shannon called Brittany at her desk.

"Can you come up here for a little bit?" Shannon asked, clearly in shock.

"Of course, I'll be right there," Brittany said. Price was their commander, the commander of all the SEALs and their enablers in the area, and if this deployment was too much for him, what did that mean for everyone else?

"Listen, there are not many times in my life where Shannon has actually needed me," Burris said, turning to her chief. "I need to go see her right now." Her chief didn't object. Back home, Shannon would come over to see Brittany with a bottle of rum or a bottle of wine when she was having a bad day. But that wasn't an option in Afghanistan, and that day was different.

Burris went up to camp around dinnertime to eat with Shannon.

"I don't wanna talk in here," Shannon said. Burris agreed. After they finished eating, they retreated to a firepit outside the JOC where they could talk privately.

Being assigned to a special operations task force, they almost never wore uniforms and usually had their hair in ponytails, which was not allowed at the time. As always, Shannon was sporting her favorite Yankees cap in addition to her desert uniform pants, pistol belt, and brown T-shirt. It was December in Afghanistan, and Shannon often complained about being cold, so she was also wearing her go-to black Patagonia puffy jacket.

They sat on the logs, listening to Mumford & Sons and staring into the dancing flames. Almost everyone else was still inside eating or working out, or on the job. They had the entire area to themselves.

"So you heard?" Shannon said without looking away from the fire.

"Yeah, I heard earlier," Brittany replied.

Commander Price's death was the final straw in what they saw as a series of unaddressed issues. They constantly dealt with the challenges of being a woman in NSW. Out of the approximately four hundred SEALs and enablers assigned to their team, there were only seven women—and Shannon and Brittany were two of them. Brittany had already been sexually harassed and assaulted during that deployment, and Shannon had faced her share of harassment too. It wasn't all bad, but they were often treated very poorly. Shannon carried that weight with her. They considered themselves tough role models, and Shannon was fierce in that regard.

"We need to make a pact to help people like us," Shannon said. "I want to help people like us who are in this community but feel like they need to be tough because they're scared of losing their security clearance and scared of retribution. Scared of people thinking differently of you, thinking that you're weak, so you bury those feelings. Then people commit suicide. Why? Because we're too scared to tell people?"

They cried together and swore to help.

"There are so many people in the special warfare community who just suffer in silence," Burris said. "If you start taking medication, you're not allowed to touch a gun or deploy for six months. It's fucking horseshit."

Shannon and Brittany both agreed to make a change. They resolved that if somebody reached out for help and they received the help they needed, they should still be able to do their job. They should still be able to deploy. Brittany saw a change in Shannon's maturity that day. She was done with the bullshit. She had seen first-hand what suffering in silence could do to even the nation's most elite warriors. It was a problem, and she would be a part of the solution.

About then, one of the Marines who worked for Shannon came out to the firepit with her ukulele. She was known for her funny improv songs, and it didn't take long before Shannon and Brittany were smiling again, their laughter echoing into the cold Afghan night.

Ultimately, there was limited time for grief, sorrow, and emotion; they lived in the Taliban's backyard. Shannon and her team did what professional warriors are expected to do: compartmentalize their emotions and focus on the mission at hand. That was the problem though, and one of the issues she aimed to fix.

By this point, the "women in combat/special operations" conversation started to make its way into the public consciousness. Debates in Congress and in Facebook comment sections raged as veterans and the general public debated whether women have the same rights as men to serve their country in combat military occupational specialties.

Some accused the military of conducting social experiments with life-or-death consequences, while others accused the detractors of ignoring women's proven success on the battlefield during the war on terror.

While the debate raged, the first female soldiers graduated from Ranger School and continued serving in combat. And there were of course people like Shannon, who had literally been selected for service at the highest levels of our nation's special operations community—but nobody knew that at the time. Internally, it was never about whether or not women belonged. It was about picking the right person for the job. Shannon and Brittany were never against women in SOF, but they were worried about women *in* SOF.

The debates about women in combat extended to the dining facility tables at forward operating bases around Afghanistan. At one particular meal, Shannon and Brittany sat at the table for dinner with a group of SEALs, and the topic came up.

The discussion revolved around science rather than common tropes, with everyone remaining civil and professional. But at the end of the conversation, one of the Team Guys looked right at Shannon and said, "Well, if all the women in SOF were like Shannon, we'd be fine."

The respect Shannon had gained over her years in special operations never led to her forgetting what was required of her, unfairly or not, to stay in the high esteem of her peers. She also held her friends and fellow female sailors to those standards. Shannon and Brittany had two rules: "Don't let Team Guys see you cry" and "Don't date Team Guys."

Shannon produced such an authoritative volume of intelligence during her Afghanistan deployment that she was awarded the Defense Intelligence Agency's HUMINT collector of the year award. The DIA's award conjures a gentlemanly scene of meeting assets for long chats and typing up reports, almost white-collar war zone work. In reality, collecting human intelligence in a dangerous and austere environment is a gritty and exhausting endeavor. She and her team conducted combat patrols to meet and cultivate potential assets. These patrols frequently required that Shannon walk several miles through the Afghan mountains just to get to the meeting location.

She was credited with producing four hundred mission-critical intelligence reports, providing advance warning on twelve attacks against Advanced Operations Base Trident, preventing thirty IED attacks, and the capture or killing of at least six enemy combatants.

In addition to her battlefield achievements, her civil affairs initiatives resulted in medical care and humanitarian supplies being delivered to at least fourteen villages in three different districts.

The SEAL team she was assigned to lost two SEALs and two regular Army personnel in combat with the enemy. The stress of fallen comrades added a heavy weight to Shannon and her team, who were already dealing with the frustrations of a war that no policymaker could realistically define success in—yet they were still asked to advance the war effort.

CHAPTER 12

THE RISE OF ISIS

TAJI PRISON, IRAQ, 2013

*T*hwoomp! *Thwoomp! Thwoomp!* The mortars sailed into the air with violent intention, impacting as a vehicle-born IED (VBIED) rammed the front gate and exploded at a prison that held dozens of violent extremists in Taji, Iraq.

"Allahu akbar!" a man cried. His eyes glazed over with the solemn acceptance of fate. He self-detonated, sending shrapnel and pieces of his flesh in every direction. A two-hour firefight between Iraqi security forces and attacking ISI terrorists followed. Al-Baghdadi's forces were attempting to free the prisoners inside.

But the attack on Taji Prison was a distraction; the real target was the infamous Abu Ghraib Prison, where a similar attack was taking place simultaneously. In the capstone effort of Abu Bakr al-Baghdadi's

"Breaking the Walls" campaign, more than five hundred violent extremists broke out of their prisons after killing twenty-nine Iraqi police officers and soldiers.[1]

This was the final step before the ISI and al-Nusra Front joined forces, effectively creating what we now know as ISIS. The death and destruction had only just begun.

ISIS rose to international fame via a campaign of terror across Syria and Iraq, with al-Baghdadi at the helm. The world watched as kidnappings, sex slaves, terrorist attacks, and the broadcast of live torture and executions headlined the ISIS land grab that put much of the world in a moral quandary: intervene in yet another Middle East conflict, or stand by as atrocities at scale took place.

By 2014, ISIS had invaded and taken by force more than 34,000 square miles of land in Syria and Iraq,[2] in an old-world empire that stretched from the Mediterranean coast to south of Baghdad. At its peak, the terror-group-turned-autonomous-nation-state was generating more than $3 million a day in revenue—mostly from the oil fields it had seized.[3]

Although ISIS and its leader, al-Baghdadi, became famous for their brutality, they owed much of their success to the media juggernaut they launched to recruit extremists, disgruntled youth, and the handicapped into their army of darkness. Whether they were involved in destroying ancient artifacts, setting someone on fire while they were locked in a cage, or straightforward armed conflict, they always made sure someone with a video camera was nearby.

Their propaganda machine would spin this raw footage into underground recruiting videos. They worked. People from all over the world joined them on their front lines. Many of them did not make it out alive, and those who did often faced legal consequences once they returned home.

Their military campaign resulted in the fall of Mosul, Fallujah,

Tikrit, and al-Qaim. Many residents in Kurdish-controlled Erbil reported that at their closest, ISIS was within a ten-minute drive of their city borders.

For Americans, the victims weren't anonymous faces from a far-off land. Kayla Mueller, an American humanitarian working in the area, was taken captive near Aleppo, Syria.

Al-Baghdadi's brand of violence was so extreme that al-Qaeda formally cut ties with ISIS. It wasn't long before ISIS announced their worldwide caliphate, headquartered in Raqqa, Syria—with al-Baghdadi as their self-appointed caliph.

Finally, on August 8, 2014, targeted air strikes were authorized. Two US fighter jets bombed ISIS artillery positions, kicking off what would become a dramatic escalation of the US presence in Iraq and Syria.

"Earlier this week, one Iraqi cried that there is no one coming to help," President Obama said in a somber statement delivered from the State Dining Room on August 7, 2014. "Well, today America is coming to help. . . . As commander in chief, I will not allow the United States to be dragged into fighting another war in Iraq," he continued. "American combat troops will not be returning to fight in Iraq."

Both Iraq and Syria, however, saw a steady escalation of American troop levels, with that trend continuing well into the next administration. The threat was very real, and the violence—the genocide—was so extreme that many nations felt a moral duty to intervene.

CHAPTER 13

SECRET LOVE

UNDISCLOSED LOCATION, VIRGINIA, 2014

Anticipation and fear of the unknown hung as thick as Virginia's humidity in July. About twenty service members met at an obscure parking lot at 8 a.m., but they didn't know anything about what was in store. What little information they did have came from a short email they'd received the night before, telling them where to be and to wear business casual attire. Everyone present had already been through the forty-day selection course for this murky unit and knew to expect the unexpected—but that didn't ease anyone's nerves.

It was only the first day of a course that would last about a year—and the exact duration wasn't clear. Joe Kent was terrified of failing, of not making the cut. For a veteran Green Beret, that was the most potent form of fear he was capable of feeling. There was no time to dwell on that, though. *Time to fake it till ya make it,* he told himself while attempting to make small talk with classmates.

Suddenly the sound of metal on metal broke the silence. Joe turned to see a blue Nissan pickup truck strike a car. His eyes focused on the driver; a gorgeous, athletic, strawberry blonde was in the driver's seat. A flash of familiarity washed over him. *I know her . . . the Vill? Maybe 2007? Shannon!*

"Eh," Shannon said without missing a beat. She looked right at Joe with cool blue eyes, grinned, shrugged, and then quickly corrected her parking. She jumped out of her truck and walked to another group of students like any other day at the office. *Damn, she's cool,* Joe thought.

He had thought about Shannon on and off over the years and returned to Iraq several times, always hoping he might run into her again at the Vill or some other outpost. He promised himself he wouldn't let her get away again.

Go talk to her—NOW! Joe thought. As he approached, their eyes met, triggering the same spark of familiar comfort he'd felt in Baghdad all those years before. This was the woman who gave him a brief reprieve from the angst of war during his 2007 deployment to Iraq. As he approached, Shannon looked at Joe like she was almost expecting to see him.

She was the one who got away, Joe thought. *But now here she is, six years later, competing for a slot in the same unit I'm trying to get into.* He wasn't surprised she found a way into the qualification course for this outfit, considering her skill sets, but it still felt serendipitous.

"I can't believe that parked car jumped out and bit your bumper like that," Joe said.

"That shit will buff out," she replied. Joe let himself laugh out loud, maybe a little too loud. Her cool, devil-may-care demeanor confirmed he was talking to the right girl.

"I'm Joe. Were you in Baghdad in 2007?"

He extended his hand, which she grasped with a firm handshake in return.

"I remember! We met in the Vill! Oh, I'm . . ."

"Shannon!" he said, maybe a little too fast. He suddenly became aware of the big grin on his face. But she looked happy to see him too, which helped ease his worry.

"We were both looking for the same shithead, right?" They easily picked up right where they'd left off all those years ago.

"That's right! Abu Abbas—or whatever his name was. Great to see you here," Joe said.

"Yeah, you too. Pretty interesting the people they invite to random parking lots," Shannon said with raised, conspiratorial eyebrows.

Her subtle humor seemed to be the limits of their flirtation—after all, they were both students selected to prove they had what it took to serve in an elite unit within the special operations community.

For the uninitiated, many serve in special operations units, but very few are referred to as "operators." Neither Joe nor Shannon would settle for anything less than the latter; this training course is what stood in their way.

The course is not for the faint of heart, nor should it be. Those who make it through the gauntlet are assigned to a unit charged with performing some of the DoD's most unique missions. For Shannon, it would mean she could finally leverage everything she learned over the years to have the most impact in the war on terror.

The selection to get this far had been anything but standard or predictable, and Shannon and Joe knew they were under the microscope and could be fired if they failed to perform or were deemed incompatible with the unit. Not only are the standards to pass the course a secret, but the itinerary is intentionally vague, leaving those attending only able to guess at what they might expect.

No one wanted the spotlight directed their way for flirting in public.

"So what happened after the Vill? Did you head home after that?" Joe asked.

"No, I got moved to Area Four and Camp Fernandez to work with the strike force. Long story short, that's how I ended up here," Shannon explained. The names of these familiar places in Iraq, where Joe had spent most of his twenties, conjured up old memories.

"If you are here for class, follow me," a dry monotone voice said from behind their formation. Joe quickly snapped out of the trance Shannon and the images of Baghdad had produced.

"Leave your cell phones in your vehicles," he said. He was a serious-looking man wearing a suit, right out of Central Casting for well-dressed government goons. Without another word, he turned away from the group and walked toward an unmarked brown building.

"Always so mysterious . . ." Shannon whispered to Joe out of the corner of her mouth, pulling it into a mischievous half smile. All Joe could do was try not to laugh too hard. He appreciated people who didn't take themselves too seriously—and in the world of special operations, that is easier said than done. Joe knew Shannon was the real deal, so seeing her crack jokes in a stressful training environment only deepened his interest in this mysterious woman.

"Here we go . . ." Joe said to Shannon as they joined their classmates, following the man in the suit.

They were led into a large classroom with a few rows of desks. On the desks were placards with only first and last names, followed by each student's branch of service insignia. No rank, no indication of military occupation. The room was sterile, nothing hung on the walls, and all the furniture looked brand-new.

"Please find your name and have a seat," the man in the suit said again in his monotone. Joe found his name and was happy to see Shannon seated directly behind him. He sat down, turned around, and made eye contact with her.

"If they give us a test, can I copy off you?" Shannon asked in a hushed tone.

"All right, let's get started," a new man-in-suit said from the room's rear. He looked a bit more personable than the one who led the students in from the parking lot, but still like a Hollywood stereotype.

The room fell silent, all eyes on him as he walked down the center of the classroom to a podium in front of the desks. Every exposure the students had to the unit up to this point was filled with a great deal of mystery. The forty-day selection preceding this course was shrouded in secrecy—most of the time, they had no idea where they were and were forbidden from divulging full names or unit affiliations to fellow candidates. Everyone was anxious to hear what would come next.

"First off, congratulations on making it this far. You are a small minority of the military chosen for this type of work and an even smaller minority that meets our standards for selection. I'm Mike, and I'll be getting all of you ready for what comes next."

Mike had everyone sign a stack of nondisclosure forms and gave a security brief about what the students could and could not tell people outside of the organization. Once that was complete, he stepped out from behind the podium, loosened his tie, leaned on the podium, and placed one hand in his pocket.

"All right, now that we have the formalities out of the way, let's talk." Mike's tone was far more relaxed than before. More casual than Shannon and Joe had heard from anyone in this outfit, for that matter.

"You all were chosen to attend this training for two reasons: how you performed during selection and your backgrounds. Some of you are from the special operations community, and some are from the intelligence community."

"For the next year, we will teach you how to combine these skills to do something very unique for our nation."

Mike intentionally arranged everyone so they weren't sitting by people they attended selection with.

"I'll be back in a bit to give out instructions for tomorrow," Mike said with a half grin as he walked back down the center aisle and disappeared through a door in the back of the classroom.

That was not the briefing anyone expected. In fact, Joe thought the day would be kicked off with some sort of evaluation or a speech about how any of them could be fired at any time. But then again, this unit was unpredictable. Joe and Shannon were both happy with the turn of events since Mysterious Mike basically said they could continue flirting with each other—professionally, of course.

The chatter in the classroom picked up after the back door closed behind Mike. Joe turned around. Shannon was already looking at him as if she was waiting—hoping—he would engage her for the get-to-know-each-other session. Looking at her, Joe could feel that spark of excitement rush over him again. Shannon looked warm and familiar—and like she was feeling the same.

"Well, you heard Mike, tell me about what you've been up to since Baghdad, and we'll combine our skills and go kick ass for America," Shannon said. Joe couldn't help but laugh. They shared the same sense of humor, and her voice was music to his ears.

"After Baghdad, I went home, back to Baghdad, then to Mosul, and took a slight detour to Yemen, then back to Baghdad. What about you?" he said, as casually as possible.

"Same story, dude, back to Baghdad, a quick trip to Basra, another Baghdad, and I just got back from Afghanistan last month," Shannon replied. She was casually naming some of the most dangerous places in the world as if reading her grocery list.

Who is she? Joe thought.

"Was all that through the NSA?" The last time he saw Shannon, she worked in the National Security Agency's section of the Vill deciphering terrorist cell phone intercepts.

"Nope, SRT," she said matter-of-factly. SRT—the Special Reconnaissance Team—was a unique unit of intelligence professionals and Navy SEALs assigned to SEAL teams to provide them with timely, actionable intelligence. Joe realized that Shannon had a knack for making it sound like doing the unbelievable was easy.

"That's badass." Joe was impressed. "I didn't know SRTs were open to females?" He'd worked with many women in combat over the years, but regulations had not yet caught up with reality, and women were still unable to serve in formal combat positions.

"Yeah, I was one of the first to try out. It's not the norm—still a boys' club," she said, rolling her eyes. Joe could see the fierce drive beneath her casual demeanor. She could have chosen to continue riding a desk, translating Arabic like the last time he saw her, but instead made a habit of deploying to dangerous places with a unit tasked with hunting and killing the enemy.

"So, how'd you get to keep going back to Iraq so much? They don't give you guys a break?" She was sharp. Joe's deployments did not follow a standard deployment tempo.

"Well, I volunteered for some, and I went warrant too, which gave me more time on an ODA and more chances to deploy."

Shannon's brow furrowed as *warrant* left Joe's lips.

"Warrant . . . like warrant officer?" Shannon asked, hoping she misheard him.

"Oh yeah, warrant officer," Joe replied. The look on Shannon's face changed quickly.

"Ah, okay." She was unable to hide her disappointed tone.

Fraternization! Fucking military rules! Joe thought, catching up to what Shannon had already figured out. Officers, even warrant officers, are forbidden from fraternizing, dating, or interacting with enlisted service members outside of work due to the military's antiquated rules about relationships. Joe was an officer, an Army Chief Warrant Officer 2 to be precise, and she was a Chief Petty Officer, a senior enlisted rank in the Navy. Despite *chief* and *officer* in both their titles and the fact that they served in different branches of service, military regulations clearly stated they were off-limits to each other.

"Alright, wrap it up with your new colleagues and listen." Mysterious Mike's voice broke the mental gymnastics of trying to find a loophole in military regulations.

The next few days featured briefings about upcoming training and administrative tasks. Shannon and Joe were put in separate groups, making it difficult to see each other very much.

At the end of the second day of briefings, they were led into a larger classroom with everyone from the training class. Shannon and Joe once again managed to find each other and started making small talk when Mysterious Mike walked to the front of the classroom, grabbed a dry-erase marker, and wrote "0500 tomorrow. Gym, dress accordingly." Mike then turned around and said, "Pretty simple instructions. See you tomorrow."

"Shit, I forgot to pack gym clothes," Shannon said. She did not have her truck either, since she rode in a government van with several other classmates to the DC area from Baltimore that day.

Perfect, Joe thought.

"I'll give you a ride to your place if you want?" Joe said in as nonchalant a tone as he could muster.

"Really? You don't mind?"

"Not at all. I'll come pick you up in an hour?"

"Sounds great! You're a lifesaver."

It was not the first-date either of them envisioned, but it would have to do. They had about an hour each way to get to know each other outside of the supervision of the training environment. It would either be awkward, or they'd click—Joe was betting on the latter.

He picked her up outside her hotel in his gray Toyota Tacoma and couldn't help but notice she looked amazing. Her radiant red-blond hair flowed down to her shoulders, and she wore a pair of faded cutoff jean shorts and a flowery bohemian-style white and pink tank top. Joe thought she looked like a model going to the beach.

Besides being one of the few women in this line of work, her laid-back demeanor and natural beauty had Joe so intrigued he almost didn't know what to say when she first hopped in his truck. Luckily, Shannon never had a hard time breaking the ice.

"Dude! I love your truck. I almost bought this same one!" she said. "Oh, and thanks for giving me a ride!"

"No worries at all. Honestly, I jumped at the chance to talk with you outside the classroom," Joe said as he pulled out onto the highway. *That should make my intentions pretty clear,* he thought.

"Yeah, seriously, fuck that judgment-zone shit, man," she said with a smile. Joe smiled back. *We are on the same page, thank God!*

"So tell me, why aren't you married with kids yet?" Her tone managed to soften the point on a sharp question.

"Ah, you know, deployments and going to selection are not great for keeping a steady home life, so no wife, no kiddos." In the civilian world, such a conversation would probably not happen, or at least not on the first date. But marrying young, having kids, and then getting divorced are all too common in the military. It is almost abnormal to have a family survive intact as long as Joe had been in the military.

"How about you?" Joe asked.

"Nope and nope. I've been trying to accomplish as much as possible before it's time to focus on kids and a family," Shannon explained. This was Joe's first exposure to her meticulous planning. Shannon had already mapped out exactly when she would have the freedom to pursue a career and adventure and when she would transition to focus on family.

"So I gotta ask, how did you get into all of this, like why did you join the military?" Joe asked. From Baghdad to one of the most elite units in the military—Joe was fascinated to hear about what he assumed had to have been a unique career.

"I'm a New Yorker. They attacked the towers, and I wanted to do something about it."

Legit! She actually gets it.

"Fuckin' A. That's awesome. Damn good reason as far as I'm concerned," Joe said.

"What about you? How'd you get here, Warrant Officer SF Joe?" Shannon asked. Here in the privacy of his truck, Joe noted a far more flirtatious tone in her voice.

"It's all I wanted to do: be a Green Beret and go to war. I was in pre-9/11, so I figured I'd get a shot at a Desert Storm or a Panama if I were in long enough. I never thought we'd have over a decade of war."

"Seriously, I never would have thought I'd go to Iraq three times and then Afghanistan—eleven years after 9/11. So, how many times did you go to Iraq?"

"Seven times. I was on my fourth trip when we met at the Vill," Joe said, trying not to sound like he was bragging.

"Did you like Iraq?" Her tone indicated it was a loaded question.

"I did. I got to work with a lot of great Iraqis over the years and felt pretty connected to the place by the time we left," Joe said. He wondered if that was the right response, but at least he'd been genuine.

"Good, because my apartment looks like Harun al-Rashid clacked off a VBIED." Shannon used the shorthand term for vehicle-borne IEDs, common in Iraq at the height of the war. It dawned on Joe that this was a woman who could throw out a hardened-veteran reference and a geeky historical reference to Harun al-Rashid—the twelfth-century caliph of Baghdad and lead character in the classic *One Thousand and One Arabian Nights*—all within the same flirtatious conversation. Joe laughed out loud. Not an easy feat.

The GPS guided Joe to the front of her apartment on Baltimore's Inner Harbor.

"So does that make you Scheherazade?" Joe asked.

Shannon's eyes lit up, excited that Joe got the obscure reference.

"Nice catch—I did not think you would pick that up!" She gently punched his shoulder. "You were close. My Iraqi name was Shaymah."

Holy shit. Shannon is THE Shaymah, Joe realized. Shaymah was something of an urban legend in the Iraqi SOF community. His Iraqi scouts always asked him if he knew a redheaded Arabic-speaking American female who went by Shaymah over the years. One of them had told him to find her and marry her.

The legendary Shaymah had a reputation for running local sources and accompanying SOF teams on raids to run interrogations in the homes of terrorists. Shaymah won the respect of the Iraqi operators due to her mastery of Iraqi slang and sharp wit. Joe heard about her so often that he thought Shaymah was possibly several women who shared the same Iraqi pseudonym. But here she was, standing in front of him.

"So you are Shaymah! You have quite a fan club in Baghdad."

Shannon didn't quite know how to receive that.

"You worked with Salah and Ahmed in the scouts, and I'm guessing you worked with the Wolf to find people willing to talk to us," Joe said. "Salah and Ahmed told me about you going out with the strike force, and Wolf raved about you being able to get information off of a few of the terrorist widows he hooked us up with."

Shannon nodded her head and blushed at this point.

"Dude, I can't believe you know those guys!" she said. They continued to reminisce about the good old days in Baghdad as they walked up the steps to her apartment. Shannon opened the door and flicked on the lights.

"You were not kidding. I feel like I just walked into a bazaar," Joe said. A watercolor painting of the Baghdad skyline with the city's famous mosques, minarets, and palm trees alongside the Tigris River hung in the entrance hallway. There was a collection of DVDs on the Iraq War and terrorism, and endless piles of Arabic books.

"I have never met anyone who owned the *Ganges of Iraq* and *Iraqi Voices*," Joe said, referencing the two obscure Arabic documentaries on her coffee table. Shannon rummaged through a drawer for her gym clothes in the next room. She walked back into the living room, shaking her head and smiling.

"Here we are six years after Abu Abbas, clicking over Iraqi documentaries and deployment stories," Shannon said. She let the comment hang. All Joe could do was look at her and grin. He was hooked.

Over the next few weeks, training intensified with a heavy workload and many travel periods for training exercises. Any free time

Joe and Shannon could find was spent meeting up for a secret date, or more accurately, mini-dates: a quick dinner, coffee, or a trail run together. They were both aware they were playing with fire due to the fraternization rules.

After a run one Saturday morning, they were hanging out on his couch, talking about nothing in particular, when she asked *the* question.

"So, do you want to have kids someday?" Shannon asked nonchalantly.

Joe looked at her. He couldn't help but visualize a real future, a home, and a life he never thought he would want.

"I never really did. I figured I'd keep deploying and stay in the game as long as possible." This had been his mantra for so long that it came out like a natural reflex. He realized he didn't mean it as soon as it left his mouth.

"Well, that's pretty fucking stupid."

"Yeah, it is, isn't it?"

Shannon leaned forward and kissed him.

"I love you, Shannon." It came out without Joe even thinking.

"Oh, thank God. I love you too, Joe Kent!"

From that moment on, Joe and Shannon were a team—odds be damned.

Joe and Shannon's courtship was unconventional. Their first year together was hectic, with most of their time spent away from each other on various training exercises where they couldn't call or text. When they did make time to see each other, they were exhausted and under stress far more often than not—but going through training simultaneously forged their relationship in fire.

By the summer of 2014, they were both done with training and ready to be a normal couple—or at least their version of normal. They took pride in their shared accomplishment, but having achieved the highest level of success, now it all had to be a secret. They looked and talked like the politicos they lived among, their actual employment a secret only they knew.

Shannon moved them into a fantastic townhouse near Lincoln Park in the trendy Capitol Hill area of Washington, DC. For the first time, they enjoyed a summer together and newfound freedom living in the nation's capital, reconnecting with friends and falling deeper in love. For Joe, coming home after an average day of work to Shannon seemed like a dream. Maybe he was excited about what the rest of his life looked like for the first time.

CHAPTER 14

THE WAR AGAINST ISIS

PARIS, FRANCE, 2015

F rench president François Hollande was enjoying the game, a friendly international competition pitting his country against Germany's football (soccer) team in the Stade de France on November 13, 2015. The stadium had the ability to hold eighty-one thousand people, but there was one person who, fortunately, didn't make it in.[1]

A man strapped with explosives was stopped by security at approximately 9:20 in the evening. After being refused entry, he backed up and then initiated his violent suicide, killing an innocent passerby in the process.[2]

At a different stadium entrance, another explosion went off. A half-hour later, another explosion erupted at a nearby fast-food restaurant. All three attacks were initiated by suicide bombers, but it was only the opening chapter of a deadly ISIS plot to kill Parisians.

All across the city, a total of nine ISIS gunmen and suicide bombers attacked bars, restaurants, and a 1,500-seat sold-out concert hall, murdering 130 and wounding more than 100 before the night of terror ended, making it the worst attack on Paris since World War II.[3]

"We fought France, we attacked France, we targeted the civilian population. It was nothing personal against them," said Salah Abdeslam,[4] the only attacker to survive. He was arrested months after the attack and sentenced to life in prison.

The massacre put the world on notice: ISIS's terror campaign was no longer limited to the Middle East.

NORTHERN IRAQ, 2015

Operation Inherent Resolve was fully underway. Coalition forces bombed ISIS forces in Iraq and Syria in an effort to stop the terror campaign in its tracks. Regardless of claims that the American escalation of military force would not include "boots on the ground," some Americans were ordered into harm's way.

The Kurdish Regional Government sent a request for assistance to the United States. They had located an ISIS-controlled prison full of hostages, and their intelligence indicated there were freshly dug graves nearby. The hostages were likely scheduled to be executed at any minute.

Sergeant Major Thomas "Patrick" Payne[5] was the assistant team leader for a special operations unit trained in hostage rescue tactics. In a video interview published by the US Army, Payne described the night he and his teammates got the call for the rescue mission. They were more than happy to oblige. Payne's element was responsible for assaulting and clearing one of the buildings in which the hostages were held, and they felt it was their duty to bring every single person held against their will home.

They launched the rescue operation on October 22, 2015. As the helicopter lifted off, they made the mental transition from soldier to warrior. The joking stopped as they ran through their last-minute checks. Some punched up the brightness in their rifle optic. Others performed one more radio check. Night-vision devices were flipped down, then back up again. Every single operator knew the stakes and believed in the mission. Failure meant that innocent people, unjustly imprisoned, would die a horrible death.

The MH-47 helicopters screamed toward the HLZ, before flaring and landing as if all one fluid motion. The ramp dropped, and the operators ran into a complete brownout caused by rotor wash. Payne, an Army Ranger who had moved on to a different special operations unit, could already hear the sounds of a gunfight in the distance. Speed, surprise, and violence of action would dictate the success of this mission.

He and the rest of his assaulters ran to their target building, with some placing ladders and moving into a blocking position. That's when the first call came over the radio that a man was down.

One of Payne's teammates looked him right in the eye and said, "Follow me!" They cut the locks on the prison doors and opened the first cell, then another. There were over twenty-five hostages in one cell and approximately eleven in another. Despite the chaos of the situation, Payne could see the hostages' faces light up. Some were crying, some were excited, but all were being liberated.

Outside, in another building, an intense firefight raged. Payne saw the flames, and heard multiple explosions over the radio, then an "urgent call for assistance."

"Hey, let's get in the fight," Payne said.

"Let's go," his teammate replied.

Payne moved to the roof with his teammate, but not for long. The enemy was right below them, but the smoke was thick and they couldn't breathe, preventing them from moving closer to the fight. The ISIS fighters knew they were there, though, and started yelling at them in Arabic while shooting blindly through the smoke. Payne and his teammate yelled back at them while returning fire and throwing hand grenades.

The enemy fighters didn't see a way out of the situation, so suicide bombers started to initiate their suicide vests, shaking the rooftop with every explosion. Payne and his teammate held their ground, waiting for the smoke to clear below.

They controlled their fear, knowing from experience that courage is contagious on the battlefield. One of the other teams was holding down the breach point, but were down to their last magazine of ammunition. Payne could see rounds passing through their uniforms, just missing flesh, as well as the same prison door that was on the building they'd already liberated.

Payne called for a set of bolt cutters. He knew he needed to make a move, and fast.

"Hey, I got you!" his sergeant major said, taking the bolt cutters from him. "Engage the enemy combatants in the back room!"

While Payne laid down suppressive fire, his sergeant major maneuvered to a small foyer and cut the top lock, gaining access. Payne then took the bolt cutters back from him.

Smoke was pouring out, making it difficult to breathe. Payne was able to cut the bottom lock, causing the prison door to come loose.

"Hey CQB! CQB!" Payne yelled, indicating they needed to move quickly and clear forward. He could hear the building starting to collapse. They were still getting shot at. Everything was on fire and hostages were still inside. The odds were stacked against them. That's when a mandatory evacuation call came over the radio. They needed to get back to the helicopters as fast as possible.

Payne's sergeant major started grabbing as many hostages as he could as quickly as he could from one room, while Payne funneled them in the right direction, playing the part of a third-base coach. He grabbed an ISIS flag off the wall and stuffed it into his pocket. The train of hostages had stopped. He moved to investigate, and noticed one of the hostages had given up. Their extreme situation had overwhelmed him, and he lost the will to live. That wasn't good enough for Payne.

He grabbed him by the back of the collar and physically dragged the two-hundred-pound hostage forward and through the breach point to get the train of hostages moving toward the helicopters again.

"Hey, you get them out of the other building," his sergeant major yelled. With the long line of liberated hostages moving in the right direction, he ran back into the smoke for one last check.

He and the other operators made a human wall to allow the last hostages to pass while they continued to mass fire on the building. At one point, they had to quit firing so the liberated prisoners would keep moving.

Payne received the Medal of Honor for his actions that night, but one of his fellow operators made the ultimate sacrifice.

Master Sergeant Joshua Wheeler, an Army Ranger-turned-operator, was killed in action during the rescue. His last words before he moved toward the sound of gunfire were "On me!"

He was the first American to die fighting ISIS. He would not be the last.

The war on ISIS was fraught with international complications, resulting in the campaign being fought mostly in the shadows—led by special operators on the ground and fierce aerial bombardments from above, supporting Kurdish fighters as well as many other interested parties who all sought to end the reign of ISIS. Despite a $10 million bounty on his head and an international effort to kill or capture him, al-Baghdadi was not deterred.

SYRIA, 2015

███████████████████████████████* is almost always the go-to outfit for hostage rescues, as they are specifically trained and equipped to conduct those types of missions around the world. American forces had been on the trail of Kayla Mueller for some time, with multiple attempts, many dry holes, some limited success in freeing other hostages, but never any luck in finding the young American aid worker.

"But we were close, so close actually," said one former operator who was on the manifest for many of those missions. Time was of the essence because they knew through other informants that Mueller was living in horrific conditions. Disturbing reports surfaced, detailing how she was forced into marriage with al-Baghdadi and kept as his personal sex slave. The man responsible, Abu Sayyaf, was the minister of oil and gas for ISIS, a high-ranking position that made him responsible for much of the militant terrorists' funding.

Sayyaf had recently forced a new person into being his sex slave. That person would know exactly where Kayla Mueller was. A mission to rescue her was immediately authorized.

"The President authorized this operation upon the unanimous recommendation of his national security team and as soon as we had developed sufficient intelligence and were confident the mission

---

* Specific unit redacted at request of DoD.

could be carried out successfully and consistent with the requirements for undertaking such operations," the White House's National Security Council statement said at the time.

Unfortunately, the weather and patterns of life of the target kept changing. The rescue team was stuck at their base in Iraq until everything lined up to actually launch the mission. In 2015, Americans didn't have much of a presence in Syria, so conducting a cross-border operation was significantly riskier than it would become in later years.

They eventually received the green light and immediately moved to execute. The rescue team flew in at night on MH-60 Black Hawk helicopters and CV-22 Ospreys. A female captain flew one of the ██ ██* aircraft. Although unconfirmed, this was possibly the first time a female pilot flew a hostage rescue mission.

Their plan was to land on the X—but in this case, they wouldn't actually be landing. As the aircraft slowed down to a stable hover, thick green braided ropes dropped from the doors of the aircraft. The operators grabbed hold and slid down to the ground below.

The rope was less than ninety feet—right in the sweet spot before the friction of their grip on the rope would cause their hands to start burning through their gloves. Once the operators hit the ground they were immediately engaged in a firefight. The assaulters quickly moved into the building, making every attempt to find Mueller before anything could happen to her.

As one operator cleared the building, he opened a closet and bumped into an enemy fighter with an AK-47 hiding inside behind his wife. They engaged in hand-to-hand combat.

---

* Specific unit redacted at request of DoD.

The struggle was intense. Fortunately, one of the other operators came into the room behind him and attempted to shoot the man, but his rifle malfunctioned. In a tense moment, he immediately transitioned to his sidearm and promptly killed the enemy combatant.

Unfortunately, although she had previously been there, Kayla Mueller had already been moved from that location. The operators did, however, rescue a different girl who was being held as a slave hostage.

After numerous rescue attempts, Kayla Mueller, the American humanitarian aid worker from Prescott, Arizona, who had been held captive by ISIS since 2013, was eventually reported dead. She was the fourth American killed while in ISIS custody.

UNITED STATES OF AMERICA, 2014

Shannon looked down at the pregnancy test. It was positive. *Holy shit. Holy shit. Holy shit!* She took a picture of the test with her cell phone and texted it to her cousin, Sharron Kearney. Sharron called her immediately.

"Are you fucking kidding me?" Sharron said.

"Are you fucking kidding *me*? We're pregnant together!" Shannon said.

"Oh my god, this is amazing. What did Joe say?" Sharron said.

"Joe doesn't quite know yet."

"Why?"

Joe was overseas.

"I'm kind of nervous. Joe hasn't exactly been excited about having kids, like how it would work with his career." Shannon was worried but excited. She knew Joe was the one. But that didn't make her any less nervous about telling him the news. After she got off the phone with Sharron, she went to the store and bought a stuffed animal for the baby's room. She didn't know if it was a boy or girl, but she knew the room would be sailor- and ocean-themed either way.

One thing she knew for certain: life was about to change in a major way for her and Joe.

CHAPTER 15

LOOK AT WHAT WE MADE

UNDISCLOSED LOCATION, VIRGINIA, 2014

I need a beer, Joe thought. It had been a long day—most of which he spent driving in a new city—and he could feel it in his back as he got out of the rental car at his hotel. He had been looking at locations a terrorist leader was using to plan attacks while determining if he was being followed. Now it was time to write a report. *That's the part they don't show you in the Jason Bourne movies,* he thought.

Fortunately, there was a pub across the street where he could grab dinner and a beer and knock his report out before catching a few hours of sleep. As he walked over, he turned his cell phone back on to catch up on life—this was just a training mission, after all.

Hey, hun, call me when you can. I love you! the text message read.

I wonder what she wants to talk about, Joe thought as he hit the call-back button. Shannon rarely called Joe while he was working; she knew firsthand how important it was not to have distractions in this profession.

"Hey!" she answered, ecstatic.

"Hey . . . What's the good news?" he said, figuring her tone might mean something good happened.

"Well . . ." She hesitated a moment. "I was gonna wait to tell you, but I can't—you're going to be a dad, and I'm going to be a mom!"

"Holy shit! A baby! This is awesome!" Joe was ecstatic. He never had an interest in kids or raising a family, but Shannon had changed how he viewed the world and what he wanted out of life. The idea of bringing a child into the world with her genuinely excited him.

"Well, this explains why you were eating salmon at five a.m. last week, and I guess we probably won't have to worry about the fraternization police coming after us now?" Joe said, unable to hold back his happiness. He and Shannon had already been researching how to get around the fraternization regulations regarding officers dating enlisted personnel. Article 92 and 134 of the Uniform Code of Military Justice is clear that even if you're married, your chain of command could still come after you. Joe called a friend at his old unit who worked in the Army's equivalent of human resources, and he reassured him that if they got married, and as long as they weren't in the same chain of command, it was unlikely anyone would pursue charging them with fraternization.

"Yeah, I guess it all makes sense now!" He could hear the excitement in her voice and could tell she had a huge grin.

"So let's get married soon," Joe said without thinking.

"Oh yeah, way ahead of you. You're good with Lake Placid, right?" she said in her all-business voice. He never asked her to marry him, nor did she ask him. When he first said, "I love you," there was a mutual, unspoken agreement they would get married and start a family at some point.

"Of course, and hey, I just asked you to marry me!" Joe laughed.

"You've had my heart from day one, Joe Kent," she said. "We are getting married ASAP!"

Shannon wasted no time planning the ceremony while rearranging their townhouse to accommodate their first baby. The Smith family had a tradition of going to Lake Placid for Thanksgiving and sometimes for Christmas, and Joe's parents lived in the area when they were first married, so the Crowne Plaza in Lake Placid, New York, seemed like an excellent venue for the ceremony.

"So you're wearing your Class As for the wedding, right?" Shannon said one day, referring to Joe's military dress uniform.

"Sure, but only if you wear yours," Joe replied. Despite being in the Army for fifteen years, he still cringed at wearing dress uniforms. They were a ton of work to keep neat and prepared, and having a squared-away uniform was never one of his strong suits.

"Hell no, I'm wearing a damn princess dress to my wedding! Can you please dress like my prince charming in your army costume?"

They both knew Joe wouldn't say no.

LAKE PLACID, NEW YORK, 2014

They opted for a small wedding, limiting the guest list to family and using a justice of the peace to conduct the ceremony. Shannon wanted to get married in the hotel lounge overlooking the lake but was not thrilled about the idea of paying several thousand dollars to rent the space. So, she devised a plan.

"Wear your Prince Charming costume and follow my lead," she

said to Joe on the morning of Christmas Eve, 2014—the day of their wedding.

When Joe and Shannon arrived in the lobby, he was in jump boots, a green beret, and all the "scare badges"—like his military free-fall wings and combat-dive "bubble"—he could fit on his green service uniform, and she wore a light pink floral pattern wedding dress topped off with a unique tiara that looked like a small crown of daisies. Her skin was radiant from pregnancy, and Joe could not think of a more perfect woman to spend the rest of his life with.

Joe appreciated their soon-to-be wedding venue. The lobby is a massive ski-lodge-style room with an equally impressive stone fireplace to the left of a vast set of windows, revealing an epic view of Mirror Lake and the snow-topped forest behind it. Their families were standing in front of the window, with the justice of the peace waiting nearby.

Shannon led Joe over to the hotel clerk and smiled big. Joe had no idea what she was up to.

"Hey, we're going to get married over by the window real quick!"

She wasn't asking.

"Uh, okay? Congratulations, and . . . thank you for your service," the clerk said awkwardly. He didn't know what else to say at the moment. All Joe could do was laugh at Shannon's plan coming to fruition.

As they approached their families, Shannon squeezed Joe's hand and whispered, "I love you, Joe Kent."

He squeezed back.

"I love you too, baby, since day one."

The justice of the peace reminded them of their vows, and they kissed. Shannon's trusty dog Fang, acting as ring bearer, ran up with their rings secured on his back. They exchanged rings and kissed again. It was a magical moment; Shannon and Joe were officially one. Their first child was on the way and they were both exactly where they were supposed to be.

Joe and Shannon's honeymoon period didn't last long. Joe had another deployment overseas coming up right after the holidays in early January 2015. Shannon was pregnant with Colt, but he wasn't due until August, and Joe was supposed to be back in June—just in time for the baby to arrive—so she was supportive and even helped him pack for his trip. This was the start of a balancing act they would need to perfect if they both wanted to continue serving at a high level. They agreed to offset their frequent deployments, so one of them would always be home for their kids.

"Unless you can carry this little guy for a bit, there's nothing you can do till game day. Be back by then!" Shannon told Joe.

But, life wouldn't be absent of challenges.

SAFE HOUSE, UNDISCLOSED LOCATION, 2014

Joe sat in a lawn chair outside the safe house that he lived in on the other side of the world. It had been a long day, and all he wanted was to hear his new wife's voice. They attempted to talk daily while he was deployed, and thanks to modern technology, they could stay in touch reasonably well. He pulled up Shannon's number on the burner phone he only used on deployments and hit send. After a few rings, she picked up.

"Hey!" Shannon answered.

"Hey, how's it going?" Joe said. "Has the baby been kicking?"

"Oh yeah, this kid will be crazy when he gets out. I wish you were here to feel the little kicks right now!"

"Me too, baby. This trip will be over before we know it. How's everything else going?"

"Good . . . I've been thinking a lot. Ya know, like, what's next?" Shannon said.

"Are you still thinking about going back to school?"

"Yeah. I think . . ." Shannon paused. She could hear a helicopter flying over on Joe's end and knew he wouldn't be able to hear until it passed. "I keep going back to Afghanistan in my head. When Price committed suicide, I felt horrible for him at first."

"Yeah, I still can't believe that happened. He was a good dude," Joe said. He knew even the best of the best sometimes couldn't escape their demons.

"But lately, I can't help but feel like . . . like how come he felt like he could just leave?"

Joe was silent on the other end. He knew he needed to let her get whatever this was out.

"But the more I've reflected on this and analyzed his position, I realize he was all alone. As the commander, he bore all of the burdens but had no one on the ground to vent to. He was supposed to be the one people came to for help, not the one who needed it."

"Yeah, I mean, the further up the ranks you go, the fewer people you have . . . you know how it is," Joe said.

"It's too much to ask of one person over and over—deployment after deployment after deployment. I know we can do better. I know *I* can do better."

Shannon gained a new perspective from her combat experiences and the long-term mental health effects she saw in herself and her teammates. She had always been interested in human psychology, or what makes humans tick, which led her to start on a degree in psychology a few years ago. But then, life seemed to get in the way of finishing.

First, it was going to selection for ██████████.* Then it was her deployment to Afghanistan. After she got back from Afghanistan, she went to OTC. She understood the magnitude of being selected to attend this prestigious unit's training course; it was a young person's line of work, and she could not wait. She figured she could return to psychology as soon as she accomplished a few more goals in the Navy. But she met Joe again at OTC, and now they were married with a kid on the way. It was time to make good on the promise of higher education to herself.

But while working on her degree, she was still dealing with the aftermath of her last deployment and a major life transition into wife and mother. She hated dwelling on stress and pain.

Her coping mechanism was turning those factors into positive actions, not just positive feelings. She developed courses of action with a well-defined goal at the end, and for her, the goal needed to serve a higher calling—not another personal accomplishment. She needed a job that was still part of the mission but allowed her to be home more often. She concluded that a graduate degree in psychology would open up a path to do that and to help her fellow service members and veterans.

So Shannon finished her bachelor's degree in psychology during the second trimester of her pregnancy and began applying to online programs offering a graduate degree in psychology. She carried their first child, ran their household solo, and acted as chief planner and organizer. Of course, she was still working full-time for one of the world's most elite special operations units.

Joe already had another deployment on his calendar for 2016, so Shannon didn't waste time trying to get their DC townhouse ready

---

* Description of specific unit redacted at request of DoD.

for Colt's arrival. But the more she worked, the more she assessed how much additional room they might need and concluded neither their townhouse nor DC, for that matter, worked. So, Shannon decided they needed to move to accommodate their growing family before Joe returned, or at least before he left again.

After a month of house hunting and analysis, she compiled a list of houses suitable for their rapidly changing lives. In the spirit of partnership, she emailed Joe her top five to include him in the decision-making, but he could tell which one she wanted. It was in Annapolis, Maryland, a small, tucked-away community overlooking the Severn River and home of the US Naval Academy. Most of the neighbors were their age and starting families as well.

Joe tried to convince her to wait until he returned so she wouldn't have to pack all their wares up and move by herself again. She said she'd think about it. A week later, she sent him a copy of the house's title to sign, and a week after, she sent pictures of their new home with everything unpacked.

Shannon, now in her third trimester, never slowed down. Preparing their new house for a new baby, she painted rooms her favorite colors, started a beautiful new garden outside, and still found time to pursue her passions outside work, education, and parenting.

She ran multiple marathons and even completed a Tough Mudder race while seven months pregnant. She filled their new home with massive, ornate mosaics that she worked on at night. A very organized person, she could do all the planning in her head, which contributed to her ability to pull off this incredible balancing act. Joe always wondered if she had the same twenty-four hours a day, seven days a week as everyone else.

Joe returned from deployment in June as planned. Shannon shuffled around the house—Colt was a big baby—making preparations and asking him about his deployment. This was Joe's ninth combat rotation, and he usually felt drained and out of place when he came home. Not this time. He had Shannon, and she was his home and his life. He never felt so good or fulfilled as he did with her.

They spent the final weeks of summer getting to know their neighbors and enjoying their new home. They both found a way to make friends with civilians for the first time in years, an odd but grounding feeling of belonging. Maybe it was a slice of the ordinary for a family that was anything but?

BETHESDA, MARYLAND, 2015

Finally, the big day arrived. Colt was on his way to join the family. Joe was terrified of Shannon having the baby while stuck on the notorious DC Beltway, so he helped Shannon into the car as soon as her contractions started.

They drove from Annapolis to Walter Reed National Military Medical Center in Bethesda, but in his haste, Joe managed to get caught speeding by a traffic camera. The ticket now makes a great souvenir in Colt's baby book.

After arriving at the hospital, Joe had no idea what to expect. He had been to several doctor's appointments, so he knew where to go, but figured everything would be different on game day. For some reason, Joe thought the dad was supposed to stand back or out of the way, maybe even in the waiting room like they often portray on TV shows. Fortunately, the doctors let him stay with Shannon the entire time.

"Joe, you doing okay?" Shannon joked. Not even her current situation could get in the way of her usual cheerful self.

Joe never received formal training as a medic but had seen some gore through the years. It felt good being in a hospital for an exciting, positive event for a change. *I've experienced enough of the other end of the life cycle for the past thirteen years,* he thought as the medical staff prepared for the birth.

"Do you want an epidural?" the doctor asked.

Shannon's contractions were underway, and they were both anxious to welcome their first son into the world.

"Nah, I think I'm just gonna suck it up," she said with a deadpan expression.

"Uh, okay . . ." the doctor responded, unsure what to think.

"No, I'm kidding," she said, laughing. "Give me them drugs!"

Joe laughed, but the doctors still didn't know what to think.

"I'm going to put my headphones on, so if you have something important to say, yank 'em out," she told Joe as her contractions got closer together. She didn't want to be disturbed by the doctors unless necessary.

She put on the headphones and cranked up her "Colt Infil" playlist that she'd prepared for the occasion. To nobody's surprise, it was mostly Iraqi hip-hop and Bollywood music. As Colt made his way into the world, Shannon squeezed Joe's hand and made giving birth look easy.

Colton Kent was born on August 11, right before midnight, which gave him the same birthday as Joe's father. He didn't cry as Joe and Shannon stared into his eyes for the first time.

"Look at what we made," Shannon said.

Joe knew immediately that watching his son come into the world was the most beautiful moment of his life. He and Shannon were no longer a couple—the addition of Colt made them a family.

CHAPTER 16

MOTHER WIFE SAILOR SPY

THE KENT HOME, FALL 2015

S hannon laid Colt on his back and started to unbutton his onesie. He had a full diaper, wasn't happy about it, and made sure anyone within earshot knew it.

"Joe, can you grab me a diaper and the wipes?!" Shannon yelled.

"Yup, on it!" Joe shouted back from another room. He and Shannon had saved up a lot of vacation time in preparation for Colt's arrival so they could savor time at home with him for the rest of the summer and into the fall while adjusting to life as a new family. Their fast-paced lives would catch up, though.

The unit slated Joe to deploy the following spring, and Shannon had been recruited into another secretive, more compartmentalized element. This element required her to attend a different high-stress selection and training pipeline when Joe was gone on his upcoming deployment.

"Okay, got the diaper and the wipes," Joe said, placing them next to Shannon. She wrestled with Colt, binding his ankles with one hand while trying to wrestle a wipe from the container with the other.

"Can you help me out here?" Shannon said, frustrated he was standing idle.

"Yes, yeah, sorry," Joe said while pulling a few more wipes out for her. Newborn baby poop never comes off easy, and the looming deployment was causing underlying stress. Before any deployment, there was much to do, but now with a new family, home life was tense.

Shannon finished wiping and then affixed the fresh diaper to Colt's bottom. Exhausted, she handed the soiled diaper to Joe to throw away.

"Here ya go, sweetie," she said, smiling and switching gears, doing her best to be the family's rock. "Relax. Enjoy the moment. You won't have to worry about diapers for too much longer!"

"Yeah, that's the problem. How are you going to do this while I'm gone?" Joe asked.

"The same way I do everything any other time you're gone," Shannon said. "Don't worry—it's only a baby. No big deal, right?"

"I don't know," Joe said. "This next trip feels different. I've never had to say goodbye to my own kid before."

"Seriously? Stressed about a deployment?" Shannon said. "I remember my first beer!"

She was spot-on, and Joe knew it. He couldn't hold in his laugh, and the mood in the room was immediately lighter. Training for war and going to war was normal for both of them. But their new life was just that: new. The transition for Shannon and Joe should have been more difficult, but with her steady, loving touch and levelheaded approach to every obstacle, it seemed to fall into place as if everything was going according to plan.

Their vacation days eventually dried up, and they returned to rigorous training schedules. They both managed their calendars so most training took place in the local area, allowing them to spend evenings and weekends together. Still, they needed help if they both wanted to continue working at a high level while raising a family.

They asked Shannon's sister, Mariah, if she could come down to help, which she was more than happy to do. By the end of the year, Aunt Mariah moved in and started helping with Colt, loving him as if he were her son and relieving some stress from the Kent family's fast-paced lives ahead of Joe's next deployment.

⚓ ⚓ ⚓

Close your eyes, and you can be," Shannon read aloud, then turned the page. "Sound asleep in an apple tree!" She could see Colt's eyes getting heavy and gave Mariah, who loved helping with his bedtime routine, a knowing look indicating he would fall asleep *any minute now*.

"For you're asleep in a cozy bed, with secret dreams in your lovely head. The end." Shannon closed the book, the same one her parents read to her when she was young, and kissed her baby's forehead. A lullaby was next. Some nights she sang "Cups" (from the movie *Pitch Perfect*) or "Stand by Me," and other nights she changed the lyrics to a lullaby about something fitting for whatever Colt dealt with that day. Tonight she opted for her favorite Irish lullaby. Her sister joined in, making it a duet:

Too-ra-loo-ra-loo-ral,
Too-ra-loo-ra-li,
Too-ra-loo-ra-loo-ral,
Hush now don't you cry!
Too-ra-loo-ra-loo-ral,
Too-ra-loo-ra-li,
Too-ra-loo-ra-loo-ral,
That's an Irish lullaby.

The bedtime routine worked. Colt was out by the song's end, so they crept out of the room. Shannon felt more fatigued than usual—it felt like more than the normal tiredness most new parents experience. She put it out of her head, chalking it up to something between *I need to drink more water* and *give yourself a break; you just had a baby.*

"Thanks, it's so nice having you here to help," Shannon said as she walked into the kitchen to fix her evening snack of rice cake with pico de gallo and avocado—her go-to option for relaxing on the couch at the end of a long day.

"He's so cute!" Mariah replied, following behind her.

"I know! I'm still not used to it!"

"So, do you still wanna go to the Eastern Market tomorrow?" Mariah asked. "That dragon costume you got for Colt last time is awesome."

"Yes! Actually, there's an artist there I need to see. I'm going to have him paint me, Joe, and Colt. We need a family portrait on the wall before Joe leaves again, and this guy's work is great." The Eastern Market was a local street fair in Washington, DC, that Shannon and Mariah frequented, and there were a few artists there she loved.

"Oh, awesome! I'm sure Joe will love it. So what are we watching tonight?" Mariah asked. It was more of a statement than a request;

they were definitely going to watch a movie tonight. Joe had a training event and wouldn't be home until late. To drive the point home, she grabbed the ingredients for Shannon's favorite drink: a Sailor Jerry with ginger ale. She was looking forward to a night of sister bonding and knew Joe's upcoming deployment weighed on Shannon. Mixing her favorite drink and being there to talk was the least she could do.

"If I'm ditching my homework to watch a movie with you tonight, then you can pick from *Republic of Embaba* or *Very Big Shot*," Shannon said. Both movies were in Arabic.

"I'm thinking something in English, maybe something from your eighties collection? Like *The Dark Crystal, Labyrinth,* or *The NeverEnding Story,* or . . . we could go more modern and watch *Pineapple Express?*" Mariah suggested.

Shannon flopped onto the couch in her living room, claiming the corner spot with the arm—the good spot—with food and her drink in hand.

"Actually, I could go for *Labyrinth* tonight. Good call," Shannon said. Mariah sat down next to her. Shannon looked over suspiciously, knowing her younger sister normally fought her for the corner spot. *She's probably glad not to be stuck watching a movie in Arabic tonight,* Shannon thought.

It was a rare night when Shannon wasn't multitasking. She couldn't sit still and focus on a movie, usually opting to half-watch while doing homework or working on one of her art projects. Tonight was different.

"So what's next after you finish your degree? Are you going to get out of the Navy and get one of those normal-people jobs?" Mariah asked as the movie started playing, and only half-joking.

Shannon took a sip of her drink and thought about how to answer for a moment.

"I don't know. I mean, it's hard for me to imagine leaving the Navy right now," Shannon said. "But I know Joe isn't going to quit deploying anytime soon either."

"Yeah?"

"Yeah. Sometimes I think about how awesome it would be to sell our house and move out to Montana," Shannon said. "Buy a few horses, maybe run an equine therapy program for vets? That would be a cool way to put my psychology degree to work. I don't know."

"I mean, sounds amazing," Mariah said. Shannon and Mariah had been talking about opening a ranch since Mariah was six years old and Shannon was sixteen. One that would offer equestrian therapy for veterans with post-traumatic stress disorder and children with emotional and developmental issues made the old idea all the more compelling.

"I would follow you to Montana if you had horses."

"But that's so far away," Shannon said. "I like the idea of Mom and Dad being near their grandki— Never trust a fucking talking worm!" Shannon quiet-yelled at the movie. On the screen, the protagonist was being given bad directions by a talking worm. Mariah laughed.

"Anway, I love Lake Placid, and that wouldn't be very far away from them," Shannon continued. "Or, I've always thought it would be cool to raise my kids on a beach. I could teach Colt how to sail, wakeboard, surf . . . You know Joe would love to turn Colt into a mini combat diver."

"And you could dress Coltie up in old-timey swimsuits!" Mariah said.

"Only if I can talk him into taking off his new dragon costume!" They both laughed at the thought. "So I guess I need to figure out if I want to do horses and psychology in Montana or be a professional mosaic artist on the beach," she said sarcastically.

"How did you even begin attempting that shit?" Mariah asked, referring to her mosaic projects.

"It's all about stress management," Shannon said. "Seriously, it's the only way I've found to channel my stress from work into something positive."

$$\text{⚓ ⚓ ⚓}$$

Months later, in the spring of 2016, Joe left for his tenth deployment, and Shannon started her new training pipeline. For most service members, the inability to communicate with family while away on deployments or sensitive training is one of the many hardships of military life. When people with security clearances get married, they don't have to deal with that problem as much. In Shannon and Joe's case, they were often able to communicate over classified networks at work, regardless of where either of them was in the world. But sometimes, even Shannon was unable to use any form of communication.

During one of the final exercises in her training pipeline, some of Joe's friends from Special Forces were tasked to play "bad guys," going after Shannon and her classmates. One morning in Iraq, he checked his classified work email and saw a short note from an old friend:

> Joe, I started my day by kidnapping your wife and putting her in my trunk.
> Have a great day.

To most, that message would be very unsettling, but Joe understood she must have been doing well if his buddy emailed him.

If not, no one would have reached out. All he could do was smile at his computer screen, happy the mother of his son, his soul mate, was crushing yet another elite selection process. *We may be weird and high-stress, but we aren't boring!* he thought.

Shannon completed training and returned home shortly after being "kidnapped" by Joe's friends. He still had three months to go in Iraq, so Shannon settled back into hardworking single-mom mode. Despite them both being well into their military careers, it was the first time either of them did something like this with a small child at home. Sure, Mariah was there to help, and sometimes Joe's parents when Shannon needed to go out of town for her pipeline training, but that only alleviated some of the guilt of being away.

"I love being over here," Joe told Shannon over FaceTime one day after she got home from training. "But this time, it feels like I'm not supposed to be here . . . like I'm supposed to be there with you and Colt."

"I know, and I wish you were home too," Shannon said. "But we talked about this. I hate to admit it, but this is your duty to the country. It's what we do. This is us. We both knew it would be like this if we had kids."

Shannon's reassuring words helped, but only so much. She was already starting to do the math in her head and knew they couldn't keep this lifestyle up for long. She also knew he would never be able to wrap his head around not deploying again. Combat was his calling.

"There's something else I wanted to talk to you about . . ." Shannon said.

"What's up?" Joe replied.

"I've been home for a few weeks and should be recovered from training by now," Shannon said. "But I'm always tired and feel like I can't get enough rest. I don't know, maybe it's going straight from training into full-time mom mode, but this feels weird."

"You should go get checked out," Joe said. "Better safe than sorry."

"I have. The doctors think it's normal post-baby stuff."

But after another month of constant fatigue and not feeling like herself, Shannon went to a different doctor for a second opinion. They diagnosed hypothyroidism. The doctor explained how her pregnancy gave her the condition and reassured her it was a common occurrence. The doctor prescribed Synthroid and told her to keep an eye on her symptoms.

Shannon went home and immediately threw herself back into work, trying to focus on anything but herself. Something wasn't right, though. She compartmentalized and drove on—the same way she negotiated every obstacle in life. But the night sweats continued, and she could tell something was off.

The night sweats, in particular, were a primary cue to Shannon the doctors were missing something. Her cousins both had Hashimoto's disease, an autoimmune disease where the immune system creates antibodies that attack cells in the thyroid, thus significantly reducing hormone production. The odds were she might have it, given her family history.

Shannon returned to the doctor with her suspicion. They tested and confirmed she had Hashimoto's disease. From that point forward, she could get the doctor's visits she needed but had to suffer through months of appointments with no improvements to her health to show, and doctors seemed unconcerned.

Mariah noticed she was becoming irritable and overwhelmed but stubbornly tried to shoulder the entire burden herself. Shannon wanted to project that she was fine and there was nothing to worry about because she didn't want Joe to be distracted or concerned while he was deployed. Everything wasn't fine, though.

Shannon went to three separate doctors looking for answers, and all three doctors told her she was okay. Finally, she saw a fourth doctor, who asked her to come in to talk about his findings.

"All right, Shannon, thanks for making time to see us today. We have some answers explaining why you've felt so awful."

Shannon nodded her head, anxious for him to go on.

"We confirmed you have thyroid cancer, which isn't surprising since your Hashimoto's diagnosis puts you at a higher risk," the doctor said, getting right to the point.

Shannon couldn't help but show emotion—tears ran down her cheeks.

"There are a few different treatment options, but the most direct way to deal with this is to conduct a biopsy and cut it right out," the doctor continued.

Shannon composed herself and straightened her posture. "Well, let's cut it out—shouldn't be a big deal, right?" she said. "I have stuff to do."

She mentioned the upcoming biopsy to Joe in a text message on her way home but didn't elaborate. She didn't want him to think it was anything other than a routine medical procedure. Joe was caught up in what he was doing in Iraq and figured it must not be a big deal if she was texting him.

The surgeon removed the cancer in one surgery, and Shannon was back to work within a day without missing a beat. On top of being a special operations combat veteran, a mother, and a wife, Shannon now added "cancer survivor" to her list of titles. She sent Joe another text message, this time with a photo of the noticeable laceration across her throat, freshly stitched closed.

Got a touch of cancer cut out, she typed in a blunt follow-up text. Joe was instantly worried. He'd had no idea it was that bad. He asked if he should get home, but Shannon insisted it wasn't a big deal and that she could take care of it.

Nothing you can do now, so just finish what you are doing there and get back to us, Shannon typed. Shannon was already back at work, planning secret operations during the day and raising their son full-time at night.

After four months of working through the problem with doctors, Shannon was declared permanently cancer-free. She didn't know it at the time, but it would still impact her life in ways she couldn't yet fathom. Her fight with cancer was short-lived, but it created a new struggle—one that wasn't so simple to defeat.

CHAPTER 17

A BRIGHT FUTURE

THE KENT HOME, FALL 2016

Joe returned home from Iraq in the fall, and Shannon and Colt were excited to greet him. Their family was whole again for the first time in over six months.

Shannon knew her husband was coming up on his twenty-year mark, which meant retirement was on the table. She didn't dare give herself hope this last trip to Iraq might be Joe's last deployment, but she couldn't help but think about the possibility. She prepared amazing dinners every night while Joe played with Colt, trying to make up for the lost time. On weekends, she slept in while Joe got up with Colt so they could hang out together. Colt had grown so much while Joe was away; he looked like Joe, but with Shannon's fair skin and reddish hair, and was becoming quite the character.

Every weekend, they invited their friends over. They worked in the same circles, so their friend groups meshed easily. Being from New York, Shannon often prepared baked ziti to feed everyone, then they all played cards well into the evening.

Joe's best friend from his old ODA, Josh Rowson, worked in the area, and Shannon encouraged him to come over several nights a week to have a beer with Joe on the back porch. She knew what it was like to come home from a long deployment and knew how important it would be for Joe to take time to decompress with friends who understood what he was coming home from. In that way, Shannon knew him better than he knew himself.

One Saturday morning in early October, she walked down their stairs, shaking her head while sheepishly looking at Joe.

"Make me a big cheesy omelet, please. I'm pretty sure you knocked me up again!" A doctor's visit confirmed she was pregnant with their second son, whom they named Josh, after Joe's best friend. They were excited to have another child and to give Colt a playmate. In under three years, the Kent family went from marriage to having two kids amid high-intensity special operations training, combat deployments, and a bout with cancer.

Shannon had recently finished her bachelor's degree in psychology and decided to return to school for her master's, working toward a future that gave her options to pursue a psychology doctorate. She heard about the military psychology program at the Uniformed Services University of the Health Sciences from a psychologist who worked with special operations forces. Once she learned how psychologists supported warfighters, she knew it was a way to merge her personal and professional goals. A PhD in psychology would allow her a more normal lifestyle conducive to raising her sons, but still in a position to contribute to her unit's mission and even help her fellow veterans who were struggling with PTSD. She was still haunted by her experience in Afghanistan and losing her commander to his demons.

She wasn't slowing down because she was pregnant. She needed time to think, to digest the escalating complexities of raising a family while both parents served in special operations. Joe often found her up at odd hours of the night, working on her mosaics while a TV show with Arabic subtitles played in the background or with a headlamp on doing a little midnight gardening in the backyard.

Her garden was an escape, much the way her art was. She would spend thirty minutes, sometimes a full hour, in her garden after work each day before coming inside for the evening. Their greenhouse allowed Shannon to work well into the night, even in the winter, tending to her plants. She grew everything from basil to zucchini squash to make zucchini spaghetti noodles, corn for the squirrels, pumpkins, apple trees, peach trees, and citronella to keep the mosquitoes away.

She loved having Colt in the garden with her and created an environment that would be fun for him to explore with a path winding through her fruit trees and flowers. Sometimes she would take the basil leaves out of their pots and hand them to Colt to put in a bag for pesto later. He ate the basil instead.

"Coltie, oh Coltie!" Shannon would say in a high-pitched mothering voice, attempting to make him laugh. At that age, Colt was always putting something in his mouth, so Shannon tried to simultaneously discourage him from eating something he wasn't supposed to while making him laugh in the process.

Whether it was a thin slice of chicken breast baked with a tablespoon of cream cheese and bacon on top or her go-to dish of spaghetti squash with tomato sauce or pesto, the garden went hand in hand with her passion for cooking. Regardless of what she was preparing, she never ran short on cheese. She put it on everything.

As the arrival of their second son drew closer, Joe's command

Shannon Kent's official Navy photo.

Shannon (*center*) posing for a group photo in costume with the cast of her high school play.

Shannon behind the counter at the local drug store, Pine Plains Pharmacy, where she worked after school during high school.

Shannon and her younger sister, Mariah (*left*), riding horses in New York.

Photos from
Shannon's
deployment to
Afghanistan
in the early 2010s.

Joe and Shannon Kent at the Navy chief's Khaki Ball in Annapolis, Maryland, in 2015. Shannon just had cancer surgery on her throat—her scar is still visible here.

Joe and Shannon out together in Washington, DC, while Shannon was pregnant with Colt in 2015.

Shannon after delivering Colt at Walter Reed National Military Medical Center.

Shannon with Josh after he was born at Walter Reed.

Shannon posing with Colt and Josh for family pictures.

Joe, Shannon, and Colt posing for a picture at Christmas in 2016.

Shannon holding Josh at home in Maryland in 2017.

Shannon training for her Appalachian Trail race with Colt in tow and Roo alongside in 2018.

UNIFORMED SERVICES UNIVERSITY OF THE HEALTH SCIENCES
4301 JONES BRIDGE ROAD
BETHESDA, MARYLAND 20814-4712
http://www.usuhs.mil

GRADUATE EDUCATION

March 1, 2018

CPO Shannon Kent
▇▇▇▇▇▇▇ Maryland 21032

Dear CPO Kent,

Congratulations, your application for graduate study in the Clinical Psychology Ph.D. Program at the Uniformed Services University (USU) has been favorably reviewed. I am pleased to inform you that you have been selected for admission to the Clinical Psychology – Military Track (CPS) Ph.D. Program for the 2018-2019 academic year.

Your acceptance is contingent upon service (Navy) approval and release for out-of-service long-term graduate training. You must be detailed, on orders, to this University as a full-time graduate student. This letter does not constitute approval by your parent service department, which must be obtained by you in a separate personnel action in accordance with the directives of that department. Students will be responsible for making their own arrangements for lodging and meals.

Please notify this office in writing (or by e-mail at ▇▇▇▇▇▇▇@usuhs.edu) of your decision to accept or decline this appointment by April 15th, 2018.

If you have any questions, please call our office at 301.▇▇▇▇ or 301.▇▇▇▇.

Thank you! I look forward to hearing from you.

Sincerely,

▇▇▇▇▇▇▇

▇▇▇▇▇▇▇, Ph.D.
Professor, Anatomy, Physiology and Genetics
Associate Dean for Graduate Education

Learning to Care for Those in Harm's Way

Shannon's acceptance letter into the Uniformed Services Health Service Clinical Psychology program.

Shannon in 2018 during her visit to Capitol Hill to solicit support for her proposed change to the regulations about officer accessions so that she could commission—or at least make it possible for others to do so.

Shannon during her race through the Appalachian Mountains, right before a major snowstorm began, which forced them to abort the race.

Shannon in a photo she sent to Joe while deployed to Syria in 2018.

Shannon at a safe house in Syria, days before her death. This is the last picture Shannon sent to Joe.

The restaurant where an ISIS suicide bomber attacked Team Manbij. Photo taken in November 2019.

Shannon's uniform top—referred to as "khakis"—with her chief's anchors visible on the lapels.

A "sea of khaki" filled the pews at the Naval Academy's chapel during Shannon's memorial service.

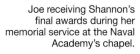

Joe receiving Shannon's final awards during her memorial service at the Naval Academy's chapel.

Each Navy chief took an anchor off of their uniform's lapel and dropped it in a jar as they filed out of the chapel.

A collection of notes and photos from Shannon that Shannon's sister, Mariah, keeps.

A variety of mosaics and other artwork that Shannon made for their home in Maryland.

The Kent family during Thanksgiving 2018, a day before Shannon left for Syria. This is the last photo the Kents took as a family.

asked if he could deploy for the eleventh time. It was early 2017, the fight against ISIS was at a peak in several countries, and the majority of the warfighting responsibility rested on the shoulders of the special operations community. Time wasn't measured in months and years but rather a never-ending rotation of training cycles and deployments. Rinse and repeat, over and over. It was common to hear things like *remember that great brewery we found two training cycles ago* or *I think we could plan to take the kids to Disney after next deployment.*

The special operations community led every fight in the war on terror, and the fight against ISIS was no different. But Joe was nearing retirement and could have said no. After all, he'd returned from Iraq only three months before and already had ten deployments. No one in his chain of command nor any of his peers would have thought less of him if he opted not to go again on short notice. But he couldn't bring himself to say no.

Shannon didn't take the news well. She worked in the same community, so there was no bullshitting her. She knew he didn't need to go and was unhappy with his decision.

"I get it. This is you. This is one of the reasons I love you. But I'm not happy about it. You'll have to figure out how to be you without this someday," she said. It felt like he'd just returned from his last deployment.

She knew that some of Joe's inability to say no was due to his sense of duty to the mission and his brothers and sisters in arms—which sounds honorable. But the truth was he couldn't resist the allure of war. At age thirty-seven, it was all he'd ever known. His entire adult life was spent either at war or preparing for it. Maybe it was the desire always to feel needed—like he was doing his part for society as a man and a warrior. Yet any rational person being honest with themselves would see family needs should come first after so many years of service to others. She knew ego was a factor too. They asked *Joe* to deploy—not just anyone—specifically *Joe*.

Even though Joe didn't want to admit it at the time, Shannon knew the military had others who could take his place. But how do you convince someone who feels more comfortable overseas in combat than at home? Of course, he was happy at home but felt the most useful while deployed. He needed to reconcile himself as either a father or a warrior, but until then, all burdens resulting from his being gone rested on Shannon—who was pregnant.

"I can't say no and make someone else go in my place," Joe said in a patronizing attempt to explain his self-righteous warrior ethos to her. "I can't do that."

The decision was final.

While Joe was gone, Shannon supported her other teammates in preparing for war. As someone trained in signals intelligence, Shannon did not always need to deploy forward to support the fight. She could hunt from the shadows and be home by six to make dinner for Colt.

Pregnant with Josh, with Colt keeping her up most of the night and Joe deployed, Shannon continued her full-time duties as a Navy chief, signals intelligence professional, mother of two, and wife of a deployed soldier. These circumstances solidified her decision to pursue a PhD instead of seeking more danger. She needed to ensure she would never leave her boys as long as Joe was still deploying. Mental health was an area the military needed help with, and she could do that without having to be in harm's way.

The essay Dr. Buechner assigned weighed heavy on Shannon. All she could do was stare at the blinking cursor, which seemed to mock her from inside the empty Word document staring back at her from the laptop. The house was quiet; coffee and her deepest thoughts were her only company.

His lecture was good, and she kept returning to the Gandhi quote he used—or was that Yoda? "Do or do not. There is no 'try.'" *That pretty much sums up how I view the world and what I do every day,* she thought. *Yeah, let's start there.*

"Sometimes the military doesn't really appreciate it when you try to change something," she typed. It was a huge understatement. "I do it all the time, and sometimes it has cost me dearly. But I'll keep doing it anyway."

So many thoughts rushed through her head as those words hit the page. A few operators in the past didn't appreciate her being in places women weren't supposed to be, but she was there anyway. There was institutional resistance to seeking help for mental health issues, but that wasn't stopping her from telling friends they needed to go to therapy. You can't effect change if you don't try, even if the odds are stacked against you. She recognized there was a time to be hard and a time to show empathy.

Shannon thought of her friend Laura, who had recently returned from a deployment where she lost friends and saw things she hoped no one ever had to see. Shannon needed to give her friend permission to be vulnerable and get help.

"You should go talk to the doctor," Shannon remembered telling her. Laura insisted she was fine.

"No, Laura, you're not fine, and that's okay," Shannon told her.

No one said no to Shannon, so Laura made an appointment and eventually talked to a doctor. It made a difference.

"Man, Shannon, that helped," Laura told her. "But I'm not going to lie, I cried like a little . . ."

Shannon interrupted and looked her straight in the eye, "Crying doesn't make you weak. You can't keep it all bottled up. That's the old way of thought and look at where it has gotten us. Look at all of these suicides."

Shannon and Laura talked about the different types of crying that day, and she convinced her friend it was okay to cry. *But we both agreed accidental angry crying is the absolute worst.* Shannon smiled, remembering their conversation.

Shannon may not have been a psychologist yet, but she knew her community and its problems well enough to help. She didn't need to wait for a piece of paper to give her permission to help fight the mental health epidemic sweeping through the military.

"The military expects people to follow the regulations and expects senior NCOs to enforce the standards and regulations," she wrote, feeling momentum building. "Well, not all of them are good or fair. I will not stop trying to change the unfair ones because that's what kind of person I am. I won't just talk about not liking something, I'll actively try to change it."

The words felt liberating to put down on paper, as if typing these statements—some in the Navy might consider them borderline blasphemous—made them exist in the real world, outside her head. She realized that what she'd learned in this master's program over the last two years changed her worldview and how she approached problems, one of the biggest being preventing good people like Commander Price from taking their own lives.

"As a senior NCO, I see disciplinary problems all the time," she wrote, then took another sip of her coffee. *How many times have I gotten in someone's face and told them to stop being such a dirtbag and to get with the program without any thought about why?* A lump formed in her throat. Sometimes looking in the mirror is hard.

"Things are no longer as black and white for me, and they never will be again. Now I look at the situation through the lens of a mental health professional. I think, *Why is he acting out this way? He's not following the most simple of regulations.* Obviously, the regulations are not the real issue here."

But the regulations are still a factor, she knew. How do you balance good order and discipline with caring for the sailors in your charge? *This is why leaders in the military do such a shitty job at dealing with this stuff,* she thought.

"When I reflect on my own 'dark times' in the military, I find that this course of study has allowed me to forgive myself," she wrote. "There was a period of about a year and a half wherein I acted rashly, recklessly, and sometimes insensitively, angrily, or inappropriately. I beat myself up over my behavior and the consequences of it. Now I realize, *Wow, I really went through the wringer. No wonder I acted out that way.*"

Shannon referred to the period leading up to and during her fourth combat deployment when she lost her internal filter and good judgment. She did things she wasn't proud of, and looking back, knew she had spun out of control and punished herself for years afterward. *That was, without a doubt, the worst period of my life,* she thought.

"But now, I marvel at what I went through and how I didn't end up worse off. I'm proud of how I've bounced back," she continued typing, hoping what was in her head translated onto the page. "I realize now that I was treated very poorly and was right to be angry during that time, and that the chronic stress of having undergone four combat deployments in six years is a load that is ridiculous for anyone to bear."

Shannon knew she was a senior leader now and had a responsibility not to keep repeating the same mistakes as her predecessors.

I would never make my people do that much, especially in such a short amount of time. Looking back, she knew that while one is always responsible for their actions, you have to ask, "Well, what did you think would happen when you put someone under that much pressure?" *It's amazing I didn't end up worse off than I did.*

"I will probably never forgive the leaders I had at the time for their blindness and what they put me through," she wrote. "They didn't even realize how many deployments I had done. They held me to an unrealistic standard and had no idea what they were doing to me because they themselves hadn't done as much as me. They also never tried to find out. They just punished me and were quite cruel. I'll never forgive them for that."

It was the brutal truth. Typing it out, saying it out loud, felt good. She knew she wasn't a bad person or an underperforming sailor. She gave the Navy and this nation so much but experienced the misfortune of working for some leaders who took everything for granted. She stared at the screen, the cursor again flashing, almost encouraging her to get to the point. *The point is, I need to be the change.*

"I will carry the lessons forward, and never let that happen to my people," she typed. "I know what it looks like when someone is starting to spiral. I know what it feels like. And now, I know what to do about it."

With that, Shannon leaned back in her chair and let out a forceful exhale. It felt as if she'd been holding her breath for the last hour. Her coffee had gone cold, but she took another sip anyway. *This is good,* she thought. *Probably more than Dr. Buechner figured he would get, but I needed this.*

She reread the essay twice to check for mistakes and then read it out loud once more. Satisfied, she saved the document and submitted it to her professor. Emotionally drained but feeling like a weight was lifted off her shoulders, Shannon closed her laptop and returned to her ongoing mosaic project. The night was still young.

⚓ ⚓ ⚓

Shannon was seven months pregnant with Josh, Joe was still on his eleventh deployment, and the basement flooded due to faulty piping. Shannon fixed the pipes and then decided to renovate their unfinished basement while she was at it.

Two weeks later, the kitchen pipes flooded the kitchen. Shannon repeated the drill, fixing the pipe but then going further to put in a new kitchen floor. Coordinating with the contractors could have interfered with her studying schedule, but she paid her tutor extra to show up early in the morning or later in the evening instead. During all the renovations, Shannon still found time to FaceTime or at least text Joe daily so he could keep up with their growing sons.

Joe's final deployment came and went. He did not save the world or win the war on terror. Maybe they didn't need him so bad after all. He started his trip home a month and a half before Josh was due. Like all his homecomings, Shannon made his return special by preparing a cooked turkey with stuffed peppers and stocking Joe's favorite beer in the refrigerator. She handed him one of those beers as he walked in the door, and Colt ran up and hugged his leg.

"Grab Colt and your beer. I'm giving you a tour of our new house!" Shannon said. She was excited to have her husband back—*maybe this will be his last one?* Despite how close she was to delivering her second child, she showed off her work in the basement, kitchen, and master bathroom renovation.

A month later, on June 21, 2017, Baby Josh was born at Walter Reed. They even made it to the hospital without a speeding ticket this time. Shannon and Joe fell into a family routine with their kids that summer. One parent would stay home with Josh, and the other would take Colt on adventures in the morning or afternoon.

They daydreamed about what it would be like to take the boys on vacation someday. Shannon wanted to write down information about different countries worldwide, put each country in a separate envelope, and then have their sons pick one. That would be where they went on vacation that year. Shannon couldn't have been more excited for life with Joe and their sons.

Joe had been promoted to Chief Warrant Officer 3 the year before, so his number for some sort of bureaucratic staff purgatory assignment would inevitably be called. He had plenty of vacation to burn and decided to quit while he was ahead, concluding what most in the military would characterize as a legendary career, the kind almost anyone who has served would envy.

He figured he could find work in the special operations or intelligence community when he retired and could continue contributing to the fight. With a plan in place, Chief Joe Kent requested to retire from the US Army and move on to the next chapter with Shannon and their two boys.

Shannon remained focused on getting into the psychology program and performed very well on her GRE—despite taking it one week before giving birth to Josh. She spent the summer getting her application in order and preparing for the upcoming interviews with the department heads of the psych program.

Shannon's preparation was rigorous: she read thousands of pages of academic journals and prepared to discuss the latest topics in psychology and military mental health. Still recovering from giving birth, she attacked this task in a very Shannon way, using late nights with Josh as a chance to read papers and make notes.

Around this same time, Mariah received a job offer back in

New York and moved out after accepting the position. Shannon researched how to get help with the kids and found an au pair named Ayelen—Ashe for short—through an agency.

Ashe was already working with another family and in the process of a rematch, when the host family looks for another nanny and the au pair searches for a different host family. There is a worldwide network where au pairs and families often trade notes on the best places to go, good experiences, and families to avoid. Ashe came with high recommendations, so Shannon scheduled a Skype interview.

"Hi, my name is Ashe. I'm from Argentina," She said at the beginning of the Skype call.

"Hey, what's up? I've actually been to Argentina three times," Shannon said in perfect Spanish and an Argentinian accent. Ashe did not expect a response in her native language when interviewing with families living in the United States. The way Shannon said *hey, what's up* was particular to Argentina—Ashe was immediately impressed.

Shannon explained how Argentina was a country she knew very well. She continued the conversation, talking about her family and the plans she and Joe had for expansion. They talked about what the hours would be like and already started making jokes about how they would like to speak with her about an extension after her year was over.

Ashe might not have realized it at the time, but Shannon had already done extensive research on her and knew she would fit in with their growing family very well. Out of the eight interviews she conducted, Ashe was the only one who asked about Colt.

"My husband and I are both in the military," Shannon explained. "We have a pretty hectic schedule and need someone we can trust because of how often we're out of town." Being a true quiet professional, Shannon didn't elaborate on what type of work she did in the military. It would be years later before Ashe found out what Shannon was really doing and why her and Joe's schedules were so busy.

They acted quickly to move Ashe out to Maryland and integrate her with the family. Shannon picked her up from the airport the day she arrived and drove her home to meet the family.

Joe opened the door, holding Colt. Colt and Ashe became quick friends. Shannon wanted her to feel comfortable and welcome and had already decorated her room. Two weeks after she arrived, Ashe flew to Oregon with them to spend Christmas with Joe's side of the family. They made her feel like part of the family, and Ashe was hooked.

They fell into a daily cadence and found a new normal. Shannon left for work early in the morning—five in the morning if she was going through training or other times at eight if it was a regular office day. Ashe stayed at home with the boys until Shannon came home around five.

After Shannon came home, they would spend time catching up on each other's days while Shannon cooked or gardened. Shannon talked about how work went, and Ashe would tell her what the boys were up to. After Shannon put the boys to sleep, she transitioned to studying or working on mosaics.

Her skill with mosaics was remarkable, and not only because they were beautiful or took immense care to create. More than that, the volume of work she completed was astounding. One of her more notable projects was a massive dinner table with an inlaid tile mosaic in the shape of a tree. It stretched the length of the table and was incredibly detailed.

One of Shannon's first mosaics was a seashell arrangement that spelled Kent. She wanted to hang it over a door but needed Joe's help. It became a classic moment almost any married couple can identify with. Shannon stood back and gave Joe directions:

"A little to the left, more, more, no, too far, come back right a little bit . . ."

Joe dutifully, maybe a bit begrudgingly, made the adjustments with the heavy piece of art held over his head against the wall.

With Joe's retirement looming and Shannon progressing toward acceptance into a PhD program, the future looked bright. Small back-and-forths about hanging a piece of art were almost charming in that it was a preview of what life could look like going forward: a happily married couple raising their kids, tackling chores around the house, and living the American dream.

CHAPTER 18

THE NOT-SO-CALM BEFORE THE STORM

THE KENT HOME, MARYLAND, NOVEMBER 2017

Shannon always looked forward to hosting Thanksgiving, and this year, she wanted to do it Shannon-style. Ali Hassoon and his family were close friends of Joe and Shannon's from their time in Iraq together, and being somewhat new to the country, Shannon saw an opportunity to bring people together over turkey and a traditional Iraqi meal called dolma . . . and take a break from her PhD board preparation.

In addition to Ali and his wife, Sarah, Shannon invited another Iraqi American family; her sister, Mariah; Joe's best friend, Josh Rowson; and a few friends from work. This Thanksgiving wasn't a typical turkey-and-football affair but a multicultural holiday with traditional dishes from wherever their guests came from.

When the day came, Shannon and the other wives worked on the big meal while Joe, Ali, and Josh drank beer and kept all the kids distracted. With everyone gathered, they broke bread over Shannon's mosaic-tree table. They ate turkey, kebab, and dolma stuffed with grape leaves, onion, rice, and zucchini, with a custom mix of spices. There were a variety of pies—including Shannon's pecan pie—and sweets alongside other traditional fares. Ali had never had an American-style pie before, but it quickly became his favorite.

"Shannon, from now on, like from this point forward, if you ask me for something, you can make it up to me by making me a pecan pie," Ali joked, though he knew she rarely, if ever, asked for help.

It wasn't the first time Ali was blown away by Shannon's culinary expertise. He even put his mom on the phone with Shannon to talk to her (in Iraqi Arabic) about what kind of spices she put in her food and what she thought was the best rice, grape leaves, and spices for making dolma. "I know a few things," Shannon responded every time Ali was surprised by her cooking.

While it looked like any other Thanksgiving gathering, one might not have guessed this one brought together a unique mix of men and women, warriors and operators, immigrants, and siblings. Everyone vowed this was the new tradition and that it needed to happen again next year.

⚓ ⚓ ⚓

After Thanksgiving, Shannon announced that she'd volunteered for a fifty-mile race through the Appalachian Mountains that Third Special Forces Group organized. "So don't plan on any work trips for mid-December," she told Joe.

"I'm happy to hold down our very warm, very dry fort with

Colt and Joshy while you slog through frozen mud on the side of some mountain," Joe said. The race was scheduled only six months after Shannon delivered Josh, and she was still dealing with a painful abdominal muscle tear that occurred during delivery. He wondered if it was too soon for her to be running up and down mountains in the middle of winter, but dismissed the idea—who was he to doubt Shannon's will to push herself?

"You know," he added, "if the weather gets nasty, most of the Green Berets and SEALs will probably go find the nearest hotel with a decent bar."

"You guys can get away with that shit, but not the chick, and definitely not the intel chick," Shannon said. "So I'm walking till it's over, or they come get me."

Joe had no doubt. The fifty-mile orienteering race on the Appalachian Trail in the mountains of North Carolina and Georgia in mid-December was something every component of the special operations community was participating in, and she saw it as a good chance for friendly competition.

Competitors would be facing thousands of feet of elevation gain, and wet, cold snow was inevitable, so the race rules required two-person teams, and that the team stay together for the entire race due to the austere conditions. Between the conditions and the likelihood of sustaining injuries being high, no one initially volunteered to be her partner. So, Shannon's commander volun-told someone from her unit to go with her.

Her partner was another intel operator like Shannon, and the rumor was they would be the only team with a female competitor, and the only team without a Green Beret, SEAL, or Raider on it. When Shannon heard this, she became even more serious about the race—now there were shit-talking rights on the line.

She prepared by taking Colt on long hikes in a baby backpack, sometimes with Joe, other times without. She went on long runs to build her endurance up as much as possible and lived by the popular mantra *proper preparation prevents piss-poor performance.* She knew if she wanted to perform at a high level during this race, she couldn't slack.

APPALACHIAN MOUNTAINS, DECEMBER 2017

The skies were overcast and drizzling rain during their ride to the point of departure. The forecast predicted it would get worse before it got better.

Shannon arrived prepared for whatever weather came their way, with trekking poles, hiking boots, gaiters to keep the moisture out, and multiple layers—including a waterproof shell. She also carried her cell phone as well as a radio to communicate checkpoints with the cadre running the race. The right gear was as essential as her physical abilities in a race like this. She wanted to represent her unit with a strong showing, but the upcoming weather compounded her pre-competition nerves.

Fifty miles is no joke on flat ground in good weather, she thought, staring out the window of the nondescript government van moving up the mountain road. *This won't be easy.*

Shannon and her partner stepped off with calm determination at the starting line. *One foot in front of the other, just like selection,* she thought. Damp leaves crunched under her boots and cold air hit her lungs.

They began the hike with light conversation, but as happens on all long walks, that eventually gave way to silence to preserve their lungs for the challenges ahead. Shannon's mind wandered. She thought about the PhD program and how important it was to complete it.

There's no way I will convince Joe not to go to Ground Branch after he retires, and the boys will need a full-time parent. I can't keep deploying if he isn't going to stop.

They moved up a steep ridge, legs pumping one in front of the other. Their boots gripped the ground well despite the wet conditions. They moved over the ridge, caught a brief view of the beautiful landscape, then headed back down into the trees again. In the mountains, what goes down must go up and up again. Over and over.

The first mile turned into five, five into ten. Day turned to night, night into day. The cold air stung their nostrils, throat, and even their lungs. Shannon was out of reception most of the time but was able to find a signal on some ridges. She used those rare opportunities to check in with Joe, who followed their progress on Google Maps.

"Hey, babe, how's it going out there? Weather looks like it's about to get rough," Joe said after picking up on the second ring.

"Yeah, it would be nice if the sun came out, but I don't think that's going to happen. How are the boys?" Shannon said.

"Joshy's sleeping and Colt is fighting sleep. So, totally normal," Joe said. "I'm telling you, there's no way all those SEALs and GBs haven't found a warm bar with cold beer by now."

"And I'm telling you, we don't have the luxury of quitting. There's no way in hell the lone intel team is pulling out! Is Joshy eating okay?"

"Definitely, he's crushing bottles. All is good on the home front. Just worry about hitting your next checkpoint—I got everything covered up here."

"Ugh, I already miss them. And I know you have everything covered. But we better get going—thanks, Joe, love you!"

"Love you too, babe."

The wind only seemed to blow harder the farther they moved. On the third day, it started to snow. At first it was barely over the rubber sole on her boots, but before long, her feet were sinking with each step. Visibility was rapidly deteriorating, but they pressed on—no one promised them it would be easy.

What if I don't pass the board? What the fuck am I going to do then? She knew the answer to her question. Life in a ███████████████████* wasn't going to slow down anytime soon. ISIS still threatened the Middle East, their offshoots continued to destabilize regions of Africa, and of course, Russia and China weren't going away anytime soon. *It's only a matter of time before I deploy again if I can't make this happen.*

They logged mile after mile, pressing on with visions of hot food and coffee inevitably waiting for them on the other side of the ridge. They used those visions as fuel for every ridge they ascended. *Just over the next one . . . and the next.* The blowing snow was so bad they couldn't see the trunks of trees ten feet in front of them. The wind punished any small amount of skin they left exposed. At one point, they stopped completely to confirm their location before moving on.

"Hey, Shan, it's getting to the point where we could walk off a damn cliff and not even know it," her partner shouted over the gusts.

"Yeah, dude, and we haven't seen anyone else. Like, not a single other team," Shannon replied. About then, their radio crackled to life.

"Shannon, this is the CP. Radio check, over."

"CP, this is Shannon, read you Lima Charlie, over."

"Roger. Listen, the commander is making a weather call. All remaining teams are being pulled off the trail at this time. What's your current grid, over?"

Shannon confirmed their current location, reading their six-digit grid location back over the radio.

---

* Description of unit redacted at request of DoD.

"Roger, okay. So there's a road crossing about three kilometers from your current position. Do you see that, over?"

"Yes, got it, over," Shannon said.

"Move to that point for pickup, time now. CP, out."

Shannon was disappointed, but accurate navigation was practically impossible at this point, and she was pretty sure she had exacerbated her lingering abdominal injury. They made it to the road crossing in under an hour, where two sergeants waited for them.

"Hey, guys, come on over. We got the heat running and hot coffee. Leadership is pulling all racers off the trail due to . . . this," the sergeant said, waving his arm in the air in no specific direction. "You and one other team are the only ones still out here!"

"Roger that!" Shannon said. Of course, she would have kept going, but rules are rules, and thirty miles through the mountains in a blizzard would have to be good enough. Besides, she definitely obtained the shit-talking rights she wanted if all but one other team already dropped out.

Shannon sent a text message to Joe when she arrived at the hotel.

We were one of two teams who stayed on the trail, everyone else traded the trail for a local pub as soon as the weather got nasty, just like you said.

I knew it! Joe chuckled, knowing few could match his wife's tenacity.

⚓ ⚓ ⚓

The Uniformed Services University of the Health Sciences (USU) Department of Medical and Clinical Psychology runs an American Psychological Association–accredited doctoral program that produces certified clinical psychologists for service in the US Navy, Army, and Air Force. The Navy provides funding for only two doctoral students per year to attend this prestigious program, and those slots are highly competitive as they are open to anyone who has at least a bachelor's degree—including civilians and enlisted naval personnel alike—and fully paid for.[1]

Passing the admissions board is crucial for acceptance into this program, but applicants must also be eligible for and meet the standards of a commissioned naval officer. This is required even if you are already serving in the Navy, as accessions standards for commissioning as an officer are different from retention standards in military regulations—the former being significantly more stringent than the latter.

Competing in the Appalachian Mountains orienteering race was Shannon's last "break" before her psychology admission board interviews, so with that behind her, she shifted back to preparing for the questions she would be asked and rehearsing her speech. She couldn't ignore the pain in her abdomen, though, and to make matters worse, she could now see a protrusion.

With her board interviews rapidly approaching, she went to the doctor to have the protrusion looked at. The doctor diagnosed it as traumatic diastasis recti, or a ball of angry, pulled muscles trying to poke out of her lower stomach.

"It's a misconception that abdominal muscles are all one muscle," the doctor explained to Shannon. "In reality, they are individual muscles separated down the middle and held together by connective tissue we call linea alba—kind of like a tendon or ligament. When you were pregnant with—Josh, right?"

"Yes, we call him Joshy," Shannon said.

"Well, when you were pregnant with Josh, that tissue expanded as he grew, and your abdominal muscles weakened. Eventually the tissue tore, allowing your underlying fat and internal organs to poke through, which is the protrusion you see."

"I'm guessing the hike through the mountains I did a few weeks ago didn't help?" Shannon asked.

"No, no, it did not," the doctor said. "As you are well aware, this is a very painful condition. I would recommend surgery as soon as possible so we can reconnect your damaged lining and start the healing process."

Shannon underwent surgery only days before she was scheduled to go before the selection board. She had a high pain tolerance and had made giving birth look easy, but after the invasive surgery, she was in great pain and had trouble walking or standing up straight. Because the incisions for the surgery were in her lower abdominals, she couldn't wear anything more than sweatpants, which were more forgiving than jeans or her uniform trousers.

The timing couldn't have been worse. Although she had already done the majority of the preparation required for the interviews, the selection board required she wear her service khakis—the formal khaki uniform specific to Navy chiefs and officers.

She didn't want anything standing in the way of her acceptance into the psych program, so she gritted her teeth and put on her service khakis on the big day. Joe took the day off work to drive her to Bethesda, where the interviews took place.

As she did her best to stand tall before the board, which consisted of several professors and active-duty psychologists, the questions began.

"Chief Kent, we've reviewed your records, and it's clear you've had a very successful career in the Navy, and frankly, we don't have many applicants come through as senior as you are," one board member said. "Why are you applying to this program now? Why would you want to switch tracks and essentially start over again at this point?"

Shannon took a beat to digest the question, even though she knew they would ask this.

"Commander Job Price was a Navy SEAL, husband, father, and someone I considered a mentor and friend. He killed himself during my last deployment to Afghanistan, and he's not alone in the path he chose. I hear about my fellow veterans taking their own lives more often every year that goes by. And why? Because they think they have no other option? Because they can't get help?"

Shannon paused. Faces of friends no longer alive flashed before her mind's eye.

"I don't know. But I know I refuse to be anything other than part of the solution to this problem. I would like to be a clinical psychologist because I refuse to sit on the sidelines of this epidemic for one more day."

The board was riveted by her words. They continued to ask her questions, but it was clear that with the right training, Shannon could be a clinical psychologist capable of understanding both mental health treatments and the perspectives of those she treated. She would know what they were going through because she'd already gone through it.

Meanwhile, Joe was at the gym at Walter Reed, killing time until she was done. He knew she had a lot riding on these interviews and was nervous for her. But he felt confident she would pass the board interviews because, well, they would be crazy not to—in his opinion. But he worried that maybe they would hold her seniority against her. At the end of the day, no matter how qualified someone was, he knew the military would want their chunk of flesh after spending so much money on putting someone through this program. Someone earlier in their career would have more runway than Shannon at this point.

Eventually he got a text from Shannon saying she was finished. He quickly left the gym, eager to hear how her interviews went, and drove back to the school to pick her up. As he pulled up, he saw Shannon in her element, smoking a cigarette and holding court for a crowd of younger female soldiers and sailors.

I am a lucky man, Joe thought.

"So they said I'll find out the results within thirty days," Shannon said as soon as she opened the door to get in.

"How did it go?"

"I think I did all right, but . . ." Shannon, her own worst critic, spent most of the ride home telling Joe about everything she thought she screwed up and how she could have prepared differently.

Joe shook off the negativity. "I know you crushed it."

The following day Joe was getting ready for work when he heard Shannon shout, "Holy shit!" She popped out of the bathroom and handed Joe her phone.

"Read that email to make sure I'm not hallucinating," Shannon said.

"Congratulations on your acceptance," Joe read. "To the Uniformed Services Health Service Clinical Psychology program!" Joe said as he hugged her.

"This is life-changing, Joe," Shannon said, wiping away a tear. "I can stay with the boys and have a job that matters. This is *everything.*"

Joe read the rest of the email out loud to Shannon, confirming the date/time stamp on the email and noting it was sent the afternoon before. The board had selected Shannon before they'd even made it home. Shannon's interview went so well it didn't require much deliberation between the panelists. All that was left to do was check the block with the officer accessions recruiters—a formality at this point.

Or so she thought.

A week later, Shannon received a call from the recruiter she was working with to commission as an officer. As she held the phone to her ear, she couldn't believe what she was hearing.

"You won't fucking believe what the Navy recruiter just told me," Shannon said as she walked into the living room.

"What's up?" Joe asked.

"They just told me I can't be an officer because I have cancer in my medical records."

"What?"

"Yeah, I guess they didn't catch it when they did their initial screening, but now that the actual paperwork is going through, my packet was flagged. They said there's 'no possible way' for me to be an officer," Shannon explained.

"There's got to be a waiver or something. There's a waiver for everything," Joe said, trying to stay positive, convinced it was a technicality that could be resolved. After all, Shannon was in excellent health and applying to be a psychologist, not a fighter pilot.

Shannon, completely blindsided, tried to comprehend the decision. The medical recruiters who screened her application did not think her thyroid or diastasis surgery was severe enough to disqualify her, and didn't say anything about the cancer diagnosis, so they never brought up any medical concerns during her application process. Technically, they should have never let her apply in the first place.

According to medical regulations for accession into the Navy at the time, a "History of Cancer with treatment within five years (except basal cell carcinoma)" is one of the conditions that cannot be waived—period.

Ironically, Shannon was still considered "worldwide deployable" as an elite special operations unit member. That means what it sounds like: According to the Navy, they could send Chief Petty Officer Shannon Kent anywhere in the world because she had a clean bill of health. However, Shannon Kent—the officer candidate—was too much of a health risk to sit in a classroom for four years or work in an office as a psychologist. The regulation made no sense.

"I'm not going to just complain about this. This regulation is stupid, and I *will* fight it," Shannon told Joe. A chief's chief, she wouldn't stand idly by while something was broken. There needed to be a fix, and she was going to find it.

Within a week, she spoke to everyone in her Navy chain of command and was emailing the Navy Bureau of Medicine (BUMED) to determine how to get around the issue. She was convinced there had to be an exception to policy or waiver. Like most issues in the military, you need to keep moving up the chain of command after every "no" until you get to an officer with enough authority to give a "yes."

While everyone was sympathetic to Shannon's situation—and even advocated on her behalf—no one offered real solutions. Most of her superiors within her chain of command seemed to think the regulation was carved in stone. "It is what it is" is a popular refrain in the military, and in the minds of many, the regulation says what it says. They advised her that if she wanted it to change, she should write her representatives in Congress.

She had a hunch that others were affected by the same regulation—and she was right. The Navy Chief's Mess, literally speaking, is the space on a naval ship specifically set aside for chiefs to eat or have meetings, but figuratively how the community of chiefs is referred to. It's a tight-knit community, so Shannon asked around the mess to see if anyone else tried to commission as an officer but was denied by the same regulation. More than ten people responded, saying the exact same thing happened to them. Even Joe reached out to the Special Forces community and discovered two personal friends whose Purple Hearts were used against them and who were denied a commission in the Army based on the same justification as the Navy regulation.

"So you're telling me, and everyone that's been fighting this war for the last ten years, that we can't be officers if we have some medical condition that's already been solved?" Shannon said to Joe. "Ya know what, I am taking this to Congress. I'm going to make them tell me no to my face."

Capitol Hill was only a thirty-minute drive from their house, so Shannon put on her best pantsuit and paid a visit to every New York State and Maryland senator and Congress member she could find, along with a few more with seats on both the House and Senate Armed Services Committees. She was as thorough in her approach to Congress as she was in combat, writing letters in both "military speak" and "civilian" so anyone could understand her proposed changes. She started gaining traction and even wrote an op-ed titled "If You're Fit for Combat, Why Aren't You Fit to Be an Officer in the Navy?"

Despite her progress, she knew nothing happened fast at this level of government, and any changes to the regulation would likely take years. The PhD program she worked so hard to get into would be off-limits until then.

Representative Walter B. Jones Jr., a Republican from North Carolina, eventually sent a letter to the secretary of the Navy urging him to look into the matter. The Navy put a few informal processes in place as a result, but no permanent changes to the regulations were made. Shannon was excited that her efforts weren't entirely in vain, but the reality of her situation started to sink in.

Her unit's next rotation to Iraq and Syria approached, and Shannon knew she was fit for combat. Since the clinical psychology program wasn't happening anytime soon, she had a choice to make. She was in an all-volunteer special operations unit, and no one forced her to do anything. If she didn't want to go, all she needed to do was say the word and transfer to a different unit. It wasn't lost on her that if her commission had been approved, she wouldn't even need to consider going to combat again.

An internal debate raged within her. Becoming a mother had changed her, but she was still a warrior trained and ready to hunt down the most evil people on the planet. She did not want to spend time away from her sons, but she also missed the unique sense of purpose only found on combat deployments.

As an intelligence professional, she took pride in her unique role in the fight. She also realized, as Joe had several years before, that she gained valuable experience over the years and learned lessons in combat that were not easily duplicated in training. If she weren't there for her teammates, those lessons might have to be relearned the hard way. The bloody way.

The war on terror dragged on over the years, and not many people sought out operational positions year after year as Shannon did over the course of her entire fifteen-year career. Most service members, both officers and enlisted alike, begin their careers on the front line of their occupation, actually plying their trade. Then, after promotions and experience, they become managers of people and resources to support the younger, less experienced troops on the front line. That's how it's supposed to work, anyway.

But Shannon, like Joe, moved from operational position to operational position, spending years honing the complex skills of human intelligence (HUMINT) and signals intelligence (SIGINT). By the time 2018 rolled around, and American special operations forces were fighting ISIS in Iraq and Syria, there were not many troops fighting at the ground level who had also done so in Iraq in 2007. Shannon knew this perspective and experience gave her more than cool stories or bragging rights. It gave her tremendous responsibility.

But what about responsibility to family? Had she not done enough already?

She frequently talked to her cousin Sharron Kearney through text messages. As the mother of kids the same age as Shannon's, Sharron was a trusted confidante—someone she could give unvarnished thoughts about motherhood to without fear of judgment or how she might be perceived. On one occasion, Shannon texted her, I'm sick to my stomach, all the other deployments didn't bother me. If it was just me, if I got killed, okay, you know, it sucks. But if I get killed, and I leave these two babies . . .

One night, texts weren't enough, and Shannon gave her a call.

"I cannot fucking leave my six-month-old baby," Shannon said. "Like, I can't, I can't do it. I need to figure out a stall tactic. I need to do something."

"How do we figure this out?" Sharron said. "Shannon, I will support you. I will lie. I will do whatever you want me to do. Just tell me what your options are."

"Sharr, I don't think I can get out of it," Shannon said. "But I don't want my boys to have an attachment disorder. Joe has been gone so much. And when he goes, and he comes, then he goes, and he comes . . . like, Colt won't snuggle."

Shannon was near tears at the idea of having to leave them, and because of her psychology education, she knew the impacts of prolonged military absences on a child. She was worried.

Shannon was still a sharp and dedicated, well-rounded operator. She kept up with her languages by watching the Arabic news every day at home. Shannon knew she needed to be strong enough to pull her larger male counterparts out of harm's way, so she attacked physical training like she did everything else: with a positive attitude, a lot of hard work, and her New York Yankees cap.

As a natural distance runner, she had impressive upper-body strength for a slim woman. She installed a pull-up bar in her bedroom and weights in the basement. She did P90X or CrossFit early in the morning while hiking or jogging in the evenings. Colt was her workout buddy, either strapped to her back or being pushed in the running stroller.

Shannon's sense of duty was ultimately overwhelming. Her unwavering commitment as a leader to both her comrades and the nation was something she couldn't shake, no matter how conflicted she felt. She came to the resolution that, with the psychology program off the table for now, she would deploy and do her job—whether that was a part of her and Joe's life plan or not.

"I just don't see any way I can avoid this deployment and still look myself in the mirror," Shannon told Joe one night after dinner.

"You and I both know there are ways to get out of going on this deployment," Joe said.

"Fuck that. It's not that big a deal. Why shouldn't I go?"

"Because you're a mother now, Shannon. We have two young boys who need you," Joe replied.

"Look who's talking," Shannon said. This wasn't the first time they'd had this conversation; the only difference was now she was the one choosing to deploy. "How many fathers have had to leave their kids behind? Why am I any different?"

Shannon and Joe weren't so different from each other. They would always go if asked, no matter what, no matter the consequence. They lived by Isaiah 6:8: "Whom shall I send? And who will go for us? And I said, 'Here am I. *Send me!*'" It was that simple for both of them, but also represented their most significant marital conflict.

CHAPTER 19

HOW DO YOU SAY GOODBYE?
THE KENT HOME, MARYLAND, 2018

As Joe rounded the corner to turn down his driveway, the last rays of light flickered off Chesapeake Bay. The fall air was crisp, accented by the smell of a wood fire wafting through the air. His dog, Roo, darted across the leaf-strewn lawn, chasing Colt, while Josh trailed behind. He tried as hard as a one-year-old could to keep up with a three-year-old and a puppy.

He watched as Colt crashed into Shannon's legs as she trimmed the top of the pergola in the yard. She stopped to look down at Colt and kissed his head before looking up at Joe. It's an image—a moment in time—seared into his mind.

She wore tan cargo pants, a red North Face jacket, and Joe's old army boonie cap with his last name on the back. *Combat casual, as always,* Joe laughed to himself. It made him proud to have her wear his old clothing.

Shannon scooped up the boys, looked at Joe, and said, "Look, boys, it's Daddy!"

Joe hopped out of his truck and walked toward his family; an incredible feeling washed over him as he took it all in. He felt this before when he and Shannon first started dating, but this feeling had grown and matured over the years after they married and had kids. For a man who once said he didn't want any children, who couldn't see a life beyond perpetual war, he was amazed at how good everything felt.

Josh leaped from his mother's arms into Joe's, and Colt jumped down so he could half-tackle his right leg. Shannon gave him a quick kiss.

"How was work?" she asked.

"Oh, another day, nothing too crazy," Joe said, knowing there was a larger conversation that needed to happen. He was the luckiest guy in the world and even felt a sense of peace—maybe even satisfaction with life in a way he never thought possible.

Satisfaction and fulfillment are odd concepts that can be the archenemy of achievement and determination. On one hand, Joe knew how blessed he was to have a family and be near the end of a twenty-year career in special operations. He should have easily, by any measurement, been happy with retiring after serving in the Ranger Regiment, Special Forces, and in ███████████████████.*
He served at the highest levels of the special operations community, in combat, during his generation's war. He knew he was fortunate to do all that and still literally be standing on his own two feet—so

---

* Description of specific unit redacted at request of DoD.

many in his line of work could not do the same. From the time he'd graduated from high school, he'd done everything he wanted to do with his life.

The problem with determination and a desire to achieve is that it's a never-ending cycle of establishing goals, pursuing them like a madman, accomplishment, then quickly feeling like you haven't accomplished enough or done enough, finding a new goal, and starting the cycle over again. This cycle is more addictive when you can wrap the next challenge in a cloak of nobility.

Deploying to combat with elite units was the ultimate accomplishment in Joe's world, so it's hard to take other challenges seriously after experiencing that brand of intensity. You were considered honorable for deploying to fight for your nation regardless of its effect on you or your family. It was and continues to be the hidden lure of war.

Joe's retirement date from the Army drew closer, but he was determined to stay in the fight. He felt like his accomplishments were not something to rest on, that he was in debt to all the friends lost in combat over the years and all the guys he knew who were still going into harm's way. With all of his training and experience, how could he stop deploying—stop doing his part—while so many were still doing theirs?

He wanted more, even if it made life hard for Shannon and his family. There was one more challenge he wanted to set his sights on after retirement: to stay in the fight as a Paramilitary Operations Officer at the CIA as a member of the fabled Ground Branch—or "GB" for short, as most in the community refer to it. GB was where legendary warriors served their nation in a covert capacity long after their military careers ended.

Joe could seamlessly transition from the military to the CIA because he already attended the CIA's operations course while still in the military. Most people know it as "The Farm." There was a catch, though: Because Joe was able to skip past much of the initial training, that meant he would be operational sooner. He needed to deploy right away, which meant both he and Shannon would be deployed at the same time—something they promised would never happen after they had kids.

As much as the CIA promised more adventure, Joe reasoned it also provided the opportunity to take their family overseas once Shannon was out of the Navy. They both loved the idea of raising their kids in exotic countries while they worked as intelligence officers. The CIA would want Joe to do paramilitary deployments for a few years before transitioning to traditional ████████* work overseas, giving Shannon time to finish her Navy career before applying to the CIA herself. Joe and Shannon previously worked alongside a few Agency couples and loved how family-oriented it was. It made it easy to see a life with kids overseas.

On that clear autumn day, Joe knew he had it all: an amazing family, a great career in the Army, and an adventurous post-Army career, all because of the support his wife gave him. He had to figure out how to talk her into one more adventure.

"Daddy, look what Mama made!" Colt proudly held up a tiny muddy pumpkin he untangled from Shannon's ever-expanding garden in their yard. "It's from the Joshy part of the garden!" he added, pointing to the section of plants closest to where they were standing.

Joe looked at Shannon. She beamed with pride—she loved her garden, and he could tell how much it meant to her to see their growing boys in it.

"There's the Colt section of the garden, the Joshy section, and

---

* Specific descriptions of Joe's work redacted at request of CIA.

the family section will be right there!" Shannon explained how she planted each section while pregnant with the boys, and now they were planting another area with her together.

Later that night, Joe and Shannon crept out of the boys' room after putting them down for the night.

"Soo . . . I have a plan," Shannon said quietly. She was happy but seemed focused; he could tell she had a lot on her mind. With her upcoming deployment on the horizon, they both did.

The preparation for combat was routine at that point. But this time, it was different, and they both felt it.

"If I buy you a drink, will you tell me?" Joe asked.

"You know my love language," she said, leaning in and lightly kissing his cheek.

As Joe mixed her Sailor Jerry rum and diet ginger ale on the kitchen counter, she pulled out a notebook and some other papers. She was the most informal-formal person he ever met. She kept a million and one projects straight in her mind while keeping notes and references readily available—a badass NCO to the core. He popped the top on a Loose Cannon IPA for himself, handed Shannon her drink, and sat next to her at the kitchen table.

"All right, so I have been scheming about what our next steps are. After this one, I'm not leaving the boys again for anything short of another 9/11," she said before taking a sip of her drink.

"Agreed. Fuck this," Joe said, lightly tapping her glass before taking a sip of his beer.

"I'm going to submit another waiver for the psych program next year," she said. "And if it goes through, I could be good to go for summer 2019, but I'm not counting on that. I have one backup, and I want one more, like two fail-safes to keep me from having to leave the boys again."

"Amen. How do we make that happen?" Joe asked, knowing she already had a plan and was just using him as a sounding board.

"The PhD is the number one option. Number two is a watch officer job at NSA." She explained. It's a hard job, but nondeployable, so she could be home while contributing to the fight. With her language and technical skills, there were several jobs she could do at Fort Meade that directly benefited national security.

"I've already met with the commander of that unit and have an invite, so it's a solid backup plan."

Joe was relieved, but he could tell everything weighed on her more each day as her impending deployment to Syria approached.

"You know, hun," she said as she leaned forward in her seat, looking at Joe lovingly as always but also tired with worry. "I'm so proud of you and support you going to GB. I get it. I've always understood who you are, and it's why I love you. You're a warrior," she said with extra strain in her voice. "But I'm tired, Joe. I'm tired of always being the one having to figure out a new path. You haven't had to change anything since we got married and had kids."

She was right, of course. She always balanced the whims of Joe's career, kids, and her career. Deep down, Joe knew he was being selfish as everything lined up in his life. He didn't want to stop to think about how his chosen career affected Shannon and the boys. Someday he might wish he had taken the time to at least acknowledge what she was going through. But not that day: he was defensive and dismissive.

"What do you want me to do?" Joe asked indignantly, as if someone were forcing him to go to the CIA immediately after retiring from the military.

"I don't know, Joe, can you think about doing something else when you retire? I mean, you just got home from your tenth deployment. You were in SF, in ████████.* You made it. Can you enjoy that and maybe focus on helping me and put the boys first?" Shannon said, her emotional dam breaking, pent-up feelings rushing out.

"Fuck, Shan, I don't know what else to do. Going to GB is the only thing I feel comfortable getting out of the Army for. Why do I get to quit deploying?" Joe said. Someday he would wish to God he could take back this conversation, but in that moment, it was what he believed after twenty years of putting the mission and his accomplishments first. So many had given their lives—why did he get to tap out once he reached some arbitrary date?

This is my calling. This is my religion, he thought.

"Look, I'll do GB for two years or so, then I'll switch to being a regular case officer, and we can take the boys to ████████† overseas," he said as if trying to sell her a used car.

"I want you here, with us, because we love you, I love you, and I need some help. I can't be the anchor all the time," she said calmly as she put her hand over Joe's. Their fingers intertwined.

"I know, Shannon, I will make it all up to you; we'll get through this next six months and reassess. If GB doesn't work for us, I'll quit."

Shannon smiled and let out a sarcastic laugh.

"Like fuck you will, Joe."

God damn it, she sees right through me.

"I love you, Joe Kent," she said as she looked him in the eyes. "You give us so much; we want you around as much as possible." She held his gaze. "You know I'm no different than you. I'm not done. I have so much more I want to do, but I want to do it with you and our boys."

---

* Description of specific unit redacted at request of DoD.

† Specific description of overseas assignment redacted at request of CIA.

The conversation wasn't going to resolve anything. Instead, it highlighted the imbalance in their relationship. She was the giver, and Joe was the taker. He did his best to give love back, but Shannon's request to live a more balanced life wasn't going to overcome his foolish pride.

"Go to GB," she said. "I'm proud of you. Hell, I brag about you all the time at work. But you need to find time for us before time gets away."

"I will, baby. I love you too," he replied, in awe of her love and patience despite his stubborn nature.

⚓ ⚓ ⚓

For the next few months, Joe and Shannon enjoyed a regular schedule as he prepared to transition to the CIA while Shannon attended an Arabic language refresher course for her deployment. Each night Shannon made elaborate dinners with ingredients from her garden. Each meal, in true Shannon style, there was an international theme.

Most evenings, Joe would come home to a house filled with the smell of Middle Eastern or Indian food cooking while Shannon played with the boys in their backyard. Shannon was an expert at making memories; every meal and every family outing was something to remember.

Shannon was never one to dabble. She was always all in.

"I'm going to make every inch of our house ours," she said one Saturday. She held Josh with one arm while pouring Joe a cup of coffee with her free hand.

"You and Joshy can stay here, and Colt will come with me to

Home Depot. I have a plan," she said with her classic look of determination.

A few hours later, Shannon and Colt returned with several sheets of plywood, an eight-foot-long two-by-four, and several fishing-tackle-style boxes full of glass and marble tiles and seashells. For the following three months, using simple materials, she spent most nights creating lasting tributes to her love for her family.

Out of the plywood, she crafted an elaborate family hearth for their fireplace. The theme blended their military lives and family. The bottom portion was an ocean scene with a scuba diver and four Maryland crabs representing their family; above it was a forest with Humvees and a family of four bears inside. Farther up, a skydiver steers his parachute.

Next, she made a sizable, elaborate wall mosaic bearing the crossed arrows of the Special Forces emblem. She worked late into the night after the kids were in bed on these projects, determined to finish the job as quickly as possible. One night, as she set up her mosaic-shaping tools, Joe was on his way to bed but stopped to ask her why she worked so hard on these projects. She brushed a lock of strawberry blonde hair off her face.

"Because when I'm in Syria, I want you and the boys to see my love for you everywhere you look." Her tone was steady and loving, as if she knew she was almost out of time but still determined to leave her family with as much of her love as possible.

CHAPTER 20

THE NEVER-ENDING WAR ON TERROR

IRAQ, 2017–2018

In July 2017, the Battle of Mosul ended, with the Iraqi Army taking control back from ISIS after fierce fighting with hard-line extremists in the historic Old City. This signaled the beginning of the end for ISIS's control of physical territory and led to many fighters and their leaders going underground.

However, the fight was not over, and ISIS had not been eliminated.

Their forces scattered, with some returning home and others bedding down to fight an insurgency. Many fled to other countries in the region to attempt reestablishing the caliphate. Notably, ISIS-K invaded the eastern Nangarhar region of Afghanistan, while other elements in East Africa pledged allegiance to the caliphate while replicating their brutal brand of violence. Al-Baghdadi was still at large, and elements loyal to him still posed a great danger. "For the mujahideen, the scale of victory or defeat is not dependent on a city or town being stolen," al-Baghdadi said in an audio recording.[1]

In recognition of this, the hunt for al-Baghdadi and his cohorts continued. American and allied special operations units did what they do best: hunt humans. In December 2018, President Donald Trump announced the defeat of ISIS and his intent to pull US forces out of the region via a tweet.[2] However, US forces are still in Iraq and Syria to this day.

Paul O'Leary served as a human intelligence collector for a special operations task force in Syria in the months leading up to and overlapping with Shannon's deployment to Syria in 2018.

"In that 2018 to 2019 time frame, ISIS was being continually pushed back. So they lost Raka, they lost Mosul. They were being pushed further and further south into the Euphrates River Valley," O'Leary said. ISIS only controlled a small amount of land in the very southern Euphrates River Valley but still had pockets in a few cities like Manbij, as well as other cities that they'd previously occupied.

Like any insurgency, they had stay-behind operatives who were shifting from the caliphate into traditional terrorist operations, which is arguably their comfort zone.

"That was everything we were focused on," O'Leary said. "Getting al-Baghdadi was the golden ticket. In fact, almost every interrogator just wanted to throw that question at every guy they brought in."

Even if it was a meaningless bottom feeder, they would still ask, "What do you know about al-Baghdadi? What do you hear? What are people saying about him? Where is he?" It was all in the hope that collectors would get a strand of something that could be turned into actionable intelligence.

Their second priority was to continue crushing the caliphate in place, or pushing them back where applicable, and getting the innocent people in the caliphate-held areas out and debriefed.

The third priority was helping the Syrian Defense Forces (SDF) stand up in their controlled areas. The SDF was key in flushing out pockets of ISIS and their sympathizers operating in the area. The removal of underground ISIS operatives was essential to regaining influence and ensuring life could return to normal. The SDF could navigate that network of enemy combatants, but that strategy also risked the possibility of SDF soldiers playing both sides.

"That was why we were continuing to do surveillance and identify networks and supply and smuggling operations," O'Leary said. "One of the big things in that area was Turkey being a funnel point for foreign fighters coming in with ISIS. They would all use these smuggling routes through Turkey."

Because of the threat level and complex multinational politics, Syria wasn't a very secure part of the world to operate in, but especially so if you didn't have a regular SDF escort. The threat was always there, creating a semi-permissive operating environment for deployed Americans. A semi-permissive environment is generally considered not safe, but the direct threat has been removed. This created a condition where most collectors tried recruiting sources who would come to the different bases they worked at and conduct a meeting that way. That's not always possible, though. Specially trained intelligence operatives were needed for the more high-risk source operations conducted outside the security of an American military base.

The battlespace was complicated by a prominent Russian contingent in the area and holdover ISIS militants under disguise and more intelligent than your average black-flag-waving foot soldier.

The geography of where Americans were operating played a role, too. Some cities had so many factions competing for power that it resulted in a secure area that was essentially an international tinderbox. There were Americans, Russians, Turks, the SDF, Syrian regime forces, and smaller militia power brokers that wielded considerable influence competing for power in a single town. Leaving a forward operating base for a meeting required people who could conduct themselves calmly during tense situations with geopolitical ramifications at stake. By 2018, there were no less than a dozen different major players in any given battlespace inside Syria, all of whom had various foes and alliances—often both.

"There was one place that I used to go to talk to people, and there was a spot during the drive over where I could look across and see the Russian flag flying on top of a government building because they were literally blocks away," O'Leary said. "I'm an old guy, so as an American soldier who started in the eighties during the Cold War, and seeing a Russian flag without optics because it's that close—in an area that I'm deployed in—is weird, you know?"

"There were always little pockets of everybody running around, running their own sources," O'Leary said. "And then when you get into the Third World, you get these underdeveloped nations that historically there are people who are really good survivors."

The "really good survivors" are typically locals with a lot of hustle who want to talk to Americans, get paid for the information they hand over, and then go talk to the Russians, do what they need them to do, and make more money. On top of that, they'll still talk to ISIS, and according to O'Leary, they're going to give ISIS whatever they need. It's not about morals so much as it is about keeping your family safe, with a roof over their heads and food on the table. For the people doing traditional source operations, they just didn't know who they were dealing with or who exactly they were talking to.

The Syrian theater was unlike any other environment the military and intelligence communities had found themselves in.

"I would make the argument that in 2000s Iraq, we had taken down the whole government, so it was a series of pockets and places that had insurgencies," O'Leary explained. "When you're dealing with the caliphate of ISIS, they legitimately had their own territory. They had tax stamps, inspectors, currency, laws, governments, and a medical system."

This created a hybrid environment that forced leaders to face local oppositional governments, insurgencies, and superpower functions in the same area, further complicated by the strange dynamic between the Syrian government, backed by Russians, and the SDF, backed by the US.

They shared a common goal, which was to destroy ISIS and get the oil fields back. But, obviously, the shared aspect of that goal disappeared when it came time to decide who would ultimately control the oil fields. "The common goal was definitely, *yeah, we need to defeat ISIS,*" O'Leary said. "We were on board with each other in that we're not working together, but we have the same goal."

Intelligence professionals and soldiers alike had to be prepared to deal with those different dynamics, from an established government to the Syrian government backed by the Russians, to a newly stood-up government within the caliphate, and then yet another newly stood-up government within the SDF.

The power dynamics at play created bias when it came to the actual gunfighting side of the war, too. In that capacity, American forces were restricted to more of an assist and advise strategy.

"You didn't have the Tenth Mountain Division running presence patrols," O'Leary said. Conventional forces provided security or conducted counter-IED training within tightly defined areas of operation. There was some direct action, but that was rare and typically only performed at the highest levels of special operations.

"Right before I went into Syria, when I was still operating in northern Iraq, one of our senior interrogators said, 'When you talk to these guys, if the information that they're giving you doesn't assist us in putting a team of operators, or a bomb, or a missile on an objective, I don't give a fuck about it,'" O'Leary said.

The mandates across the region were similar for everyone working in an intelligence-gathering function. It wasn't a traditional intelligence operation per se, but rather a problem set that required creative solutions and an emphasis on data-driven results. They only needed the information leading directly or indirectly to the destruction of ISIS assets, capturing or killing ISIS leadership, and the eventual dismantling of the caliphate.

TUNISIA, 2018

Tunisia is beautiful. It boasts Mediterranean beaches only a stone's throw from Italy, and a thriving economy with a tourism industry envied by most African countries.

Tunisia is also a fault-line country in northern Africa and the Arab-Muslim world. Its strategic location on the southern Mediterranean Sea makes it a neighbor to Europe and a vital trade port for the African continent.

On December 17, 2010, Mohamed Bouazizi set himself on fire outside the provincial government building in Sidi Bouzid.[3] The twenty-six-year-old street vendor died in protest. The flame he lit did not die with him but instead was the spark that ignited the Arab Spring all across North Africa, with ramifications that rippled throughout the globe.

By 2011, President Zine El Abidine Ben Ali resigned and fled the country after twenty-three years in office.[4] The ousting of the longtime dictator made the Tunisian people feel like they had a real voice in their government.

Terrorists attacked Tunisia with ferocity in 2015. Twenty-two people were killed in an attack at the Bardo National Museum,[5] and later that year, thirty-eight people died while at the Sousse beachfront.[6]

Neighboring Libya crumbled to the point that human slaves were sold at auction in open markets.[7] The instability affected the entire region.

After Tunisia, the Arab Spring was not so kind to the nations it swept over; varying degrees of chaotic wars still linger in Syria, Libya, and Yemen. Egypt did not fare much better, trading revolution for a cycle of coups and instability.

Tunisia's land border with Libya to the east complicated its stability and desire to keep radical Islam at bay. Since the US had assisted varying tribal and popular groups in Libya in their efforts to topple the regime of longtime dictator Muammar Gaddafi, Libya had slipped into tribal warfare and chaos. ISIS exploited the chaos and took over several towns in Libya, establishing another foothold for the caliphate. Libya's chaos threatened the stability of the region, in particular its secular, prosperous neighbor to the west, Tunisia.

The government of Tunisia works in close cooperation with the US government to this day to increase its ability to combat terrorism. But to combat terrorism, you have to find it, and this is where Shannon's skill set was needed. As Shannon began her predeployment training for Syria, she was asked to lead a small team to Tunisia to support the US mission in that country.

Shannon's trip to Tunisia was going to be short; she and her team were only needed for two weeks. As she packed her suitcase at home, Joe drove to the airport to pick up his mom, who would give him a hand while Shannon was gone.

Joe was happy for her. He knew that getting selected for a "hot fill" (unplanned short deployment) was an honor and that commanders don't randomly staff those types of missions with whoever happens to be in the office that day. They send their best.

Shannon and Joe viewed her trip to Tunisia as a practice deployment ahead of the big one to Syria. The boys would say goodbye to Mom, settle into a routine with Nana, and see Mom come home shortly after the goodbye. Shannon and Joe would also get into the deployment routine of communicating via text message and Face-Time chats so the boys could see her and hear her voice as much as possible.

They had done that drill for two years in a row, except usually Joe was the one deployed. This time it was his turn to stay back with the kids and keep the house running. He probably needed the two-week warm-up more than anyone.

A short time later, Shannon Kent and her partner, Blake, arrived in-country. No weapons. Just clothes and a backpack.

Their official mission was to provide Department of Defense linguistic support to ██████████████* because they were both Arabic linguists, and the ██████████† didn't have any at that time. Shannon also spoke French, which helped with translating documents. Any other aspects of their work in that country remain highly classified.

They went during Ramadan and stayed in a swanky hotel but couldn't go to restaurants because everything was closed down for the religious holiday. Shannon, always eager to experience local culture and food, was disappointed but found that some Muslim restaurants were still open to serving them.

---

* Specific roles and responsibilities redacted at request of CIA.
† Specific entities redacted at request of CIA.

It was trial and error. Some people got angry, but Shannon was able to bring them back down from the brink by speaking to them in their language, only talking in Arabic or French. They would try to speak English to her, but she wouldn't have it. This would happen at the hotel, the hotel restaurant, shops—basically, anywhere Shannon went. Some retailers would give her free merchandise because they were so taken aback by her ability with language.

Shannon's forte was negotiating with merchants in the local bazaars. Blake was happy just to pay full price and get out of there. But Shannon would really get into it with the merchants and eventually walk away with a ton of stuff and a big smile.

On one hot afternoon during the trip, Shannon and Blake returned from a mission. According to Blake, they were in a tiny car stuck in bumper-to-bumper traffic, and it was "hot as fuck" outside.

"We had a plan, it didn't work, whaddya gonna do?" Shannon said. It's the kind of advice that is prudent for anyone in Shannon's line of work but easily applicable in any area of life. They turned the Arabic language radio up and rolled their windows down to find some sense of relief.

It turned out everyone on the road was listening to the same radio station: Tunisia was playing England in the World Cup. When Tunisia made a goal, the whole road and every vehicle on it erupted. The highway essentially transformed into a block party.

"Oh my god, this is the greatest cultural experience I've ever had!" Shannon yelled. She soaked up every minute of it. No matter where she went, Shannon wanted to be culturally inclusive and participate in the local traditions.

Tunisia was an adventure for Shannon in more than just that experience with the World Cup. She had an upcoming deployment a few weeks away, so she made Blake wake up with her at six every morning to run on the beach. She didn't want to run by herself, as the beach was covered in trash, homeless people, and overturned boats. Despite the lackluster scenery and potential for a bad situation, Shannon couldn't have been happier to be running on the beach. She needed to be in peak physical shape so she could hold other people who weren't up to her standard accountable. Running was also a way for her to deal with her nerves about the upcoming deployment.

"Don't do anything your gut tells you not to," Blake said, offering some advice of his own. "You have authority. You're a singleton." She was basically a one-person operation. He wanted her to remember they don't just let anyone have that level of autonomy.

Her trip to Tunisia came and went, with Shannon and Joe able to talk daily. Joe got the practice he needed holding down the fort. He had his mom and their supernanny, Ashe, so he was far from a single parent—but it was still a very new world for him.

Shannon came back from Tunisia conflicted. She was excited to be back in the game after a five-year pause for training courses and pregnancy. Getting back to the real work of combat missions was invigorating for her. She was professionally excited to go to Syria and help track down ISIS. But at the same time, she was a mother, and the thought of being away from her sons for any length of time—let alone six months—felt unbearable to her.

She felt anxiety about deploying but knew she had a mission to train for. So, she did what everyone in the profession of arms does: compartmentalized the anxiety and focused on the task at hand. Seeing things from a new angle, Joe wondered if their ability to compartmentalize emotions was a blessing or a curse. Emotional compartmentalization is a necessary survival trait in their line of work, but at some point, it inhibits real communication.

CHAPTER 21

LIVING UP TO THE ANCHORS

WALTER REED NATIONAL MILITARY MEDICAL CENTER, 2018

When Shannon was promoted to chief petty officer years before, it was a major milestone in her Navy career—something any sailor is proud of achieving. A "chief" is revered in naval lore and tradition, and although percentages vary, approximately 25 percent of all applicants Navy-wide will be selected for promotion to chief petty officer in any given year.

At Shannon's promotion ceremony, the speaker talked about what a distinguished sailor Shannon was, and how she performed all of her duties with grace and class and went above and beyond to meet the requirements to serve all of her sailors. Shannon even teared up when the chief's anchors were pinned on her uniform.

Shannon Kent was a leader, a chief in the greatest Navy the

world had ever known. That title came with a lot of responsibility. She took immense pride in her khakis and the anchors adorning them. They meant more than just looking good. As a seasoned chief, she was charged with selecting the next generation every year during "the season."

This initiation is not unique to special operations but something all naval enlisted personnel must go through to reach the rank of Chief Petty Officer. In the Navy, there are E-7s, and then there are Chiefs. It is a brutal process meant to identify the best sailors for service as the branch's enlisted leaders, and Shannon took this responsibility seriously.

The process has been a naval tradition for 126 years, ever since chief petty officers were part of the Navy. Every unit runs its "season" differently, but it always entails physically and mentally demanding tasks that revolve around developing leadership and teamwork. They teach future chiefs that it's not about them anymore; now they are in charge of something bigger than themselves. Often the chief's selects will face a final gauntlet before pinning that will push them physically and mentally. The anchors are earned, not given, and every chief in the Navy has to live up to what they represent every day.

For Shannon, being a chief in the United States Navy was not about being a hardened warrior or special operator but someone who cared deeply about her sailors and worked to develop them, protect them, or fight for them. But she wasn't thinking about any of that as she drove toward Walter Reed. Instead she was running errands in preparation for her upcoming deployment. In this case, picking up enough of her medical prescriptions to last her through the trip.

The fluorescent hospital lights and sterile walls at Walter Reed National Military Medical Center didn't offer any comfort. James was supposed to be at an appointment but was restlessly walking the hallways instead. He was an intelligence professional who spent most of his career assigned to the US Navy's special warfare units and had deployed multiple times to combat theaters. But he had demons that were eating away at him.

He had been going to appointments to address some of his issues ever since he returned from his last deployment that summer, but still felt alone and isolated. His depression was worsening.

His appointments at Walter Reed were the only help he could find, but he couldn't get any treatments to work. Even though his providers had the best intentions, he was no closer to solving his problems than before his treatments started. He just couldn't turn the corner. At the end of his last treatment regimen, there was a gap of over six weeks before he was able to check back in. It seemed, to James, that everything was spiraling out of control.

It's a familiar story in the special operations community, even if it's not talked about as often as it should be: mental health issues stemming from the stress of the job, and repeated deployments, take their toll. At some point, something has to give. Many of James's issues had begun four years prior. But, in retrospect, that was just the beginning of an eternity spent trying to fix clinical depression, anxiety, and a lack of emotional range and awareness that felt like one big ball of yarn in his head that he couldn't untangle.

For people in that state of mind, isolation can be deadly. He often avoided people in his life, but when he did try to reach out to friends, he found most of them too busy with their own lives. Family, work, and the daily stress most adults endure have a way of overshadowing what are often thinly veiled attempts from friends to reach out. The most common reaction from friends and family when they lose someone to a mental health crisis is *I had no idea they were struggling* or *I knew they were going through a rough patch but didn't know it had gotten so bad.*

The problems compounded over time. After a while, James stopped reaching out altogether and sank into quiet desperation. No one knew how far he had fallen. It seemed like his emotional decline and ensuing isolation were reaching the point of no return. He considered taking his own life—like many veterans struggling with mental health, he couldn't see a way out of the endless pit he found himself in.

According to a study published by the US Department of Veterans Affairs, veterans who deployed overseas had a 41 percent higher suicide risk than the general US population.[1] In fact, in the active-duty military, with approximately 7,000 service members killed in action and over 30,000 dying by suicide, there have been over four times the amount of deaths by suicide as deaths in combat.[2]

Possibly more disturbing, a study commissioned and published by the US Special Operations Command (USSOCOM) and conducted by the American Association of Suicidology showed that suicide rates in the special operations community are about 27 percent higher than the rest of the US military.[3] Special operators make up a large part of the military's most deployed and combat-experienced service members. When you add in the stresses of finances, marital strain caused by time away from family, and compounding medical issues, it's no surprise that the SOF demographic is disproportionately affected by mental health issues and the suicide epidemic.

As James turned a corner down yet another hallway, he saw a familiar face. Shannon was walking down the corridor opposite him. He appeared calm on the outside, but inside he was panicking. There was nowhere for him to duck and hide. James had known Shannon for almost ten years; they'd first met while both were assigned to

Naval Special Warfare, working in the same troop, drinking, and deploying together. Shannon made James feel like part of her family, not just another coworker—as she did with all of her friends.

Unbeknownst to Shannon, she was one of the first to support James while he struggled with mental health ailments and was likely responsible for him still being alive. She had always been there to help him, encourage him, and be the tough leader who gave even tougher feedback. She coached him and put things in perspective for his traumatized mind. But the years went by, and they both continued with their lives. Although they had kept in touch, bumping into each other at various assignments and training events, it had been a while since they had last seen each other in person.

Now Shannon had caught James off guard, lost in the anonymity usually granted while walking the hospital corridors. She was the one person who could hold him accountable to himself, and there was nowhere to go.

"James? Is that you? Oh my god!" Shannon said, shrieking as her face lit up with excitement. She closed in for a tight hug before James could get a word out. It was the same reaction he received on previous deployments whenever their paths crossed, usually catching him after he returned from some remote outstation. Shannon would greet him every time, the same way, with the same kind of genuine enthusiasm. He was happy to see her again after randomly bumping into her at the hospital, even though he may not have admitted it to himself at the time.

"What's it been? Three, four years now?" Shannon asked.

"Yeah, I think since that course we did together in DC in 2014. You introduced me to Joe, and we got Chinese food, I think?" James said.

"That's right. Wow, it's been too long. What are you doing here? Have time for a quick coffee? I'm just here picking up prescriptions for my next trip—walk with me and we'll get coffee and catch up," Shannon said in her force-of-nature way. She sensed James had been restlessly walking the hallways and she didn't want to allow him an opportunity to turn down her invitation.

They stopped by a cafe on the way to the pharmacy. She treated him to a small drip coffee as she ordered one of her customary caffeinated sugar bombs. James smiled, with waves of nostalgia overcoming him. They continued to the pharmacy, where Shannon checked in and received a ticket marking her place in line. She was there to pick up enough Synthroid to last her through her upcoming deployment to Syria, so they settled in for what was likely a long wait.

"So, how's life been?" James asked, diverting the conversation away from him.

"We're staying busy. Joe is in and out of town, and the boys are growing fast. I had a little snafu with cancer—don't worry, that's all taken care of—and I tried to commission so I could get a PhD and become a psych for the Navy, but that didn't work out. Still fighting that, actually. But anyway, that's why I'm going on another deployment."

"Bloody hell, I'll take your word for it that the cancer wasn't anything to worry about. But why wouldn't the Navy let you commission? That's crazy." James was bewildered. If anyone was fit to be a naval officer, it was Shannon. She stood out to him as one of the best he'd ever served with among a sea of bad managers posing as leaders. She encouraged him to pursue advancement in the Navy, fought for him to get slots to career-advancing schools that would make him a more effective intelligence professional, and even encouraged him to screen for the same elite special operations unit she was trying out for during a previous deployment together. Even though James didn't always see the benefit, he appreciated that she saw potential and cared enough to encourage him. But, maybe most importantly, she wasn't a leader who stood idly by while others in their unit made poor decisions that compromised morale and mission.

"It's all because of the poorly written medical regs," Shannon said. "It looks like it's going to literally take an act of Congress to change. But anyway, how's life been for you? Tell me all about what's going on with you these days!"

Shannon wasted no time turning her attention back toward James. He initially tried to avoid the real issues, being purposefully casual, and joking or being outright dismissive of his problems.

Midway through the conversation, he knew it was futile to keep masking what was really going on. Shannon had always been able to see right through him, so he might as well be up front and honest.

"Shan, I don't really know what to say," James said. "It's been hard. I'm still dealing with depression and anxiety attacks. I'm still fighting fibromyalgia and chronic pain. I lost a friend last month, someone I considered a mentor. I was passed over for promotion . . . again. I feel like . . . I feel everything and nothing simultaneously."

Shannon's demeanor changed. Her friend was in a bad place, and she needed to be equal parts compassionate listener and professional human intelligence collector to find out what exactly was going on. She had a way of getting information out of people, and not just on the battlefield. Her worst fears were confirmed when he eventually disclosed the most severe challenges he faced: disillusionment, isolation, and emerging thoughts of suicide.

"What are you doing about this? Have you talked to anyone? Have you asked for help?" Shannon said, with urgency in her eyes.

"I'm in therapy," James said. "I'm doing weekly treatments for the depression. But I don't feel like anyone actually understands what I . . . what *we* deal with. And it's not like I know how to fix these things. I'm just doing the best I can with what I have. But it feels like everything is catching up."

Shannon knew James was going through something that could overwhelm even the strongest resolve. She didn't need to look at the statistics to see what was happening to her brother in arms, right in front of her. She had seen so many friends lose themselves to their minds and past trauma. She never forgot that day in Afghanistan when she vowed to fix whatever led Commander Price to take his own life. Sitting with her friend James at the pharmacy that day, she saw an opportunity to make a difference, and it didn't require a PhD.

Shannon showed James nothing but compassion as he talked, listening intently and lending the ear he sorely needed.

"Have you talked to anyone in your chain of command yet? Are they aware of what's going on?" Shannon asked. James's situation was serious, and she needed to put on her chief's anchors—figuratively speaking—and encourage James to do the right thing. He saw the physical change in her eyes and in her facial expressions. The tenor and timbre of her voice changed from someone catching up with an old friend to a genuine, urgent concern for that friend.

"They don't know anything," James said.

"James, you need to be selfish for once. You need to think about you and what's best for you. You need to go tell them. Please. Or anyone as long as you get help."

"There's that in-your-face demeanor," James said. But he knew she wasn't judging him or trying to be pushy. She genuinely wanted him to live when he was losing the desire to.

"Please promise me you're going to get help, that you're going to tell your team, your command," Shannon said.

"I will," James said. Inside, he wasn't so confident. But when everyone else had turned away from him, she looked him in the eyes and addressed his pain head-on without a blink. He couldn't ignore that.

They talked for a while longer, but eventually the conversation ended after her prescription was ready. Shannon didn't forget about their discussion and the promise she made James make. She had a hunch he might drag his feet on following up.

Shannon didn't want to leave anything to chance. Her friend's life may have depended on it. Before James had a chance to approach his senior chief, Shannon made the first in a series of phone calls, relaying an urgent message for a sailor in need of help. She talked to everyone who might need to be involved, and James eventually checked himself into the emergency room to be evaluated. He was released the same night.

Although he was initially angry with Shannon for making those calls before he had a chance to make the choice for himself, he didn't hold on to that anger for very long. He knew her decision set him on a more positive path that he's still on to this day.

Sitting in the hospital, sharing a cup of coffee with Shannon, and having a brutally honest conversation became one of the most important events of James's life. It's possible James would not be around today if it weren't for that unplanned, somewhat serendipitous meeting. Because of her leadership and friendship in the face of a possible tragedy, she proved tragedy is often preventable with a simple phone call or by grabbing a coffee and talking frankly.

CHAPTER 22

SEND ME

THE KENT HOME, 2018

Joe had just put the boys down to sleep when he walked into an ambush in the kitchen.

"You're getting all my shit," Shannon said as she filled out the paperwork every service member must complete before deploying to a war zone. This included instructions for what to do in case of death.

"What?" Joe responded, genuinely puzzled.

"You're getting all my shit, and I want Hindu last rites," Shannon stated just as firmly, but this time with a smile that she struggled to keep down. Joe knew the drill with this paperwork, and dark humor was the coping mechanism of choice when dealing with tough subjects like this.

Shannon and Joe were doing their best to reckon with the fact that she was deploying to a war zone once again. Joe still didn't want her to go. He was attracted to her because she was a warrior, but now she was the mother of his children. Deep down, he didn't think she had any right going to war.

Joe was conflicted about these feelings and knew it was a double standard in their relationship. He deployed three times as a father himself and recognized the hypocrisy of it all. He also knew his first deployment with the CIA was coming up and that it would over-lap with Shannon's, further complicating their situation. The boys would have to stay with their grandparents during that time.

"Shannon, I know you feel like you need to do this, but . . . these boys need you here," Joe said.

"I know," Shannon said. "But I'm not the first parent to go to war. You know I need to do my part."

As worried as Joe was, he knew she was right. Ultimately, he was in love with and proud of her.

"I'm no different than you, Joe," Shannon said. "I just want to do my part in the fight at the highest level possible."

⚓ ⚓ ⚓

The first annual multicultural Thanksgiving was in 2017; that year, it was purely experimental. In 2018, it was a bona fide event you didn't want to miss. Shannon was still fighting the Navy over their decision to block her from commissioning, but her de-ployment to Syria was only a few days away. The looming combat rotation cast a shadow over their Thanksgiving festivities, and suffice it to say there was more to talk about than pecan pie.

While Shannon and Ali were in the kitchen preparing food to put on the table, they caught up on life. She told him about how she was denied a commission in the Navy, and how she went to Congress about it. They eventually started talking about her upcoming deployment.

"I'm not scared or concerned or anything," Shannon said. "There's just something different about this one, and I can't put my finger on it."

Shannon was annoyed that the details of her deployment had changed multiple times within the last two weeks.

"I was supposed to go to Baghdad, and then I found out I was supposed to go to Erbil," Shannon explained to Ali. "And now I just found out I might go to Syria, probably? Or stay in Erbil? I don't know. I'll find out soon. I'll just do it. But it's so fucked-up."

Later, over dinner, she brought up the same concerns to her other friends, Sarah and Alia.

When it came time to say goodbyes, Shannon tried to reassure everyone the family would be okay, and that their kids would be fine. But the hugs were a little tighter than normal, and it felt like Shannon knew something no one else did. Maybe it was because she was leaving within the week that the goodbye felt different.

"I'll see you guys soon!" Shannon said. "These next few months will fly by!"

⚓ ⚓ ⚓

Shannon went out with friends two nights before her departure, doing what she could to have a last hurrah—or at least make it look that way. Maybe she was trying to push the pain of leaving her kids down—to dull the sensation from the sharp knife she felt in her side. Shannon called her cousin Sharron the following evening, the night before she was to leave, her voice raspy from too much alcohol and cigarettes.

"Sharr, I don't know if I'm doing the right thing," Shannon said. "I just like the way Joshy smells after bath time."

She was not at peace with her decision to go on another deployment. But she'd already put on her proverbial war paint. Duty to country and duty to family are almost always mutually exclusive. A warrior like Shannon was rarely afforded the satisfaction of tending to one without sacrificing the other.

"It's only eight or nine months, like another pregnancy. It'll be over in no time," Shannon said, more to herself than Sharron. She had a job to do, a job she loved, but she was forced to choose between her love of family and devotion to duty for the first time.

The time had come. Shannon's three-year-old, Colt, was old enough to understand his mom was going to war. "Momma, no fight bad guys," he told her.

This trip—her fifth to an active combat zone—was different in that Colt and Josh would be at home without their mom for a significant period of time, and she knew deep down that the work she was going over to do was not exactly safe. She would be conducting intelligence operations on behalf of the US ██████████████████ █████████████████████████.* This would mean going into contested territory in unmarked vehicles, often with nothing more than her wits and a pistol on her hip.

Shannon gave her boys one final kiss, still struggling internally about leaving. She and Joe enlisted his parents to watch the boys while they drove to Shannon's point of departure.

"Will this be the last time I see the kids?" she asked Joe as they began their drive.

---

* Description of specific unit redacted at request of DoD.

CHAPTER 23

CIGARETTES AND LIES

SYRIA, 2018

Shannon maintained her composure. The Sheikh didn't seem alarmed by the gunfire outside, so she mimicked his disposition, waiting for a sign from Scotty. Any sign.

"Fuckin' kids . . ." Scotty cursed under his breath as he reentered the room moments later. Shannon was relieved. Leave it to teenagers to rip off a few celebratory rounds from an AK-47 at the worst possible time.

Okay, let's get this back on track, Shannon thought.

Before the interruption, Shannon had referenced ISIS as *Daesh*—an Arabic word for ISIS despised by their followers.

The Sheikh didn't react. It would have been a red flag had he been offended—but he also just might have a good poker face. His body language indicated he was relaxed as he leaned back in his chair.

"It is my honor to host you, my dear, and regarding Daesh, it was my duty and honor to fight them. Unfortunately, we had no choice." As he replied, he waved his hand to someone behind Shannon. She knew Scotty was covering her back, so she kept her attention on the Sheikh.

When meeting with sheikhs, there is a predictable sequence of events, and she knew he was likely gesturing for chai and sweets to be served. Like clockwork, a young man in a flowing dishdasha, or man dress, entered the room with a steaming chai pot and glasses.

As the young man poured the sweet golden-brown tea into over-size shot glasses half-full of sugar, the Sheikh pulled out a cigarette and gestured to Shannon to offer her one. *You read my mind, old man,* Shannon thought to herself. She was taking everything in, analyzing every detail in real time while establishing rapport. Ulti-mately, she needed to see if this guy would help her track down ISIS leaders in this area.

Before she leaned forward to take the cigarette, the young man pouring chai gracefully handed Shannon a pack of Rothmans with a golden lighter. Shannon smiled and said, "Shukran."

Classic Arab hospitality, she thought. *You don't just get a cigarette. You get a whole pack.* Part of Shannon wanted to cut to the chase and point-blank ask the Sheikh how much money he needed to give up al-Baghdadi. The pressure from the shooters to produce actionable intelligence constantly hung over her. Despite her years in this pro-fession, that feeling never went away. But experience overshadowed impulse. It was time to enjoy a smoke and some chai.

Shannon lit her cigarette, took a deep drag, let out the smoke, and continued the conversation.

"Since Daesh fell, has your area been peaceful?"

She knew the area had been far from peaceful but wanted to determine how the Sheikh felt about the current security situation. This could give her more color on the Sheikh and reveal what he did or didn't know, what he was willing to discuss, and how he viewed the world. Shannon needed this data to guide her plan to engineer the Sheikh to help track al-Baghdadi. The art of intelligence collection lies in seeming natural and not like an agenda-driven interrogation.

"Embers under the ashes," the Sheikh replied as he exhaled smoke from his cigarette and stirred the chai in his cup. The small metal spoon clanging against the glass cup made a slight but distinct sound that Shannon had spent hours listening to over the years while engaging in conversational jujitsu.

"When Daesh controlled land, we knew where they were," he said. "Now they could be anywhere. The danger is not as constant, but they are still here." *At least he was being close to honest,* Shannon thought. *He didn't say things were fine; he acknowledged that Daesh was in the area. Now we can play ball.*

"Is Daesh attacking people in the area or just using your area to hide?" Again, Shannon knew the answer to this question, but there had been attacks against some of Daesh's more outspoken enemies in the area. Shannon wanted to determine how the Sheikh felt about attacks against his people. If he was defensive, that could indicate he was working with or sanctioning ISIS. If he was angry about the attacks, that could mean a willingness to work with Shannon to remove ISIS fighters from his area.

"There are attacks, but not all attacks are Daesh. Daesh can hide anywhere; they are like water. They spread and disappear," the Sheikh said. He was dancing around the question. Shannon knew better than to expect a clear-cut answer in the first minutes of a conversation. Arabs were the masters of speaking in metaphors while saying yes and no simultaneously.

"Who else is attacking your people?" Shannon asked.

The Sheikh frowned.

"The militias, the Kurds, and the regime. The real question is, who is not attacking us?"

The Sheikh's tone was more emotional now, and Shannon could almost feel his frustration. Her research before meeting him was not just to make her an expert on current events in his area; it was to help her see the world from his point of view. Putting herself in his shoes helped her understand what he wanted and how to manipulate him.

She knew the Sheikh and his tribe were at the mercy of geography. The Sunnis of Syria and western Iraq had an Iranian-backed Iraqi government to their east, Syria's dictator Assad to their west, Kurds to the north, and vast nothingness to their south. Their choices were to live under the rule of one of their rivals or unify and fight. Unity was complex; as much as the tribes mistrusted outsiders, the Sunni tribes of western Iraq and eastern Syria were far from homogeneous.

ISIS had capitalized on this tribal disorder. The sheikhs could not protect their people, but God and the Islamic State could. That was ISIS's appeal to the Sunni masses, and nothing breeds success like success. So once ISIS took a few Sunni towns in eastern Syria, the Sunnis of the region saw their chance, and the rest was history.

ISIS's appeal faded as a draconian interpretation of sharia law was implemented, and US intervention made living in ISIS-controlled territory a death sentence. With ISIS's power waning, the sheikhs, like the source Shannon was talking to, saw their opportunity to regain the power they lost to ISIS. So the sheikhs moved in to fill the void ISIS's departure caused in the average person's life.

They still had to thread the needle with ISIS, only fighting them when there was no other option while retaining a stable of hardened fighters for use against the regime, the Shia militias, or the Kurds. ISIS was dangerous, but if used tactically, they were effective.

Shannon understood why the Sheikh could view ISIS as a potent tool. She had to find a way to make him see that working with the US was more beneficial, maybe not forever, but long enough to take some of ISIS's key leaders off the battlefield. For survivors and power brokers, alliances were business deals that lasted as long as they were profitable.

"You really are surrounded here. I can tell you and your people are strong to endure attacks from every direction," Shannon said with a hint of empathy that sounded genuine, letting the statement hang as she sipped her chai. The sweet tea contrasting with the bitter aftertaste of a cigarette tasted like work, a taste she subconsciously associated with trying to get humans to tell her what they knew.

The Sheikh squared his shoulders and pridefully lifted his chin. Men appreciate being told they are strong, especially when a woman says it.

"Your strength is why the American government sent me to meet with you. We know you would do anything to protect your people," Shannon said, driving the compliment home.

"It is my duty. As long as this land has been Muslim, my tribe has cared for this area. I would do anything to protect my people," the Sheikh said as he leaned in.

"We are here to work with you, as a team, to get rid of Daesh," Shannon said, holding eye contact. "So your people can live in peace." She told the Sheikh what he already knew: the Americans wanted to use him as an informant.

Shannon described the relationship as working together, playing to the Sheikh's ego, but couldn't bluntly ask him to give her the locations of ISIS leaders. That would insult his pride, and the conversation would end there. So the dance continued even though she was confident he would eventually do just that.

"Of course, I will do what I must and work with you and American forces," the Sheikh replied. Shannon remained silent. He had more to say—she could see it in his eyes.

"But you must know there are many false rumors about who is Daesh in this area," the Sheikh said in a more passive tone.

Got it. You want to keep your goons, Shannon thought. *Fair enough.* He was concerned America would come after anyone who previously fought for the terror group, but that was not the case. If she had not spent most of her adult life trying to make sense of this region, she might not have been able to find empathy for members of such a vile and evil group as ISIS.

Shannon's empathy wasn't genuine, though, at least not in the sense that she could actually find common ground with members of the notorious terrorists who were responsible for untold amounts of death and destruction in the area. Instead, she had honed an emotional pathway to get into the mind of her prey. Like a hunter stalking an animal for miles to get the perfect shot, Shannon had the savvy and endurance to gain a source's trust.

She knew he had his own militia that employed most young men in his tribe. Being a militant was probably the most stable profession a young man could have in this part of the world.

"There are those who fought to keep Assad and Iran's militias out of our area and those who came for the caliphate," the Sheikh said. "They are very different."

Shannon nodded.

"I understand, and more importantly, the US government understands."

"I am happy to hear that," he said. "If you understand that, you must understand the dire situation with Iran's militias in this area. Will you help us fight them?"

He lit another cigarette and offered one to Shannon. She lit it and took a deep drag, thankful for nicotine and the pause it provided to collect her thoughts. She anticipated this topic and was very familiar with Iranian-backed militias. She had cut her teeth targeting them thirteen years ago and had seen Iraq's sectarian battles from almost the same vantage point she sat in now, sitting across from tribal leaders and militants, trying to make sense of it all.

But she did not have an answer. US policymakers gave the military effort in Iraq and Syria the mandate of destroying ISIS, not getting into a conflict with Iran. As a result, operators like Shannon found themselves playing equal parts diplomat and commando.

"I understand. I know firsthand what Iran is capable of," Shannon said. The Sheikh nodded and leaned back. He appeared relieved she understood more than just ISIS.

"But before we can address Iran, we must stop Daesh's leaders from hiding in this area, particularly foreign leaders," Shannon said authoritatively. "This is the first step for our partnership." Speaking confidently was critical to ensuring the Sheikh saw her, and thereby the US government, as a viable partner.

"I understand, and I am worried about Daesh as well. Real Daesh, led by foreigners, have tried to assassinate me several times."

Nothing like a few car bombs in your front yard to encourage cooperation, Shannon thought. This was precisely why she saw him as a potential ally: he was already fighting for his life. The US government wanted to help him be effective. *Help us help you.*

"So yes, I am happy to work with you, but I need you to help us with Iran," he said again. His voice betrayed his exhaustion.

"Absolutely," Shannon said. *We'll work out the details on Iran . . . later.*

She was happy they had a verbal agreement. That kind of progress was uncommon for a first meeting but not good enough for Shannon. She came for actionable intelligence on al-Baghdadi so he could be killed or captured, and she wasn't going to leave without it.

"I'm very happy you are with us," Shannon said. "Your concerns about Iran will carry more weight with my superiors in Washington, DC, if you can help me locate a Daesh leader today."

There it is, old man. Give us the goods, and I'm your link to policy makers, Shannon thought. It was a high-stakes sales pitch. If the task force took out al-Baghdadi in this area, the cat would be out of the bag that the Sheikh defected from ISIS and was no longer a neutral player. The stakes just doubled for him.

Shannon took another drag. *Thank God Arabs still smoke; this would suck without nicotine.*

He raised his eyebrows, his mouth straightened, and drew a deep breath. He understood the ramifications of what Shannon was asking him to do. His resilience in the face of ISIS earned him some wiggle room. However, telling Shannon precisely where their leaders were located would undoubtedly turn their full ire against him. Shannon could see his concerns.

"We understand the position you will be in by helping us. We can help keep you safe," Shannon said.

The Sheikh exhaled slowly.

"What can I do to help?" he asked, finally.

Hell yes, now we're talking.

"We need to find a leader—he goes by al-Baghdadi. We think he's hiding in this area," Shannon said. The Sheikh didn't blink; his mind was likely racing. She didn't ask for any run-of-the-mill militant but one of the most wanted men on the planet.

"I have heard of him, and I am sad to say that he is in this area," he replied carefully.

The sound of mumbled Arabic and furniture being moved in a nearby room disrupted Shannon's momentum. A young man appeared to her left, probably in his midtwenties, wearing a green and black Adidas tracksuit and a pair of spotless white Nike shoes. He sported a well-trimmed jet-black mustache, and a silver Beretta pistol in a leather holster under his left shoulder.

As he walked past Shannon, she was bombarded by the smell of strong cologne. The Sheikh was right out of Central Casting for *Lawrence of Arabia,* and this dude, probably his son or nephew, looked like he just walked off the set of *The Sopranos. You can't make this shit up,* Shannon mused.

She glanced over at Scotty, who remained calm as always. They had both been at this too long to get jumpy about a gun at a meeting. A pistol, especially a silver one, was standard Arab bling, a status symbol more than anything else.

The interruption allowed her to focus on the activity in the adjacent room. It sounded like lunch was underway. Once the scent of the young man's cologne had faded, she inhaled the distinct smell of beef kebabs, lamb, saffron rice, and fresh flatbread. There were many aspects to not like about being deployed to the Middle East, but its cuisine was not one of those things—at least for Shannon.

The young man leaned in to speak in a hushed tone with the Sheikh, who then looked up and said, "This is my oldest son, Khalid. We would be honored if you and your colleagues joined us for lunch."

"Sounds great; thank you for your generosity," Shannon said. "It's an honor to meet you, Khalid." As much as she wanted to get al-Baghdadi's location and get back to base, she knew adhering to cultural norms would pay off.

She and the Sheikh stood and walked into the next room, with Scotty and Khalid following behind. There was a huge dinner table overflowing with food, a large pile of saffron rice in the center, kebabs, lamb shanks, dolma, and a grape leaf dish—Shannon's favorite—flanking the spread. Around the table's perimeter were small vegetable dishes, Fanta sodas, and Pepsi. Shannon knew Arabic culture as well as their language, and sharing food was a must for a host while enjoying the food was how the guest showed gratitude.

"This all looks incredible, Sheikh. Thank you so much, and I apologize in advance if I eat all the dolma," Shannon said in Arabic with a devious smile. Her Arabic, with humor, made the Sheikh genuinely laugh.

"It's my honor. Let's eat, and you can tell me how you learned our language. It's like you were raised on water from the Euphrates."

With that, Shannon, Scotty, Khalid, and the Sheikh dug into the food and made casual talk. This kind of tactical patience separates professionals from amateurs in high-stakes intelligence collection. Shannon was confident she would get what she needed, eventually.

CHAPTER 24

FIND, FIX, FINISH

SYRIA, 2018

Shannon learned Khalid was in charge of the Sheikh's militia during the light lunch conversation. Afterward, the Sheikh invited her to the same room they were in before for more tea and another cigarette. *Back to business,* Shannon thought.

"I'm very grateful for your hospitality and cooperation, Sheikh," she said while stirring her tea.

The Sheikh nodded and motioned for Khalid to approach. Khalid had an iPad-style tablet in his hand and passed it to the Sheikh, who sat it on the edge of his desk so Shannon could see. Google Maps was open with a pin dropped on a location.

"Here is where al-Baghdadi may be hiding. It's one of a few places he uses in this area. The village is called Nahir Al-Heliwi," the Sheikh said as he pointed to the dropped pin. The village's name translated to "The Pretty River."

Shannon clicked on the pin and wrote down the coordinates.

"Do you know which house in the village he is staying in?" Shannon pried.

He nodded and again motioned for Khalid. This was clearly his area of expertise. Khalid sat next to Shannon and zoomed in on the map, revealing individual structures.

"Here and here." Khalid pointed to two residences in the southeastern corner of the village. "We don't know all of the ISIS members, but their leader calls himself the Caliph Ibrahim, and they kicked out the families who owned the houses previously."

Khalid is sharp, Shannon thought. Being able to report detailed information was not a skill most sources possessed.

"How did you find out about this?" Shannon needed to understand the genesis of Khalid's information if she was going to ask the shooters to risk their lives on it.

"The owner of the houses was evicted and came to us for help last week," Khalid said. Shannon wrote down the additional coordinates in her notebook and confirmed them on GPS as he talked. At this point, this was the most substantial lead she'd had on al-Baghdadi since arriving in-country. But the physical location was only one part of the equation.

"How does Daesh defend these homes and the village?" Shannon asked with an extra edge to her voice. "Are there IEDs on the road? Roaming guards? Has Daesh rigged the houses to explode?"

She knew her brothers would be in harm's way later that night. This information could save their lives.

"Ah, yes," Khalid said. "Here and here," he said as he pointed to IED locations at the small village's only entrance and exit roads. "And there are guards on the roofs."

"Do you know who lives across from the homes that he uses?" Shannon said while continuing to take notes. "Do you think they can tell you when al-Baghdadi will be home?" Knowing a terrorist's hideout was worthless if he was not home when the shooters kicked his door in. Knowing exactly where a target was and when he would be there was the "fix" part of the operation Shannon was working on.

"I can call the neighbor across the street, Ali Jasim," Khalid said with a nod. "He has a kerosene business and goes door-to-door each evening selling kerosene bottles—even Daesh needs gas."

Perfect, Shannon thought. *His location can be fixed.* Before a raid could be conducted, Shannon had to develop a way to ensure al-Baghdadi was home. This was known as the *trigger,* meaning the confirmation would trigger the raid.

"In the coming days, I will call you in the evening," Shannon said. "Will you be able to send Ali Jasim to al-Baghdadi's house to confirm he is home?"

If there was any confusion about Shannon's intent, the tone and specific nature of her questions made it evident she was formulating a plan targeting the leader of ISIS. The stakes were rising by the second.

"Yes, I can. If I ask Ali Jasim, he will be able to walk over with a kerosene bottle to sell," Khalid said.

Found. Fixed. And a trigger to boot!

She was happy but not done. The best plans can fall apart without a contingency plan for communication. Shannon's primary plan relied on her communicating with Khalid via cell phone and Khalid communicating with Ali Jasim via cell phone. The cellular networks were pretty reliable but solely relying on cell phones to trigger a raid was begging Murphy's law to enter the complex planning process.

"Can you drive the white Suburban in your driveway to Ali Jasim's house each night?" Shannon asked.

Khalid looked puzzled. "I can. It is normal for me to be in that area," he cautiously replied.

"I need you to go there if our cell phones do not work," Shannon said forcefully. They were past the negotiation process at this point. It was time for everyone in the room to understand she wasn't fucking around. "I need you to park your Suburban in front of Ali Jasim's house here." Shannon pointed at the spot on Khalid's tablet. "If there is no cell phone coverage and al-Baghdadi is home, lift the hood on your Suburban. We will look for the signal at ten p.m." Shannon explained.

"Ah, I see. I can do that," Khalid replied. He seemed impressed.

Shannon sat back and sipped her chai. *There. Found, fixed, and trigger set with communication contingencies. Time to get the hell out of here and give the shooters the good news,* Shannon thought.

"That is very helpful, Sheikh. What other areas is Daesh using that we can help you with?" Shannon asked. A good HUMINTer always asks for a little more.

"There are so many more, but if you find this one, the rest will follow," he said.

Fair enough. It was just the first meeting. She knew getting any information from a first meeting was a big deal. Getting a possible location for HVT No. 1 was huge.

Everything would still have to be verified against other intelligence before moving forward with an operation, even though commandos were standing by, ready to pounce. Human intelligence is just that: human. It was always possible the source was lying or using misinformation to target a rival, which caused Shannon to view all unverified information with skepticism. In this case, what the Sheikh and Khalid were saying passed her initial bullshit detector. She was confident she had enough to paint the X for the shooters.

"You're right. This is a great place to start. We will be in touch soon," Shannon said. "Thank you very much for the hospitality and your help."

"It is my honor to host you and my duty to work with you and American forces," the Sheikh replied.

Shannon rose, knowing no Arab host would rise before a guest. Once on her feet, she shook hands with the Sheikh and Khalid before turning to see Scotty by the door, making eye contact with him before following him out the house's front door.

In the courtyard, the sun shone brightly and was doing its best to break the chill from the winter day. Shannon saw Jake outside the courtyard entrance in their car with the engine running, ready to hit the road. Shannon and Scotty bid goodbye to their hosts and climbed inside the vehicle. Jake slowly pulled away.

They took a different route home than the one they came in on; the most dangerous part of the day still lay ahead. After any operation, be it a source meet or a raid, there is a massive adrenaline dump once the big event is over. At that point, it's easy to forget you are still a target as long as you're outside your base. Shannon, Scotty, and Jake knew this and immediately switched from meeting mode to scanning the area around them for threats.

There was much more traffic in the village and on the highway back to base at this time, which was both a blessing and a curse. More people on the street meant there were more casual observers to see the American trio exit the house and drive off, but once they were clear of the house, they would blend into the sea of traffic and people, making them hard to spot—or target.

"Things were pretty chill out front; I didn't see anything we needed to address," Jake reported, as he had done so many times.

"Cool," Scotty replied sarcastically. "Pretty chill except for . . . oh, that's right, those kids deciding to do a SPENDEX in the middle of our meeting." (*SPENDEX* is military speak for spend exercise, which refers to instances when there is excess ammunition at the end of a training block that must be used, so it is fired rapidly and often without any training value.)

Shannon smirked as she removed her ball cap and pulled her purple kaffiyeh over her head, giving herself a local profile. Two men up front and a woman in the back seat was a typical profile that would not attract a second glance from casual observers.

Jake held up a dip can for Scotty while keeping his eyes on the road. Scotty kept scanning outside the window while he took the can and popped three fingers of Copenhagen into his lip.

"Shan, you should have to take a dip for hotboxing in that damn room. Those haji smokes are brutal," Scotty said, his gaze fixed on the street outside the car.

Shannon was also scanning people on the streets, looking for threats.

"Oh, that bothered you?" she asked. "I figured you were just working on your sweet SEAL breath-holding skills."

Scotty rolled his eyes and Jake laughed out loud.

A few minutes later, they were a mile away from the Sheikh's house, and Jake was fighting the heavy midday traffic just like the locals. In the sea of humans, no one seemed to give them a second look.

Shannon's mind was going a million miles per hour. She was running through all the ways she could verify the source's information. But, due to her level of expertise, her day would not be over when they returned to base. In the intelligence world, there were two main functions: collectors who literally collected information from humans; signal analysts who looked at images; and regular analysts who reviewed the collected data and determined what information was accurate and what it meant.

Shannon had been trained as a signals intelligence analyst and collector before she found her way into the world of HUMINT, so she knew how to use databases and direct other intelligence resources. Unfortunately, not many collectors had analytical expertise, and even fewer analysts had any idea where the information they read came from. Nevertheless, Shannon loved verifying her own information and using her knowledge of the larger intelligence picture to focus her work.

As they pulled into the base and relaxed a little, Scotty and Jake talked about hitting the gym and watching a movie.

"Shan, you going to the matrix meeting?" Jake asked with a smile.

"Hell yeah, you guys are welcome to come and look at those sweet intel reports. Maybe help me with my nightly book report?" Shannon said as she climbed out of the car and stretched.

"Yeah, we'll meet you there," Jake replied sarcastically while walking toward his trailer.

Returning to base meant it was time to start a crucial part of intelligence work: the documentation. If it's not written, it didn't happen. Worse yet, the knowledge would not be known to all and fully leveraged against the enemy. SOF had received well-deserved publicity for hunting and killing terrorists over the past two decades; some even called it an industrialized killing machine. That sounded sexy, but professionals like Shannon and her team knew it was actually a learning and dissemination machine. The famed commandos of SOF needed to go to the right place at the right time and catch the right bad guy to be effective.

Collecting, analyzing, and disseminating information was critical to the fight. Those drawn to SOF are typically aggressive type-A personalities who have no issue taking on their assigned tasks, but frequently have problems communicating with each other and sharing valued information. Early in the war, this meant different elements in SOF and the intelligence community were not sharing critical pieces of information that could have resulted in capturing or killing key terrorist leaders had there been a more collaborative system.

In 2004, General Stanley McChrystal recognized this. So he shifted SOF culture from a tribal mentality to a Silicon Valley–like culture where information sharing and intelligence became valued as much as an operator's physical prowess. McChrystal put intelligence collectors and analysts forward with the operators and demanded collaboration. This was the real reason SOF became the famed manhunting machine responsible for decapitating al-Qaeda's brutal franchise in Iraq.

As tired as she was, Shannon headed toward the office to call the shooters waiting on the flight line to inform them of her plan and that they could be hitting the target as soon as tonight if she could verify everything in time. She still needed to type up her intelligence report and research what the source had told her.

As she was mentally plotting her tasks for the evening, a booming voice behind her shattered her thoughts.

"Shan! What'd ya got!"

She turned to see Jim, the senior shooter, dressed in full combat gear. He had been waiting for her to return. Shannon was glad he came to her; one less thing to do that evening.

"I have coordinates to al-Baghdadi's suspected location, and a trigger worked," Shannon said. "We might be able to roll as soon as tonight." Shannon tried to sound calm and professional, but her huge grin and the spark in her blue eyes gave away her pride just enough to be contagious.

Jim immediately grinned.

"Fuck'n A. Tonight it is. Tell me when he's home and down for the evening."

"Will do. I have locations of two IEDs and guards as well; let me get it into a brief for your guys," Shannon said.

"Roger," Jim replied. "I'll send my assault team leaders to your office when you're ready for 'em."

"Cool. See ya in a few."

Before she entered the secure office, Shannon detoured toward her room. Lucky for her, she had a twenty-foot daily commute. She picked up her personal phone to see what was going on back home. A picture of two happy little boys playing in her backyard in Maryland greeted her when she opened her messages.

Hi mama, we love you! The message was from "The Hubs," which is how Shannon had Joe saved as a contact in her phone. Shannon smiled and checked her watch. *Damn, too late to catch them now.*

Love you guys, back on camp safe & sound. Off to type for a bit, love all of you! Shannon wrote back. She placed her phone on her bed and walked back to the office.

Time to plan another raid on yet another suspected location for al-Baghdadi. Hopefully, this was the one.

CHAPTER 25

SAVING MANBIJ

MANBIJ, SYRIA, 2018

Shannon scanned the sidewalks, streets, rooftops, and open gates as the convoy snaked toward downtown Manbij. At this point in the war, Manbij wasn't necessarily safe so much as it was stable. Or maybe just quiet . . . for the time being. Kurdish forces backed by the American military had successfully driven out the Islamic State in 2016, with a relative calm following. But was it the kind of calm that comes before a storm?

There were simple indicators Shannon looked for while driving toward a target. For example, people walking by might hold up one finger, meaning they support ISIS. Or they would hold up two fingers, like a peace sign, which stood for the YPG or YPJ—groups actively fighting ISIS. Supporting them meant you did not support the Islamic State. For Shannon, keeping an eye on local sentiment in any given area was part of the puzzle.

The convoy eventually rolled to a stop after entering the bazaar district. Shannon looked at Scotty.

"Ready?" she asked, reaching for the door handle.

"Let's do it," Scotty confirmed. Shannon swung her door open, stepped into the busy Manbij bazaar, and immediately scanned her surroundings. Scotty followed suit. He may have been one of the only people in the theater who knew everything Shannon was doing during her Syria deployment. Some missions were just the two of them meeting a source in the middle of nowhere. Other times, like this mission, they linked up with American forces working in the area.

Those troops usually didn't know Shannon or who she worked for, but she was friendly and demonstrably good at her job, so they were happy to help. Throughout the war on terror, service members deployed overseas grew accustomed to people dressed in civilian clothes showing up out of nowhere, asking for a ride somewhere, or intelligence on something, or maybe a few shooters to hop in a truck and roll out without asking too many questions. Were they CIA? Or from the task force? Perhaps some organization no one knew about yet? Rumors could, and often did, run rampant.

"Hey, Jon, we're gonna get going; not sure how long this guy will stick around. Either way, we shouldn't be long," Shannon said to Captain Jon Turnbull, a Civil Affairs officer in charge of Cross-Functional Team (CFT) Manbij, and the convoy commander who escorted her and Scotty into town that day. Although they had sent emails back and forth for weeks, their first in-person meeting was earlier that day, back at the grain silos. Unfortunately, they didn't have time for more than a quick handshake before departing for the mission.

"Roger, we'll be here," Jon said. Cross-functional teams were somewhat of a hodgepodge of special operations and conventional soldiers, combining the unique skill sets of Civil Affairs, Psychological Operations, and Special Forces soldiers with the security that local partner forces and American infantry units provided.

Jon's small team operated out of a cluster of grain silos on the edge of Manbij proper. Their only backup was a small unit of soldiers from the US Army Third Armored Cavalry Regiment at a small camp to their west. It was outlaw country, and his team had broad authority to stabilize and rejuvenate the small northern city of approximately 300,000 that would eventually be cited as the model for what Syria could look like post-ISIS,[1] despite being at the crossroads of international tensions between Syria, Turkey, Russia, and the United States. There were legal limits to what his team could do, though.

They weren't technically qualified to perform intelligence-gathering activities. But they did have access and influence in the community and collected information accordingly. This is where Shannon came into play. CFT Manbij was an excellent source of leads for her, so she planned to make Manbij a regular stop during this deployment to keep tabs on what they had in development.

Of course, she still chased her own sources and could use the CFT's routine activities as cover to slip into town unnoticed—which seemed to be working great so far. There was also the added benefit of the CFT's assigned Green Berets being available to help if a mission ever went sour.

Jon's team set up security at the bazaar while Shannon and Scotty slipped away to conduct their meeting. Being so close to the market, Jon saw an opportunity to buy local food for the team. His favorite local treat was called manaeesh, a snack similar to a small pizza made on pita bread. Top it with Nutella and it was the perfect boost of energy for a long afternoon in Manbij.

He picked up a couple of dozen manaeesh at a restaurant down the road from where the convoy was parked, and by the time he arrived back at the trucks, Shannon and Scotty had already returned. Jon's team started to regroup while they ate, but it didn't take long to devour the delicious snacks.

"Hey, do we have any more for these guys?" Shannon asked, referring to the Syrian security force attachments, or "the Dirty 30" as they called them.

"No, I bought enough, but you ate them all," Jon said, only half-joking.

The soldiers weren't complaining, but the situation didn't sit right with Shannon. Before anyone could stop her, she ran down the road toward the bazaar—on her own.

She returned carrying as much manaeesh as she could get her arms around for the Syrian soldiers. It was a simple gesture but garnered immediate respect. The Dirty 30 recognized she didn't need to get them food but were impressed with how fearless she was in her effort to make right by them. Jon's CFT even noticed it helped with their own rapport-building efforts with the Syrians.

It wasn't just the SDF soldiers that Shannon looked out for. On other visits, she often brought snacks and other items of convenience and luxury for Jon's team, making sure they were taken care of too. Their trust and respect were just as crucial to Shannon as the Syrians.

⚓ ⚓ ⚓

What the fuck? What is going on? Why are you only showing us boys' schools?" Jon asked Saheel, clearly frustrated and feeling like the Manbij education director was trying to hide something. They sat at student desks in a classroom with Shannon listening nearby, observing the man closely. As part of their charter to establish the government's legitimacy, Jon's team often visited everything from hospitals to schools to ensure essential public services ran smoothly. This school was only fifty meters from the bazaar they had visited for Shannon's last source meet in the area.

"I'm not showing you only boys' schools, but in all of Syria, only boys go to school. Girls are not allowed to go to school," Saheel replied.

Even after ISIS was removed from power, their mandate to bar young girls from attending school remained quietly in effect for fear of remaining underground terrorist cells. This was the case not just in Manbij but all of northeast Syria, and anywhere ISIS once ruled.

"Well, yeah, but ISIS isn't here anymore," Jon said. "In theory, you guys are in charge and want to change, right?"

"We tried three years ago," Saheel said.

In 2015, the United States–led coalition moved into Manbij, kicking out ISIS and establishing a city council that promoted Western ideologies. ISIS was gone, and the Americans established a permanent presence in the city. Life seemed to be returning to normal, and the citizens of Manbij were ready to go back to work and put their kids back in school.

"We had our first girl come back to school. She sat right here," Saheel said, motioning to the children's chair Jon was sitting in. He explained how the girl attended school for about a month without issue—no threats or reasons for concern were ever brought to the school administrator's attention. The Americans were here now, after all. Saheel conducted business as usual.

"One day, a man entered the school and walked the hallways," Saheel said, his face taut in an attempt to control his emotion. The look on Shannon's face betrayed her: she knew exactly where this was going.

"He wasn't wearing a uniform, and the faculty assumed he was a parent looking for his child," Saheel continued. "As he passed the classroom the girl was in, he stopped. He entered the room, enraged, and began punching her in the face over and over . . ."

Saheel paused. This was the side of war Americans never hear about. This was the all-too-common story of what happens when evil is left unchecked outside the view of news cameras.

". . . before grabbing her hair and dragging her outside. I . . . we, the teachers . . . the students tried to stop him." It was clear at this point the man was an ISIS thug, sent to strike fear back into a community that was getting too comfortable in the caliphate's absence.

"He forced the young girl down and bent her over the fountain in the school's courtyard," Saheel said, motioning out the window. Shannon's jaw clenched. She couldn't cry, scream, or do anything but sit and listen to this man's story. Saheel's eyes stayed dry, and although he was physically there with Jon and Shannon, it was clear he was somewhere else much darker.

"He shot her in the back of the head. He left her body in the fountain for her parents to retrieve."

Shannon loved the young girls she met in Syria and certainly didn't need extra motivation to hunt down the people responsible for these atrocities, but the look on this old man's face and the story he told served as a stark reminder of the stakes at play.

Saheel explained that though ISIS was not in charge, they were not gone. The story spread across the region and resulted in parents being too scared to send their daughters to school, which is why Jon hadn't seen any girls during his other school visits.

"He said that if they catch another girl in any school anywhere in Syria, they will do the same," Saheel said. "And next time, they will kill every person inside the school, including children and faculty. So, girls don't go to school in northeast Syria."

Shannon turned to Jon, and although nothing had been said, Jon knew exactly what she was thinking. They needed to do something about this if they wanted the mission in Manbij to be successful. Not just because it was the right thing to do but because they needed the cooperation of the locals.

Correcting this issue became a point of pride for CFT Manbij, who needed to show that the local government was in charge, despite the continued presence of ISIS. They began the process of putting girls back in school almost immediately. In addition, the Special Forces soldiers started training the SDF to guard schools and ensure, at minimum, a gun truck was permanently stationed inside every school's courtyard.

Jon met with the Ministry of Education for the Civil Administration of Manbij and promised that his team could and would protect any girls who want to return to school. His guarantee of security instilled the confidence parents needed to send their young girls back outside the home to receive an education.

The fountain on which the student was executed remained a constant reminder of the horror that happened that day. So CFT Manbij destroyed it with a sledgehammer while everyone watched, and the US Agency for International Development (USAID) eventually purchased a new fountain featuring figurines of girls holding umbrellas under the water to serve as a memorial.

Improvements were happening in Manbij. Their work with the school near the bazaar proved the coalition could back their words with action and make good on the promise to secure facilities and promote education. Many challenges were still ahead, and pockets of ISIS still existed in Manbij. But suddenly, tips about ISIS operatives became much more frequent, and Shannon's work in the area started to pick up.

Weeks later, CFT Manbij returned to the school to check in and evaluate progress. Shannon and Scotty talked while Jon enjoyed a Coke as schoolchildren ran around during their break from the classroom. A young girl approached.

"Thank you for helping," she said in Arabic, then started speaking rapidly. Jon knew some Arabic but was not fluent and couldn't keep up with the young girl.

"Jasmine, can you translate?" he asked. Ghadir Taher was a Syrian-born American fluent in Arabic and worked as one of CFT Manbij's dedicated interpreters. They called her Jasmine, after the Disney character, which she leaned into by pinning a picture of Jasmine on her door so the rest of the team would know where to find her.

While talking to the girl, she broke down sobbing. Shannon noticed and sat down with Ghadir to help calm her down. A few of the schoolgirls walked over to hug her.

Shannon turned her attention to the young girl Ghadir was talking to, translating and summarizing what she said: "Thank you for helping her and her friends come back to school and keeping them safe," Shannon translated. "But she wants to know if you will keep her safe at home. There's a mean guy that hurts her that lives down the road."

The young girl, who looked like she was between six and eight years old, continued talking, describing the molestation and rape of her and her friends. Shannon tried to hold back tears, but hearing the firsthand account was too much.

"We need to help her," Shannon said. It wasn't just that the kids needed to be saved from horrendous acts; this activity was a calling card for ISIS. Whoever was doing this was likely connected to the people Shannon was hunting.

Later, they went to the young girl's house to speak with her parents. Ghadir translated for Jon as Shannon talked to the parents in their native tongue over tea.

"Your daughter describes a very evil man. Are you familiar with him?" Shannon asked. The father looked embarrassed; the mother looked away. There was no verbal reply, but that was all Shannon needed.

"Do you know where he stays?"

"He lives nearby," the father said.

Shannon took notes on specifics. He was a commander who showed up seven or eight years prior with Daesh. He hosted parties where he and his friends would get rowdy and order children in the neighborhood to come to his house. He was feared, and no one could stand up to him. Shannon pieced together that he was likely a bomb manufacturer or stored bombs at his home.

Shannon thanked the parents before leaving their house. As they walked back toward the convoy, Jon asked her what she thought.

"We'll take care of it," Shannon said.

Days later, elements of the Syrian Defense Forces raided the house of a Syrian commander in charge of all ISIS fighters in the area. It's unclear how involved Shannon and Scotty were, but Jon believes they ultimately took control of the prisoner and ensured he would be transferred somewhere conducive to eliciting more information from him to fuel more follow-on raids. The value in taking someone alive is the information they provide. Sometimes a single thread can lead to the dismantling of entire networks.

CFT Manbij's convoy of Land Cruiser SUVs with guns on top were running jamming systems to prevent any IEDs from exploding as they pulled up to the only hospital in Manbij: al-Firat Hospital, which translates to Euphrates Hospital in Arabic because it sits west of the Euphrates River.

This hospital was unique because it was commensurate with a level 2 hospital in the United States, offering ultrasounds, EKGs, X-rays, and medical professionals capable of administering dialysis treatments—a significant capability, particularly with frequent pediatric dialysis diagnoses in the area. Because of the advanced level of care available, anyone in the coalition could be treated there in an emergency. In fact, if you search for it on Google Maps, you'll see a soccer field with a stadium in the field next door. The area was designated a helicopter landing zone (HLZ) suitable for medevac flights.

Shannon, Scotty, Jon, and the rest of their team dismounted in front of what seemed like an entire hospital staff who had come out to meet them. Two people, Dr. Reem and the hospital administrator, Mona, came forward to greet the Americans.

"MarHaban, as-salaam'alaykum," Shannon said before immediately striking up a conversation with them in Arabic as if they were long-lost friends. Instantly, any barrier that existed was torn down.

"How are things going?" Shannon asked.

"Follow me," Dr. Reem said.

She took the group of Americans into the hospital for a tour and inspection of the medical facility. Dr. Reem was a pharmacist by trade, so they took a left on the first floor of three into the pharmacy.

"Look at all this space for medicine," she explained. "I just wish we had medicine to fill the space."

"I think that's something we can help with," Jon said.

He wrote down a list of all the medicine they needed, which he would later deliver to USAID and the US State Department. Dr. Reem continued, showing them the emergency room. Having a trauma department was a critical capability, given the state of affairs in the area.

Finally, they descended into the hospital basement. It was damp, cold, ominous—even creepy, with stale air and no lights. The soldiers used lights at the end of their rifles to sweep across the walls. They discovered ISIS graffiti everywhere. They kept moving through, eventually entering a room with a large hole in the ceiling.

"When the coalition took over three years ago, Daesh used the hospital as a staging point, knowing Western forces would not target a hospital," Dr. Reem explained. Civil infrastructure was strictly off-limits to the coalition, and most commanders knew that if they bombed it, they would eventually have to rebuild it. But with ISIS consolidated at this hospital, something had to be done.

"They attempted an assault to rid us of Daesh, but the Daesh soldiers retreated down here, knowing anyone who chased after them would be an easy target," Dr. Reem continued. "They tried many tactics to coax them out of their hiding spot, but nothing worked. Daesh knew they might be surrounded but felt secure."

Eventually an American advisor suggested using a "bunker buster" bomb, a type of explosive specifically designed to puncture structures without exploding at first contact, instead using a delayed detonation for deeper penetration. This would allow them to eliminate the barricaded enemy fighters without destroying the entire hospital.

The strike worked as promised. The threat was instantly eliminated.

"It's gruesome, all these spirits in here," Jon said.

"I see dead people," Shannon whispered. Gallows humor is as natural in war as death itself. That's right when they found a fridge with Arabic markings on it.

"What's that mean?" Jon asked.

"Land mine," Shannon replied. Did Daesh leave something behind before they died? They called the Explosive Ordnance Disposal (EOD) technicians to inspect the suspected unexploded ordnance. Threats like this needed to be approached with utmost caution. The EOD technicians, Staff Sergeant Jarred and Sergeant Darius, arrived and worked diligently to remove the explosive, which was eventually taken out to a field and blown in place.

Dr. Reem led them out of the basement and to the top floor, which was empty except for ISIS graffiti, flags, and propaganda posters.

"Why is this up here?" Shannon asked. "Why hasn't this been taken down, Dr. Reem?" Dr. Reem's eyes welled up with tears. Shannon hugged her and did her best to comfort her.

"What's going on?" Shannon asked again softly.

In a story that was becoming hauntingly familiar, Dr. Reem explained that after they dropped the bomb on the hospital, wiping out the ISIS fighters barricaded there, the militant terrorists still had a presence in the area. A few fighters eventually came back to enforce their will, just like at the school.

"My husband was the chief surgeon at this hospital," Dr. Reem said, composing herself. "One day, Daesh came back, demanding that he perform specific unethical procedures. He declined, which insulted them."

Her speech accelerated; Shannon did her best to relay what she was saying to the rest of the group.

"The militants grabbed her husband and dragged him out to the parking lot," Shannon said. "They forced Dr. Reem onto her knees right in front of him and forced her to watch . . ." Something caught in Shannon's throat. She took a second, then continued.

"They shot her husband in the head. He died instantly."

For years, Dr. Reem was tortured with nightmares from witnessing her husband's murder, and the prospect that they could return again someday. ISIS was hell-bent on proving they might be down but definitely not out.

"The propaganda is still up because they were ordered to keep it there by the same people who killed her husband," Shannon said. "They promised to hunt down and kill anyone that defied the order."

Without saying another word, Shannon, Scotty, and other members of CFT Manbij walked over, grabbed the posters, and ripped them off the wall one by one.

"If they ask who did this, tell them they can find us at the grain silos south of town," Shannon said without an ounce of hesitation in her voice.

Shannon lit the pile of propaganda posters on fire right there in the hospital. Her compassion and reassurance calmed Dr. Reem and instilled confidence in her.

"Thank you," Dr. Reem said, with tears still in her eyes.

CFT Manbij later refurbished that floor, adding five hundred more beds to the hospital's capacity, two more rooms for surgery, and an ultrasound machine.

⚓ ⚓ ⚓

During her deployment, Shannon used running and music as a way to relieve stress, both from war and the anxiety induced by being so far from her family. Usually she combined the two by putting in headphones and taking off. There was no limit to the miles she could cover with a good playlist, especially on deployment, when her only other option was to catch up on the never-ending reports she had to write.

Some of her favorite bands were the Killers, Dropkick Murphys, Coheed and Cambria, Lana Del Rey, and her Spotify running playlist ranged from Limp Bizkit's "Break Stuff" to "Humble" by Kendrick Lamar, with Fleetwood Mac and Britney Spears mixed in for good measure. She also listened to songs released by her fellow veterans, like Mat Best's "Bitch I Operate." But sometimes Shannon just sang made-up cadences and lyrics in her head.

Since Shannon spoke so many languages, she listened to music from many other cultures. She knew there were few better ways to stay sharp on the modern use of a foreign language than to listen to music sung in that language. A variety of Arab music could fuel her for miles; it helped that Shannon genuinely enjoyed it.

Nothing was better than following up a postmission run than late-night conversations with her cousin Sharron. There was always work to do, more reports to write, and analysis to perform, but the lure of escaping back home through conversation with one of her best friends was always tempting. One night, instead of laughing about their retirement plans that included opening a goat farm to sell goat cheese, they talked about how they had grown over the years.

"When you are overly hard on yourself about decisions you make or things you've done, you need to ask yourself, *What would my best friend say?*" Sharron told her. "Because they wouldn't think you were a failure. They would be proud of you and support you, and celebrate your accomplishments."

"That's how I'm trying to live my life," Shannon said. "I ask myself, *Would I regret not doing this if it was too late to have another chance?*"

CHAPTER 26

WHOM SHALL I SEND, AND WHO WILL GO FOR US?

MANBIJ, SYRIA, 2019

The war against ISIS was a grind, and January 15, 2019, was no exception. Shannon sent a quick text to Joe, also on deployment but in a different part of the world, telling him she was going out and "I love you" before meeting up with Scotty to make the long drive out to the grain silos.

She had a source meet planned for the following day that couldn't wait, and a new Special Forces ODA had just rotated in at CFT Manbij, so there would undoubtedly be a few new faces to meet.

When they arrived, Jon—or Captain Jon, as Scotty liked to sarcastically call him—introduced a few of his new teammates. Among the new arrivals was Jon Farmer, a salty Special Forces warrant officer from the Fifth Special Forces Group's ODA 5311; and Devin Clarke, a human intelligence collector also from Fifth Group. He had just completed a previous deployment to Afghanistan with ████* but was now attached to Farmer's ODA as an interrogator and Arabic linguist.

Handshakes were exchanged all around and Shannon mentioned her husband also hailed from "The Legion," which was the nickname for Fifth Group. After chatting about how small the world was, they started reviewing the plan for the following day's mission.

"All right, Shannon, what do you need from my team on this one?" Jon asked, looking over a map of the area. "Are we just going in with our security guys shadowing you?"

"I have a meet in town, near the school," Shannon said. "He knows I'm coming. I'm meeting him at his house and need your people set for security nearby. It should look like a normal patrol in the area."

"Yes, ma'am," Jon replied.

By this point, Jon had been out with Shannon and Scotty a few times and developed a kind of shorthand with them out of familiarity. He was more than happy to go on these escort missions because of the intel and ensuing results they regularly produced. He knew the task force Shannon represented had the resources and ability to hit targets if something big came up, and Shannon was definitely working on something big.

Shannon confidently delivered her CONOP, or concept of the operation, in great detail and described exactly what she needed to get out of this mission. She had primary and secondary options for every aspect of the planning and confidently rattled off a set of directives, making sure the new additions to CFT Manbij understood every

---

* Specific unit redacted at request of DoD.

detail while staying open to other ideas and incorporating feedback where it made sense. She was clearly running the show, which was unique in the predominantly male special operations community—but if something didn't sound right, she let them know.

"I'll be in the lead truck this time," Jon said. The movement into town would be a ground convoy, and ironing out the order of movement was important.

"Actually, we recommend you not be the lead truck," Shannon said. "Just in case."

"Why?" Jon pushed back.

"Lead truck always gets hit first, Captain Jon," Scotty jumped in. "We'd be better off having the convoy commander in the back to control the situation and move people along."

Jon acknowledged that was great advice but knew he was the one who had memorized the roads and neighborhoods of Manbij. As a former mapmaker, he even made a few maps of Manbij earlier in their deployment, and knew how to get from point A to point B in almost any scenario in which they might find themselves.

Jon insisted, reasoning he now had people way better than him on the radio, like Clarke and Chief Farmer, to control the situation if something came up. Shannon and Scotty didn't like the decision, but they moved on with the planning. Sometimes mission success requires compromise when working with other units.

After the back-and-forth about tactics, they decided Shannon would join Jon in the lead vehicle, and Clarke would drive the second vehicle with Scotty and Chief Farmer. Their "Dirty 30" from the Syrian Defense Forces (SDF) would take up the rear in gun trucks, rounding out the order of movement.

"We're gonna head out from the grain silo here," Jon said, back briefing the CONOP and laying out his navigation plan. "And take a left turn onto the main road and drive to the traffic circle about five hundred meters away. We'll take the second exit from the traffic circle, going north. Then we'll drive the ring around Manbij for about one point five miles until we hit the Civil Administration of Manbij building."

That's where the local government operated out of—it was located in a large compound and well protected. The school, Palace of the Princes restaurant, and bazaar with the great manaeesh were all in the area. Shannon's target was nearby, so they decided to park outside the school, as they'd done before.

"With the primary parking in front of the school, our alternate will be in front of the restaurant," Jon said. "It's a great location for what we're trying to do. It has a vacant second story perfect for pulling security, and besides the main road, there's only one alleyway leading up to the spot where we'd be parking."

After the briefing was complete, a few of those going on the mission the next day gathered for food and tea around the inside of the grain silo to wind down for the evening. After a while, most of the Green Berets filtered out, while Shannon continued to listen casually as Clarke and the 'terps talked.

Clarke didn't know much about Shannon other than she was DLI trained like him; he graduated in 2018, while she graduated a long time ago by his estimation. He figured she would have lost her proficiency by now, but the interpreters claimed she was a 3-3, one of the highest language ratings you can attain. A 3-3 means you know the language well enough to be mistaken as a native speaker. They sang her praises earlier that day, saying she was the best non-native Arabic speaker they had ever met, and that she spoke five other languages in addition to English and Arabic. As an Army human intelligence collector, Clarke maintained four dialects in Arabic, so that kind of praise coming from interpreters who run into linguists like him all the time was a big claim to make.

He wanted to see for himself, though, assuming she might have learned the formal dialect at best. He and Jasmine started talking in Arabic, trying to bait Shannon into joining the conversation. She saw the discussion for what it was and recognized it as an opportunity to build rapport.

She joined in, speaking fluent Iraqi Arabic, which was the dialect Clarke was trained in—but he noticed she clearly took it upon herself to study the language independently and above any standard taught formally. Her accent and language ability blew him away, and it became obvious why everyone liked her. The way Shannon drank tea while speaking a foreign language made it seem like she was a few beers deep, comfortable and talkative—something you just can't teach.

For Clarke, the exchange was a bizarre yet very laid-back mix of pre-mission jitters and happy-hour vibes with undertones of balancing professionalism while not being too serious. Shannon mentioned she was from upstate New York and provided other clues about her life back home but was too vague to satisfy the curiosity of the four or five people still there sipping tea, who were all mystified. Clarke thought she must be CIA, but nobody knew her actual affiliation.

In the Army intel community, people like Clarke often think of themselves as the Army's version of a CIA case officer, which is probably too strong a characterization. Through his conversation with Shannon, he found out what she was actually doing in Syria and how she synthesized different means of intelligence collection and analysis, performing next-level work that would make anybody in his community jealous. It was intimidating: here was a beautiful American woman who was clearly very competent at her job, could throw on a hijab and slip right into Arab society with relative ease, but still had a great, natural personality. By talking to a young intel professional like Clarke, Shannon changed his perception of how language could be used, what was possible in the military intelligence career field, and the places he could go in the future.

Clarke didn't know where she came from or who she worked for, but he was sold. He and the others on the team exchanged contact info with her, asking if she could help guide them on how to get where she was. Whatever Shannon was doing, that's where they wanted to be, because she was clearly at the top.

MANBIJ, SYRIA, JANUARY 16, 2019

The grain silos CFT Manbij called home were bustling with people preparing for the day's mission on a chilly, overcast Wednesday morning on January 16. It was winter in Syria, so everything seemed muddy and damp, devoid of sunshine. Shannon wore her black North Face hiking pants, a down jacket, and a scarf around her neck to block the brisk wind that day—but which could easily be repurposed into a hijab if the situation required it. Most weren't wearing plate carriers as they were reasonably comfortable in this location, but still packed them in the vehicles—just in case. Shannon didn't carry a rifle, instead opting for a Glock pistol tucked into her waistband. Scotty carried an H&K 416.

CFT Manbij departed from the silos at approximately 11 a.m. local time. There were two American vehicles in the convoy: Shannon and Jon in the lead vehicle while Clarke drove the other with Scotty and Chief Farmer. Jasmine, two more American Green Berets, and sixteen SDF soldiers following in gun trucks rounded out the rest of the manifest.

Their convoy tried parking at the school as planned, but the situation on the ground dictated a move to their alternate location, outside the Palace of Princes restaurant. After parking their vehicles to deliberately make it difficult for anyone to walk up unnoticed and slip an IED under their trucks, Clarke moved to the restaurant's top floor and established overwatch for most of the market.

On the sidewalk below, Shannon and Scotty synced watches and reaffirmed the exact time everyone was required to be back.

"All right, Jon, we'll be back no later than 1100 Zulu. You know what to do if we're not back by then," Shannon said, confirming an abbreviated five-point contingency plan commonly used throughout the military.

"Roger, we know the plan. Good luck, guys," Jon replied.

Clarke watched as the routine patrol departed, with Shannon and Scotty breaking off to move toward their destination. He didn't know exactly where they were going or who they were meeting, but such was life on a Shannon Kent mission.

Clarke had been to the restaurant on two previous occasions and was comfortable conducting his own low-level source operation by talking to a few visitors in the restaurant. Shannon might be doing the big stuff, but Clarke wanted to pitch in by establishing rapport with locals while maintaining visibility from the second floor. He struck up a conversation with the restaurant owner and got his business card, tucking it away for future use. You never know who you might need, and having friends in the area is better than enemies.

Pulling security during the daytime in a bustling city market is nerve-racking. They were surrounded by two- and three-story buildings all with their own windows and doors that could open at any time. You never know what's truly going on or who might be watching you from afar. Clarke felt uncomfortable but couldn't put his finger on what it was. There were more Arabs in this Kurdish-owned store, but that wasn't necessarily indicative of anything since many properties in Bandar were like that. Clarke was receiving a lot of looks, though. More than usual. *Am I being discreet enough?* he wondered.

Then he noticed something outside the window. Four or five guys were literally staring him down, not talking. They didn't seem very friendly, but they weren't doing anything that could be considered hostile either.

Little did he know, ISIS had started planning an assassination in December 2018. They wanted to use a suicide bomber to hit the American soldiers in Manbij who had been causing so many problems, so they imported operatives from Aleppo who linked up with local contacts in Manbij that were already patrolling the city, looking for a chance to attack. They finally saw an opportunity on the sixteenth of January.

Clarke moved back down to the street so that one of the Green Berets could go inside and use the bathroom. As the Green Beret came back out to relieve Clarke, they saw Shannon and Scotty on their way back to the restaurant along with the rest of the element that had been out on a foot patrol.

They regrouped out front as the vehicles were prepared for movement. Clarke was standing next to his truck, ready to go, talking to one of the Green Berets and an SDF soldier.

At 12:38 local time, just as the team was about to get back in their trucks and drive back to the grain silos, a man approached their position from south of the market. He walked right past Clarke toward the restaurant entrance, where the rest of the group stood. Without warning, he detonated a hidden suicide vest within feet of Shannon, Scotty, and the rest of their group.

ISIS later claimed responsibility.

Clarke felt an incredible force push him back, like a 200-mile-per-hour gust of hot wind hit him. A person, three feet to his front, fell straight back like a stiff plank—his face was immediately devoid of life. The explosion threw Clarke back anywhere from four to twelve feet—he can't quite remember but knows it was a significant distance. His pants were torn up; his face and hand were covered in second- and third-degree burns. He survived, but his injuries would eventually require multiple surgeries.

The ODA's junior weapons sergeant and junior engineer sergeant were positioned farther away and were among the few Americans outside the immediate vicinity of the blast. A driver in another vehicle was also protected from the explosion. Everyone else was exposed, standing in the open and very close to where the bomb detonated. Paper flew everywhere. Hot ash covered everything. There was mass confusion in the street. There was blood.

Clarke started scrambling to check bodies in an attempt to identify his teammates, but the first few people he found were Syrian. No one was responsive. For a moment, he couldn't find any other Americans still alive. Finally, he found a body with the black Patagonia jacket Chief Farmer always wore. But the nature of his wounds made further identification impossible at the scene.

Okay, there could be a follow-on attack, Clarke realized, trying to process what was happening right in front of him. He moved inside a store next to the restaurant because the restaurant itself was completely blown out. The shopkeeper asked him if he was okay and offered him water, but Clarke's mind was still racing. He told the shopkeeper to look for Daesh and to let him know if anything happened in the next thirty seconds.

Thirty seconds transpired without incident, so he went back outside. Of course, the threat of a follow-on attack wasn't completely gone, but he could be more confident after taking a tactical pause to let the situation develop, ensuring he didn't miss anything by rushing through a chaotic scene.

One of the Green Berets was already taking accountability of the survivors and the dead. He was surprised Clarke was alive. They set up a casualty collection point and started working on reestablishing communications.

That's when something amazing started happening. It seemed like everyone in Manbij rushed toward them, trying to find a way to help. The people of Manbij knew who these Americans were. They were the people who sent their girls back to school, who made the streets safer for their children to play in, the ones who cared enough to shoot when it was time to shoot and hug when it was time to hug. They were the protectors.

And now, the locals wanted to return the favor in their time of need.

The initial rush of people worried Clarke, though. The situation was still chaotic, and losing control seemed like a worst-case scenario. He kept his cool, despite clearly being in shock. He watched as the locals started picking up bodies while pointing out the Americans among them. Unfortunately, the other Americans died in a manner that made identification challenging. Chief Farmer was the only one they could identify with any degree of certainty. How can you know you haven't left anyone behind if you don't know who still needs to be accounted for?

One of the Syrians ran up to Clarke.

"There's a woman underneath this car," he said.

That's my vehicle. It must be either Ghadir or Shannon, Clarke thought.

He looked closer. It was Shannon.

Clarke kept moving, now focused on trying to find Ghadir.

"Have you seen Ghadir?" Clarke asked the other Green Beret. He still hadn't received confirmation she was dead and hoped she'd found a way to survive the blast.

"She's gone, man."

Clarke cursed the gods. *How could they just leave like this?*

"They're dead," the Green Beret repeated. He could see Clarke was having trouble coming to terms with the reality of what just happened.

But it was starting to sink in. Clarke grew angry. Trauma manifests itself in many ways, and Clarke went through it all. These were people he—and everyone—thought were untouchable.

The gravity of the situation was settling on the survivors, but there was still work to do. They popped a red smoke grenade, and a helicopter started circling above moments later. It had only been a few minutes since the terrorist detonated his suicide vest. Although that felt like a lifetime on the ground, Clarke was impressed with the response time of the helicopter, considering America's light footprint in Syria at the time.

He could see the door gunner from the ground, which was mildly reassuring. They couldn't talk to the helicopter crew, though. They were still in the casualty collection point trying to find a frequency on their radios that would work. They couldn't hear anyone; the blast had throttled their system so hard that they lost comms. Clarke did his best with no "Echos"—shorthand for Special Forces communications sergeant—to work their magic.

Finally, he broke through and established radio contact. The pilots relayed instructions on what they needed to do next. The longer they stayed in the same place, the more they risked enemy fighters showing up to make the situation worse than it already was.

Clarke and one of the Green Berets who spoke Arabic started talking to a few nearby locals, asking for directions to the hospital. Then an emergency vehicle appeared out of nowhere, and Clarke recognized it as one that would be going to al-Firat Hospital, the same one Shannon had visited before. Shannon and the others, both dead and alive, were loaded in the emergency vehicle before it sped off. Jon, who was gravely injured and in need of immediate medical care, was among the people who made it on for the ride to the hospital.

Senior Chief Petty Officer Shannon Kent—a loving wife, daughter, sister, friend, and mother of two—was killed in action alongside Special Forces Chief Warrant Officer 2 Jonathan R. Farmer, loving husband and father of four; former Navy SEAL Scott A. Wirtz; and Ghadir Taher, an American working as a civilian interpreter. Eleven Syrian nationals also died in the attack, with another eighteen wounded.

At this point, it had been at least thirty minutes since the explosion. There was no way to lock down the area or secure it—especially considering the limited resources they had at their disposal. Knowing that the gravely injured and dead were en route to the hospital, they decided to move there on foot since help was unlikely to arrive in a busy marketplace. The hospital wasn't too far away if driving, but walking there after surviving a bomb detonation was significantly more difficult.

They gathered all the sensitive equipment and weapons left from the dead and wounded and even found Scotty's H&K 416 and plate carrier. It was a lot of equipment for Clarke and the two remaining Green Berets to carry on a long movement, but they were alive and determined to make it to the hospital.

They walked maybe a hundred feet from the blast site before the shrapnel started bothering Clarke. His ankle wasn't holding up well either. He was exhausted, and the adrenaline was starting to wear off.

Then, seemingly out of nowhere, people started yelling and running away from them. They saw what was causing the commotion: SDF soldiers rolled up in the local police bureau's BearCat tactical vehicle, along with two American special operations soldiers in the back. It was a saving grace. He and the two other surviving Americans jumped in the back and headed straight for the soccer field.

Jon's boss at the task force, Colonel Jeff, was flying over Manbij on his way back from visiting another unit in the area when the explosion happened. At 12:50 local, he could see smoke rising from the Manbij market area and heard radio calls inside the helicopter shortly after.

"We've been attacked!" the soldier yelled on the other end of the radio, unaware if anyone could hear him. His transmissions were cutting in and out, but Colonel Jeff deciphered that Cross-Functional Team Manbij had experienced a mass casualty event with multiple dead and injured.

"We hear you, we're coming," Colonel Jeff said, hoping the young soldier was receiving on his end. It didn't seem so.

"Head toward the smoke," Colonel Jeff said into the helicopter's internal communication system, giving directions to the pilot. He could now see red smoke in addition to the smoke from the blast, and flashing lights from emergency vehicles moving in that direction. He and the other task force leaders on board were experienced special operators and had a flight medic on board as well. They weren't afraid of a fight and knew they could help. No American would be left behind under any circumstance.

After making a pass over the blast site, the helicopter landed on the soccer field near the hospital at 1:09 local. Colonel Jeff hopped out along with the rest of his team; he and his senior enlisted advisor ran toward the blast site, while the others moved toward the hospital to see if any Americans had come in yet. On their way, they stopped an ambulance and found Jon inside. They redirected the ambulance to the soccer field. After talking to Manbij security officials, they found out the other Americans were split up and taken to multiple medical facilities in the area.

They found and identified Scotty at the al-Hekmat clinic approximately two blocks from the blast site, Chief Farmer at al-Firat Hospital, and Jasmine at the al-Barkel Hospital. They prepared everyone for travel and started moving out to the helicopter waiting on the soccer field.

Within minutes of leaving the soccer field, Colonel Jeff and his teammate were able to link up with local Syrian security forces and found Clarke and the two Green Berets. They picked them up and headed back to the soccer field. To Clarke's relief, he found Captain Jon Turnbull at the soccer field still alive.

At 3:46 local, they identified Shannon at al-Firat Hospital. Less than four hours after the explosion, the last American was accounted for and secured on a helicopter en route to an American forward staging point near ▉▉▉▉▉.* It would take a total of four helicopter trips to get everyone out.

For days, weeks, and even months after, American special operators pursued targets uninhibited as a result of the suicide bombing. Those responsible for the deadly attack in Manbij were swiftly killed or captured.

UNITED STATES OF AMERICA, JANUARY 2019

Shannon and her two best friends growing up, Cassandra and Claire, maintained a group text over the years to keep in touch.

---

* Specific location redacted at request of DoD.

At 11:41 a.m. on January 16, 2019, Cassandra texted the group a screenshot of a news story she found, titled "ISIS-Claimed Attack in Syria," followed by another text, Shan, just saw this so I'm checking in on you. Is everything OK?

Same. Hoping you and yours are safe. Xx, Claire replied.

Cassandra could see a notification on her screen that her first message had only been delivered to one person.

The last time Claire had heard from Shannon was just three weeks prior, when Shannon texted her Happy birthday Claire Bear! The day after the group text message, when she saw a social media post from Shannon's sister, Mariah, confirming her death, she immediately crumpled into a ball and called Cassandra, not wanting her to find out via the news.

Cassandra was standing by her car in a parking lot, about to walk into daycare to pick her kids up, when she answered Claire's call. She heard the words come over the phone, but all she could do was lean against her car and silently cry, wishing what she just heard wasn't true.

⚓ ⚓ ⚓

Molly Geraci, Shannon's friend in boot camp, had just finished teaching a yoga class when a friend called to ask if she was tracking what happened in Syria.

"No," Molly said. "I'm not really following the news. What's up?"

"There was an explosion in Syria, and they're saying a female chief petty officer was killed, you think—"

"No." Molly immediately cut her off, not even wanting to entertain the thought. "It's not her. We would have probably heard by now."

Molly and Shannon had kept up with each other over the years. Their birthdays were only three days apart, so they made a tradition of calling each other with a piece of celebratory cake in hand. They got married on the same day, both on Christmas Eve, and in fact, Molly had just called Shannon shortly before she deployed to Syria to ask for a letter of recommendation for a school application. The more Molly thought about it, the more she wanted confirmation that Shannon was safe. The next day she reached out to a different friend whose husband was actively serving in Special Forces. She thought he might have the inside scoop, since no names of the fallen had been released yet.

"Hey what's going on with Shan—" Molly said.

"It's her," her friend said before she could finish. Molly sank to the ground. Her friend kept talking, but she couldn't hear anything. She couldn't believe it. *It can't be her.*

Shannon's friend James was aware of the attack in Syria too, and heard a rumor that Shannon might have been one of the fallen. He texted Shannon's sister, Mariah, to ask if it was true. No response.

The next day, while sitting in a briefing on base, he received a text message confirming the terrible news. He started shaking and became nauseous and claustrophobic. He had to get out of the room.

These were the first ripples in a shock wave about to crash through the Navy, and Shannon's friends and family around the world. Her husband, Joe, had already received the news while deployed to an undisclosed location.

CHAPTER 27

THE WORST DAY OF JOE'S LIFE

UNDISCLOSED LOCATION, JANUARY 16, 2019

The morning started like most overseas: Joe woke up early to get in a workout before the day got rolling. Before heading to the gym, he always texted Shannon to see what she was up to. Her last text was, going to Manbij, I'll txt when back, love you! That was normal, so he got on with his day.

Joe left the States in early January for his first deployment as a CIA paramilitary officer and was fortunate to work for one of his best friends, Rocco. They were on an ODA in Fifth Group together and had remained close since 2005.

Later that evening, Joe returned to the office after a mission to check in with Rocco. As he walked in, he noticed that Rocco looked somber.

"Hey, guys, why don't you give Joe and me a minute," Rocco said, indicating he wanted everyone to leave the room. They obliged.

Shit, what did I screw up? Joe thought.

"Hey, man, there's been an attack in Manbij on the task force," Rocco said. "Two females are KIA. That's all we know right now. We are trying to get names—do you know where Shannon is?"

"Fuck. Manbij, she's in Manbij," Joe replied. She was not the only female in the task force, so he could not be entirely certain it was her. He ran back to his room to get his phone, hoping for a text saying she was safe.

No text.

Joe ran back to the office. He had her office number in Syria and her work email. No answer on the phone and no email from her either.

There was nothing else to do but wait.

At one point, Rocco looked up at Joe from his computer screen. He stood up and walked over.

"I just got an email, brother." Rocco didn't want to say the next part. He had tears in his eyes.

"It was Shannon. She was killed. I'm so sorry, man."

Joe couldn't comprehend the words.

Rocco embraced him. He knew Shannon well and had spent many nights at their house swapping war stories and playing with the boys.

Joe felt numb for a moment but quickly realized he had to get home to the boys. That was where he was supposed to be. He had been in the military for long enough to know the notification process had already been set in motion. He immediately contacted the Navy casualty affairs officers and asked them how long he had until the Navy notified Shannon's parents in upstate New York.

Just two hours. *Fuck.* He needed to call immediately and tell them before some Navy chaplain they had never met showed up on their doorstep. He tried calling Shannon's dad, but the call went to voicemail. Joe tried to get him a few more times, but he was probably working in a police building where phones were not allowed.

So he called Shannon's mother, Mary. She always figured she would somehow intuitively know if something had happened to her kids. Unfortunately, she had no idea whatsoever. She was happy to hear from Joe—he had recently mailed her a beautiful picture collage of Shannon and the kids on canvas for Christmas. That was the first thing that popped into her mind when she saw his name on the caller ID.

Oh my god, he sent us this great Christmas present, and now he's calling just to talk! I love this guy! she thought as she picked up the phone.

"Hey, Mary," Joe said, sounding tired. The connection was spotty, so he would need to be blunt.

"How are you doing, Joe!" Mary said.

"Not too good."

"What's going on?" She thought he was going to say something was wrong with the kids. Maybe the boys were sick, or the au pair was ill, and perhaps she needed to help?

"I'm so sorry, Mary. I'm so, so sorry."

She still did not get it.

"What's going on, Joe?"

"There was a suicide bomber in a marketplace where Shannon was."

Before Joe could finish, Mary was already rewriting what he said in her head.

Shannon was there, but she's okay, she thought. *She was hurt, but she's okay.*

"Shannon was killed," Joe said. "The Navy will be at your door in an hour to officially inform you. I'm coming home as soon as I can. I'm so sorry."

"Oh, no. No, no." Mary started crying. "I'm sorry, Joe."

"I'm so sorry, Mary," Joe said. All he could do was apologize in return. "I'm so, so sorry."

"Maybe it isn't her; we don't know it's her," Mary said. "Maybe it's another woman. It could be another woman. Right?"

"It wasn't. It was her," Joe said, wishing she was right.

Shannon, his wife, the mother of his children, was dead, and no matter how much he wanted to change that fact, he couldn't.

Joe called his own mother afterward and repeated the conversation he had with Shannon's mom. He got off the phone as soon as possible. His compartmentalization was kicking in and remained on for quite some time. There was a lot to do before he could grieve.

He had to get home before her remains arrived at Dover Air Force Base, in Delaware. He had to be there to receive her. He had to be with his boys—that's what he needed, and it's what Shannon would have wanted.

As he went through everything in his head, worrying about returning to the States in time, he received a message from Aaron, a good friend of his and Shannon's. Aaron said he was stationed at a base near Shannon's and was now escorting her remains home.

"I'm so sorry, brother. I can't fucking believe this. What do you need? Is there anything I can do?" he said.

"Thanks, brother. I'm scrambling to get home before her. Any way you can drag your feet a bit?"

"No worries at all," Aaron replied. "I'll hold the aircraft in Europe until you give me the thumbs-up that you've cleared the Atlantic."

Joe felt much better about getting back, knowing he had Aaron escorting Shannon home.

Rocco quickly arranged Joe's air travel back to the States, and he departed later that day, flying to Europe and then on to the US. Rocco accompanied him to Europe but had to turn around there to go back to work. He had to get back to the mission.

As Joe flew, the conversation he had with Shannon about going to Ground Branch and the stress he placed on her haunted him. The drinks, the look in her eyes . . . *like fuck you will* . . . Her words played on a loop in his head, and all he could do was say, "I'm sorry, baby," to the void and hope she understood. He regretted not having the clarity and honesty to fully reciprocate the love she so readily and unconditionally gave him. *I'll always be eternally in her debt.*

In Europe, Joe was met by another old friend, Nick, from the same ODA he and Rocco were on so many years ago. Joe's immediate supervisor from the US, Tom, was traveling with him. From notification until Joe's dad picked him up at the airport back in the US, Rocco, Nick, and Tom stood by his side. His brothers stood by him and gave him more strength than he'd ever felt before.

After Joe arrived home, his best friend, Josh, and his first team leader in Special Forces, Trevor, were at his doorstep, ready to get Joe and his family to Dover the following day. Both Josh and Trevor were former members of the same team Rocco and Nick were on with him. None of them had been in the same unit in fourteen years, but when tragedy struck, they came together without hesitation.

Joe felt like the weight of the world was on his back. As the surviving spouse, all decisions regarding Shannon were up to him, so he was barraged almost nonstop for the first several weeks. Having Josh and Trevor there gave him strength and forced him to step up and do his best to hold himself together in those initial days, weeks, and months after losing his wife.

Joe's parents had supported every aspect of his life since he was born, and now with the worst happening, both worked overtime to be there for him and his sons. This continued daily.

Dover is an Air Force base in Delaware where fallen American service members' remains are returned to their loved ones in a somber ceremony known as a dignified transfer. For Joe, the transfer was a surreal experience. He was so inundated with tasks that he could not publicly show the pain that is still raw and churning inside him to this day.

On a bitter cold, overcast January day, Joe's family, along with Josh, accompanied him to Dover to attend the dignified transfer. They were guided to a small waiting area after arrival, where they waited until it was time to go to the flight line to watch the flag-draped casket holding Shannon be removed from the military cargo plane.

Driving out to the flight line felt familiar to Joe. He had carried caskets of his friends onto aircraft like the one they were approaching too many times to count, but this time he felt like he was in the wrong place. Now he was a Gold Star spouse, not a teammate of the fallen. This was his new life, but he had no idea how to play that role.

Shouldn't I be doing something, not just standing here? he thought as he stared at every movement of the honor guard. Shannon was home, but now what?

Joe was emotionally numb for Dover, her memorial service at the Naval Academy, and her interment at Arlington National Cemetery. Being numb is a natural survival mechanism hardwired into operators; without it, he probably wouldn't have been able to function.

CHAPTER 28

FAIR WINDS AND FOLLOWING SEAS

UNITED STATES NAVAL ACADEMY MAIN CHAPEL, 2019

News of Shannon's death spread with intensity. As the Department of Defense later claimed, Kent's team wasn't on a routine patrol that day.[1] As many news outlets reported, they weren't out for a leisurely lunch at a popular kebab restaurant frequented by Americans. The people closest to Shannon knew she was responsible for finding ISIS cells and their leaders, fixing their location in time and space, and providing that intelligence to her peers at ████████████████████████████████████* or to pilots who would perform kinetic strikes with GPS-guided missiles.

---

* Description of specific unit redacted at request of DoD.

Joe knew she wasn't a part of the "going out to lunch crowd," as some reports said. He would know. Around the world, operators in the shadows uttered curse words under their breath, and intelligence professionals who specialize in predicting the seemingly unpredictable were shocked to their core. Friends, family, fellow sailors, and anyone Shannon had ever touched were beside themselves. Some didn't believe it at first. Others, for their own sanity, didn't want to believe it.

A thousand sailors, hundreds of other service members, dozens of New York State police officers, and many family and friends filled the pews at the Naval Academy's chapel in Annapolis in memory of Senior Chief Petty Officer Shannon Kent. Having her memorial service at the Academy's chapel was a big deal: she was the first enlisted sailor in US Navy history to be given the honor. Before Shannon, the last person to have their memorial there was the late senator John McCain.

Every chief in the United States Navy felt the sting of losing one of their own. Shannon deserved a sea of khaki at her memorial service, and hundreds of chiefs wearing their khaki uniforms filled the pews at her memorial service. It's what she would have wanted.

Shannon's legacy was established immediately. A few days before her memorial service in Annapolis, the Navy officially amended the regulation she had fought so hard to change in the wake of her commission being denied.[2] They named the change in her honor, and there have already been sailors approved to commission because of it. A campaign was launched to convince the Navy to name a ship in her honor,[3] the DLI in Monterey renamed the area outside its naval barracks as Kent Navy Yard,[4] and eventually she had a star on the NSA's memorial wall and a post office named after her in Pine Plains, New York.[5]

Shannon wasn't unique because she died in combat. She

was special because of the life she lived. Her time with the ████████████████████* is a period of Shannon's career that simply can't be discussed in detail. Most of what we know comes from her award citations. Senior Chief Petty Officer Kent received the Defense Meritorious Service Medal for expertly leading "a joint-service special mission detachment that was responsible for planning and executing sensitive technical operations in combat zones and strategic locations across four theaters of operations. Specifically, Chief Kent prepared personnel for deploying in support of Operations Inherent Resolve and Enduring Freedom–Horn of Africa in defense of our nation, which resulted in the capture or kill of over 500 enemy combatants."

The citation describes how she spearheaded a partnership with the FBI, expanded the capabilities of a sensitive joint program, and introduced a new capability to the NSA that closed a crucial mission gap. However, her Bronze Star citation probably best sums up her contributions: "Her achievements will have a lasting impact in combating enemies of the United States."

In total, Kent answered her nation's call and deployed to areas of operation around the world a total of eight times.

Many of her teammates, most of whom will remain nameless due to the sensitive nature of their work, bravely stood up to speak to the massive crowd, hoping to shed light on the kind of person Kent was. Her senior leaders spoke of her prowess as an intelligence professional and praised her leadership as a chief.

"For the CT community, we do not often think of ourselves as a frontline force. We are the nerds who toil away diligently to enable

---

* Description of specific unit redacted at request of DoD.

the fight," one sailor said while speaking at the podium. "We would not be here today if this was true."

James, her longtime friend, wrote about how she saved his life—not on the battlefield but in the halls of Walter Reed.

"I lost one of the strongest bonds I ever had on January 16, 2019," James said. "I owe her a debt too large to be repaid, so I must try to honor her and her tenacious and feisty spirit, her raw strength every day from here on. I love you, Shannon. You were truly the best of all of us. Thank you for my life."

The passionate recounting of Shannon's life by her friends and teammates was moving, but words alone could not do justice to the essence of her soul, and that feeling was palpable in the chapel. The effort was worthwhile, though. The stories shed light on one of the most extraordinary women to ever wear her nation's uniform and undoubtedly inspired many in the room.

Standing with family in the front pew, Joe stared ahead as everyone talked, a Gold Star pin on his lapel.

After the service concluded, the chiefs who filled the chapel in a sea of khaki filed out, taking an anchor off their uniform and, one by one, dropping it in a bowl held by a stoic Navy chief standing at attention.

CrossFit Hyattsville is honored to host a Hero WOD for Shannon Kent on Saturday, May 18th. We will offer two classes that morning, one from approximately 8:00–9:00 a.m. and one from 9:30–10:30 a.m., followed by a potluck celebration.

James, Shannon's friend from the Navy, took the loss hard. His sister checked on him one day and let him know she went to a local CrossFit gym and asked the owner if she would design a Hero WOD, or Workout of the Day, in honor of Shannon.

The CrossFit coach arranged everything and put the information out on Facebook and tried to get people to come. Shannon's sister, Mariah, and the Kents' au pair, Ashe, came. Mutual friends from the unit Shannon was with were there too. There were two iterations, and although not an official Hero WOD—it was designed in-house—it was meaningful to everyone in attendance.

The workout memorialized her age at the time of her death, thirty-five, and the date she died, January 16, or 1/16. It was completed in teams of two or three, for time (forty-minute time cap):

3 Rounds:
35 Lateral Burpees over Barbell
35 Hang Squat Cleans (95/65)
35 Toes to Bar
35 Wall Balls (20/14)
116 Calorie Assault Bike

3 Rounds:
35 Lateral Burpees over Barbell
35 Hang Squat Cleans (115/80)
35 Toes to Bar
35 Wall Balls (30/20)
116 Calorie Row

Friends, colleagues, and service members who had never met Shannon, from all over the world, on FOBs and COPs, safe houses, and embassies, took part in the WOD. James ended up doing both iterations, wearing full kit for the first, then loaning his kit to someone else for the second.

Photos of Shannon were printed out, laminated, and hung on the wall of the gym. James brought guacamole cheese for the occasion, Shannon's favorite. "It was like a little altar for the event," James said. "Shannon was watching us do her WOD."

After the WOD, James walked up to the front of the gym to say a few words. That was not the easiest thing to do for him, but explaining who she was and why everyone was there was important.

Shannon was laid to rest in Section 60 at Arlington National Cemetery, in Arlington, Virginia, a few weeks later. Section 60 is inhabited mostly by service members killed in action in Iraq and Afghanistan, including Navy Cryptologic Technician First Class Steven Phillip Daugherty—one of the three special warfare sailors Shannon knew who were killed in action on her first deployment. Section 60 is known as "the saddest acre in America."

The ceremony was a quiet, private affair. Much to Joe's surprise, she had indeed requested Hindu rites. Her request was obliged.

Joe Kent had spent two decades serving in elite units across the US Army. Now, months after retiring, he joined a small group of Gold Star husbands, charged with figuring out what the future looks like without his wife and best friend by his side. He knew he would need to transition into life as a civilian and as a single father. It seemed like a lot to take on at once, but then again, he has Shannon's example to look to for inspiration.

EPILOGUE

Today, Manbij is fully self-sufficient and independent. CFT Manbij removed approximately twenty-five violent extremists from the area, eventually leading to 1,500 captured or killed ISIS fighters.

According to Captain Jon Turnbull, two thousand girls went to school the day after the explosion. Five hundred beds were added to the hospital, and the surgical capacity was doubled. The pharmacy was stocked and generators were operational.

They restored power to 450,000 people in northeast Syria and rehabilitated public utilities in the area, most notably restoring the sewer system.

"Long story short, our greatest success was that we denied ISIS the ability to govern in that area," Turnbull said. Shannon and Scotty were two of the most important people Turnbull worked with. "Shannon played a direct role in every single one of the terrorists caught."

CFT Manbij showed the people they didn't have to listen to or fear ISIS. They proved to the people they could turn to the coalition and their local government for counsel and governance, protection, and security.

⚓ ⚓ ⚓

D addy, can we read another book?" Colt asked as sweetly as possible, a solid ploy to prolong bedtime. It was a normal Saturday night for Joe and his family—well, their new normal.

A few months after Shannon died, Joe bought a house back in Oregon a few blocks from his parents so they could help with the boys. Colt, in particular, clung to Joe's mom and never let go after Shannon deployed.

It was strange being back in his hometown, living as an adult a few blocks from his childhood home. Some days it felt like his twenty years in the Army were a dream; some days it felt like being back in Portland with his sons was the dream. Joe figured that weird, misplaced feeling was part of his so-called new normal.

As Colt picked out another book, Joe checked the baby monitor to see if Joshy had fallen asleep, and sure enough, he was sleeping soundly.

"Daddy, this one is about fire trucks!" Colt said as he held up a book and jumped back into his dad's lap. *He is getting so big,* Joe thought. "Daddy, fire trucks have big ladders—I'm going to climb up the ladder all the way to heaven to see Mama."

Damn, I was not expecting that, Joe thought. Colt has had more and more questions about Shannon as he's grown older.

Just then, Joe's phone buzzed. It was from a friend deployed in Syria. *Shit,* he thought, *someone is dead.* Text messages from friends who are deployed rarely bring good news.

Joe looked back at Colt, who was still talking about his fire ladder to heaven. "Mama loves you with all her heart, buddy," Joe said as he kissed his head and took a deep breath before opening the message. It said:

Tonight is for Shannon. We got him, he self det'ed like a bitch, no U.S. KIA or WIA. Thinking about you and your sons. Love you brother.

A month after her death, US-backed Kurdish forces arrested five members of ISIS.[1] They were believed to be involved in the January 16 attack that resulted in Shannon's death.

In a series of raids, Shannon's fellow warriors took out target after target, killing or capturing those responsible, methodically striking them down from the shadows. The violence America's warrior elite is capable of knows no bounds. If you take one of theirs, they will take ten of yours. And so it was.

Over time, they continued Shannon's work, up to and including finding, fixing, and finishing ISIS founder Abu Bakr al-Baghdadi and his key leaders. There were direct correlations between operations on the sixteenth of January and the lethal strike that killed al-Baghdadi.

The death of the man ultimately responsible for the suicide attack in Manbij wouldn't bring Shannon back. But knowing a price was paid for her and her teammates' deaths was reassuring. The world is a better place without such evil in it. The world is a better place because Shannon Kent made her mark.

VETERAN NONPROFITS

Dear Reader,

If you would like to support organizations that support US military service members and American military veterans, we humbly recommend the following nonprofits who have, time and again, been there when we needed them most:

- » Special Operations Warrior Foundation
- » Navy SEAL Foundation
- » Green Beret Foundation
- » Third Option Foundation
- » HunterSeven Foundation
- » Folds of Honor Foundation
- » Global War on Terrorism Memorial Foundation
- » National Medal of Honor Museum Foundation
- » Tunnel to Towers Foundation
- » Best Defense Foundation

GLOSSARY

Abu Ayyub al-Masri (AAM)—An Egyptian who led al-Qaeda in Iraq from approximately 2006 to 2010.

Abu Bakr al-Baghdadi—An Iraqi militant who eventually became the leader of ISIS, leading them from approximately 2014 to 2019, and renowned for his brutality.

Abu Musab al-Zarqawi (AMZ)—A Jordanian-born jihadist who trained terrorists in Afghanistan and eventually became Usama bin Laden's right hand, and leader of al-Qaeda in Iraq from 2004 to 2006. He was known for his brutality.

Abu Umar al-Baghdadi (AUB)—An Iraqi-born militant who eventually became the emir of the Islamic State of Iraq, leading the terrorist organization from 2006 to 2010.

Air support—Assistance provided to ground forces from the air, typically using either fixed-wing or rotary assets.

AK-47—Originally developed in the Soviet Union, the AK-47 is a gas-operated assault rifle that uses 7.62×39mm ammunition and is renowned for its resilience in all operating environments.

Al-Iskari Shrine—A Shia Muslim mosque approximately seventy-eight miles outside of Baghdad. Originally built in the year 944, it is among the most famous Shia shrines in the world.

Al-Sijood Palace—An Iraqi landmark located in the Green Zone overlooking the Tigris River. This palace is notable because it belonged to the former dictator of Iraq, Saddam Hussein.

Ansar al-Islam—A Sunni Islamist terror group primarily based in Kurdistan, a semiautonomous region in northern Iraq.

Baathists—Members of the Baath party, an Arab political party originally founded in Syria, but most notably led by Saddam Hussein's Iraqi faction of the party during his dictatorship.

Bed-down location (BDL)—The location where a high-value target most often stays the night.

Belt-fed—A fully automatic belt-fed machine gun.

C-17—According to the US Air Force, the C-17 Globemaster III is capable of rapid strategic delivery of troops and all types of cargo to operating bases or forward bases in the deployment area.

Camp Bucca—A US and coalition military installation that was in the vicinity of Umm Qasr, Iraq, and known for its internment facility.

Chief petty officer—Usually referred to simply as "Chief," this is the seventh enlisted rank in the US Navy (pay grade E-7) and a significant promotion during a service member's career in the Navy.

Concept of the operation (CONOP)—A CONOP is a document or verbal directions that clearly express what the commander's intent is and how to accomplish it using available resources. A CONOP is often used in place of a full operations order when planning a military operation in a short amount of time.

COP—Combat outpost. These are small bases where service members live and conduct combat operations out of.

Counterinsurgency (COIN) doctrine—NATO defines counterinsurgency doctrine as a comprehensive civilian and military effort made to defeat an insurgency. The use of *COIN* as a term entered the American zeitgeist after General David Petraeus adapted his version of it for use during the height of the Iraq War.

CQB—The acronym for close quarters battle, which is a particularly dangerous form of combat usually confined to enclosed spaces like buildings or houses, and may require engaging the enemy as close as an arm's length away.

Cross-Functional Team (CFT)—Specialized team that brings service members and civilians together from different backgrounds to accomplish a specific goal.

Cryptologic Technician–Interpretive—Known as CTIs, these are the Navy's linguists, a specific rating within the cryptologic technician field, responsible for analyzing foreign language materials.

Cryptologist—According to the US Navy, the general role of a Cryptologic Technician (CT) is to collect, analyze, and report on communication signals using a variety of technical equipment.

Cultural Support Team (CST)—The US Army stood up CSTs in 2010 to support special operations forces by specially assessing, selecting, and training select female volunteers to engage other females when it is deemed culturally inappropriate if performed by a male service member. CSTs often came from a medical or military intelligence background and would serve as attachments to special operations units at the tactical level in a deployed environment.

Daesh—A derogatory term used to reference ISIS.

Deck of cards—During the invasion of Iraq, a deck of cards was issued to US troops featuring the names and faces of the coalition's most wanted individuals, usually Baathists loyal to the previous regime. For example, Saddam Hussein was the ace of spades.

Defense Language Institute—Located in Monterey, California, and formally known as the Defense Language Institute Foreign Language Center, DLI is the Defense Department's premier language and cultural training center.

Divan—Padded furniture or pillows commonly lining the walls of long, narrow rooms found in many Levantine homes.

Explosively formed penetrator (EFP)—A special type of shaped explosive charge specifically designed to penetrate armored vehicles but with a longer standoff distance than standard shaped charges. EFPs were used by insurgents in Iraq to great effect, often hung from bridges and angled down to take advantage of the soft armor on top of American military vehicles.

Find, Fix, Finish, Exploit, Analyze, Disseminate (F3EAD)—Initially adopted as just find, fix, finish, the F3EAD targeting methodology is an intelligence cycle used to great effect by special operations organizations in the war on terror, and typically resulted in lethal action, such as drone strikes or direct action operations.

Firefight—When opposing forces exchange gunfire.

FOB—Forward operating base. Larger than a COP, a FOB is a secure military base used to conduct operations and may hold thousands of troops.

Frogman—A nickname commonly used to refer to a Navy SEAL.

General Purpose–Medium tent—A standard tent used by American military forces that requires four people to set up and provides 648 square feet of floor space.

Glock—A semiautomatic pistol designed and produced by Austrian manufacturer Glock Ges.m.b.H. and fielded by many American special operations forces.

Glock 19—A popular compact semiautomatic handgun produced by Glock. The Glock 19 Gen 4 MOS (Modular Optic System) has been fielded to special operations forces as the MK27 MOD 2.

Graduate Record Examinations (GRE)—The GRE is a standardized test used as an admissions requirement for many graduate schools in the United States.

Green Zone—Also known as the International Zone, this 5.6-square-mile area in Baghdad, encompassing palaces and monuments from the Saddam Hussein regime, was a secure place for government and military officials to meet, and held up to thirteen military forward operating bases at the height of the war in Iraq.

Grid reference guide (GRG)—Small maps featuring overhead imagery of a specific location and buildings labeled in a way that makes them easy to identify.

Ground Mobility Vehicle (GMV)—A modified Humvee fielded by US Special Operations Command.

Heckler & Koch 416—A gas-operated, piston-driven, select-fire rifle that is chambered for 5.56x45mm NATO ammunition and has been popular with special operations forces for its accuracy and reliability in austere conditions.

Heckler & Koch UMP 45—A submachine gun chambered in .45 ACP, with an effective firing range of 65 meters.

Helicopter landing zone (HLZ)—An area specifically designated for military helicopters to safely land.

Hellfire—The AGM-114 Hellfire is a precision-guided air-to-ground missile employed by both manned and unmanned aerial platforms.

High-value target (HVT)—A person or resource whose capture has been deemed by a military commander as critical to the success of the mission.

Imam—A leader in the Muslim faith.

GLOSSARY

Improvised explosive device (IED)—IEDs are "homemade" bombs made to destroy, incapacitate, harass, or distract, most often in the context of a terrorist attack. IEDs became synonymous with the war on terror as one of the largest killers of coalition troops.

Individual Augmentee (IA)—A US Navy sailor who supports other Navy, Marine Corps, or Army commands while on temporary orders. IAs typically return to their home unit once they complete their assignment.

Iraqi Counter-Terrorism Force (ICTF)—A high-level Iraqi special operations force that reports directly to the prime minister of Iraq. The ICTF has expanded in recent years to become the Iraqi Counter-Terrorism Service.

ISIS, or Islamic State—Founded in 2013, ISIS (also known as Da'ish or Daesh) is a militant Islamist group and formerly unrecognized quasi-state that was unique in that it controlled land and instituted its own brand of government in those areas. ISIS follows the Salafi jihadist branch of Sunni Islam.

Islamic State of Iraq—Led by Abu Musab al-Zarqawi (AMZ) and known as the al-Qaeda branch in Iraq, among other names, it was responsible for the insurgency in Iraq after the US invasion in 2003.

Jackpot—The radio call used to signal that the primary individual a strike force was after has been caught and identified.

Jamaat Jaysh Ahl al-Sunnah wa-l-Jamaa—An Iraqi Salafi insurgent group during the Iraq War. The group aligned with al-Qaeda in Iraq in 2006, which helped establish the Mujahideen Shura Council.

Joint operations center (JOC)—A secure area where military mission planning takes place, typically in a field or deployed environment.

Kaffiyeh—A traditional headdress worn by men in many parts of the Middle East.

Kinetic strike—A euphemism for military action using deliberate lethal force.

Landing on the X—When a strike force lands directly on the target during a raid, as opposed to "offsetting" and walking in.

Lima Charlie—A phrase using two letters from the military's phonetic alphabet, most often used during radio checks, meaning "loud and clear."

Magazine—An ammunition storage device that feeds rounds into the chamber of a repeating firearm.

Mermites—Field food rations typically delivered in large green plastic containers, often including hot food. Mermites are considered an upgrade from Meals, Ready to Eat (MREs).

Mk 48—A gas-operated, open-bolt, belt-fed machine gun produced by FN America and chambered in 7.62x51mm NATO. Popular with special operations forces as a lightweight area weapon.

M2 .50-caliber heavy-barrel machine gun—A belt-fed, recoil-operated, and air-cooled machine gun that has been in use by American forces since World War II.

M4A1—A lightweight, gas-operated, air-cooled, magazine-fed, selective-rate, shoulder-fired carbine rifle chambered in 5.56x45mm NATO and popular with special operations forces as a fully automatic variant of the M4 carbine widely issued to the US military.

M-81 igniter—Used in conjunction with time fuse or non-electric shock tube to initiate the detonation of an explosive charge.

Naval Special Warfare (NSW)—Comprising less than one percent of the US Navy, NSW is the naval component of US Special Operations Command (USSOCOM) and the parent organization for Navy SEALs and Special Warfare Combatant Crewman (SWCC).

Navy SEAL—The foundation of naval special operations, Navy SEALs are an elite maritime commando force responsible for a wide variety of missions. Navy SEALs are authorized to wear the SEAL Warfare Insignia, or "Trident."

Network-centric warfare—A military doctrine that leverages the "network of networks" or "team of teams" concept to flatten bureaucratic military hierarchies, bringing sensors, commanders, and shooters together to reduce operational pauses and increase the speed combat operations can be conducted.

900 Division—A special recruit division in Navy boot camp for performing musical pieces and drill routines.

Noncommissioned officer (NCO)—NCOs are enlisted leaders who serve as the principal advisor to commanders and are largely responsible for training and discipline. They are considered to be the backbone of US armed forces.

Non-electric shock tube—A plastic, hollow tube containing a thin layer of energetic materials that attaches to an explosive output on one end and a firing device on the other.

Offset infil—When a strike force lands or parks away from the target, usually at least one kilometer or more away, and walks the rest of the distance.

Operational Detachment Alpha (ODA)—A twelve-man US Army Special Forces team. Also known simply as an "A-team."

Operator—A term used to identify a military service member who is assigned to one of the military's most elite special operations units. Technically, in this context, operators are only service members who have passed the Operator Training Course for their unit, but in pop culture, the term is used to describe anyone in special operations.

Operator Training Course (OTC)—A military training course for service members who have passed selection for the US military's most elite special operations units.

Pandur—An Austrian-made armored personnel carrier primarily used by US Army special operations forces in the context of this book.

Pattern of life (POL)—An analysis of the behaviors and movements of a particular individual over a period of time.

Petty officer—The Navy noncommissioned officer equivalent, encompassing pay grades E-4 to E-9.

Post Exchange (PX)—A shopping center on military bases for service members similar to a mall.

PVS-14—Single-tube night-vision device issued to American military forces.

Raid—A surprise attack against a position or installation for a specific purpose other than seizing and holding terrain.

Ready room—An area, typically in a deployed environment, where service members keep all of their equipment. This is also where they will "kit up" when it's time for a mission.

Remington M870—One of the most popular shotguns ever produced, it is commonly used by the US military for breaching applications.

Sensitive site exploitation (SSE)—A search of a specific location or area in order to find items and information of intelligence value.

Sheikh—An Arab leader, usually refers to the leader of a tribe, family, or village.

Shock and Awe—References the opening salvo of the 2003 invasion of Iraq, where the primary objective was to overwhelm the Iraqi military with superior firepower and speed.

Shooters—In special operations, this term usually references the main effort element primarily responsible for clearing an objective.

Special operations forces (SOF)—The collective and somewhat generic term used to refer to all special operations units regardless of branch of service.

Special Reconnaissance Team (SRT)—A dedicated intelligence-gathering unit within Naval Special Warfare that provides actionable intelligence to Navy SEALs.

Task force—A temporary organization created for a specific mission, usually bringing many different military elements together.

Team Guy—A nickname commonly used to refer to a Navy SEAL.

US Army Special Operations Command (USASOC)—USASOC is the Army component of the US Special Operations Command (USSOCOM), and is responsible for Army special operations forces, enabling them to conduct worldwide special operations in support of the geographic combatant commanders, American ambassadors, and other agencies as directed.

US Special Operations Command (USSOCOM)—The Defense Department's unified combatant command responsible for all American special operations forces.

Vehicle drop-off (VDO)—The area where military vehicles will stop to allow their passengers to get off and move toward the objective.

Village stability operations (VSO)—VSOs combined elements of unconventional warfare and foreign internal defense to support a broader counterinsurgency (COIN) operation, usually at the local/village level.

NOTES

CHAPTER 1: HUNTING HUMANS

1. "USSOCOM Celebrates Its 30th Anniversary," United States Special Operations Command, April 19, 2017, https://www.socom.mil/ussocom-celebrates-its-30th-anniversary.

CHAPTER 2: YES, I CAN

1. Jared Cooper, "Learning Disability or Vision Problem? Why Your Child May Be Misdiagnosed—and What You Can Do about It," Eastidahonews.com, July 26, 2015, https://www.eastidahonews.com/2015/07/learning-disability-vision-problem-child-may-misdiagnosed-can/.

CHAPTER 4: BIRTH OF A TERRORIST MASTERMIND

1. Paul Kamolnick, *The Al-Qaeda Organization and the Islamic State Organization,* US Army War College, Strategic Studies Institute, 2017, https://apps.dtic.mil/sti/pdfs/AD1070598.pdf.
2. Janine di Giovanni, "Who Is ISIS Leader Abu Bakr Al-Baghdadi?" *Newsweek,* December 8, 2014, https://www.newsweek.com/2014/12/19/who-isis-leader-abu-bakr-al-baghdadi-290081.html.
3. Kamolnick, *The Al-Qaeda Organization and the Islamic State Organization.*
4. Kamolnick.
5. Andrew Thompson and Jeremi Suri, "How America Helped ISIS," op-ed, *New York Times,* October 1, 2014, https://www.nytimes.com/2014/10/02/opinion/how-america-helped-isis.html
6. Terrence McCoy, "How the Islamic State Evolved in an American Prison," *Washington Post,* November 4, 2014, https://www.washington

post.com/news/morning-mix/wp/2014/11/04/how-an-american-prison
-helped-ignite-the-islamic-state/.

7. Richard Barrett, *The Islamic State,* Soufan Group, November 2014, https://
ciaotest.cc.columbia.edu/wps/tsg/0032688/f_0032688_26581.pdf.

CHAPTER 5: LINGUIST IN TRAINING

1. Jason Fagone, *The Woman Who Smashed Codes: A True Story of Love,
Spies, and the Unlikely Heroine Who Outwitted America's Enemies* (New
York: Dey Street, 2018).

2. Sonia Purnell, *A Woman of No Importance: The Untold Story of the American Spy Who Helped Win World War II* (New York: Viking, 2019).

CHAPTER 11: LIFE AND DEATH IN AFGHANISTAN

1. Nicholas Kulish and Christopher Drew, "A Deadly Deployment, a
Navy SEAL's Despair," *New York Times,* January 19, 2016, https://www
.nytimes.com/2016/01/20/world/asia/navy-seal-team-4-suicide.html.

2. "In Memoriam: Kevin Ebbert," *Times-Standard,* December 9, 2012,
https://www.times-standard.com/2012/12/09/in-memoriam-kevin
-ebbert/.

3. Kulish and Drew, "A Deadly Deployment."

CHAPTER 12: THE RISE OF ISIS

1. Suadad al-Salhy, "Al Qaeda Says It Freed 500 Inmates in Iraq Jail-
Break," Reuters, July 23, 2013, https://www.reuters.com/article/us
-iraq-violence-alqaeda/al-qaeda-says-it-freed-500-inmates-in-iraq-jail
-break-idUSBRE96M0C720130723.

2. "After the Caliphate: What Next for IS?" BBC News, November 27,
2018, https://www.bbc.com/news/world-middle-east-45547595.

3. Luay al-Khatteeb and Eline Gordts, "How ISIS Uses Oil to Fund Terror," Brookings Institution, September 27, 2014, https://www.brookings
.edu/articles/how-isis-uses-oil-to-fund-terror/.

CHAPTER 14: THE WAR AGAINST ISIS

1. "Paris Attacks: What Happened on the Night," BBC News, December 9, 2015. https://www.bbc.com/news/world-europe-34818994.

2. "Paris Attacks: What Happened on the Night."

3. Lori Hinnant, "2015 Paris Attacks Suspect Claims Deaths of 130 People Was 'Nothing Personal,'" PBS, September 15, 2021, https://www

.pbs.org/newshour/world/2015-paris-attacks-suspect-claims-deaths-of
-130-people-was-nothing-personal.

4. Hinnant.

5. US Army, "Sgt. Maj. Thomas P. Payne: Master Valor," YouTube, September 3, 2020, https://www.youtube.com/watch?v=Dq8mzrFr_0w.

CHAPTER 18: THE NOT-SO-CALM BEFORE THE STORM

1. Walter Reed National Military Medical Center, "Navy Psychology Training Programs," accessed September 1, 2023, https://walterreed.tricare.mil/About-Us/Navy-Psychology-Training-Programs.

CHAPTER 20: THE NEVER-ENDING WAR ON TERROR

1. "Islamic State Chief, in Rare Speech, Urges Followers to Fight On," Reuters, August 22, 2018.

2. Coutney Kube, Carol E. Lee, and Josh Lederman, "U.S. Troops to Leave Syria as President Trump Declares Victory over ISIS," NBC News, December 19, 2018, https://www.nbcnews.com/news/us-news/u-s-troops-leave-syria-president-trump-declares-victory-over-n949806.

3. Thessa Lageman, "Remembering Mohamed Bouazizi: The Man Who Sparked the Arab Spring," Al Jazeera, December 17, 2020, https://www.aljazeera.com/features/2020/12/17/remembering-mohamed-bouazizi-his-death-triggered-the-arab.

4. "Ben Ali Flees amid Unrest," Al Jazeera, January 15, 2011, https://www.aljazeera.com/news/2011/1/15/tunisias-ben-ali-flees-amid-unrest.

5. "Tunis Attack: Gunmen Kill Tourists in Museum Rampage," BBC News, March 18, 2015, https://www.bbc.com/news/world-africa-31941672.

6. Farah Samti and Carlotta Gall, "Tunisia Attack Kills at Least 38 at Beach Resort Hotel," *New York Times,* June 26, 2015, https://www.nytimes.com/2015/06/27/world/africa/gunmen-attack-hotel-in-sousse-tunisia.html.

7. Nima Elbagir, Raja Razek, Alex Platt, and Bryony Jones, "People for Sale: Where Lives Are Auctioned for $400," CNN. November 15, 2017, https://www.cnn.com/2017/11/14/africa/libya-migrant-auctions/index.html.

CHAPTER 21: LIVING UP TO THE ANCHORS

1. US Department of Veterans Affairs, "Suicide Risk and Risk of Death Among Recent Veterans," 2009, https://www.publichealth.va.gov/epidemiology/studies/suicide-risk-death-risk-recent-veterans.asp.

2. Thomas Suitt, "High Suicide Rates Among United States Service Members and Veterans of the Post-9/11 Wars," Watson Institute for International and Public Affairs, June 21, 2021, https://watson.brown.edu/costsofwar/papers/2021/Suicides.

3. "Psychological Autopsy Study of Suicides among United States Special Operations Forces," United States Special Operations Command, n.d., https://www.socom.mil/FOIA/Documents/Psychological%20Autopsy%20Study%20of%20Suicides%20among%20United%20States%20Special%20Operations%20Forces.pdf.

CHAPTER 25: SAVING MANBIJ

1. Rebaz Hesen, "Manbij: A Model for the Future Syria," ANF News, September 10, 2019, https://anfenglish.com/women/manbij-a-model-for-the-future-syria-37533.

CHAPTER 28: FAIR WINDS AND FOLLOWING SEAS

1. Tom Bowman and Steve Inskeep, "U.S. Soldiers Killed in Attack in Northern Syria," *Morning Edition*, NPR, January 16, 2019, https://www.npr.org/2019/01/16/685827979/u-s-soldiers-killed-in-attack-in-northern-syria.

2. Claudia Grisales, "Navy Revises Rules in Wake of Linguist's Death in Syria," *Stars and Stripes*, February 6, 2019, https://www.stripes.com/veterans/navy-revises-rules-in-wake-of-linguist-s-death-in-syria-1.567504.

3. Diana Correll, "Navy Cryptologists Urge Service to Name Destroyer after Shannon Kent, the Navy Cryptologist Killed in Syria," *Military Times*, January 24, 2020, https://www.militarytimes.com/news/your-military/2020/01/23/navy-cryptologists-urge-service-to-name-destroyer-after-shannon-kent-the-navy-cryptologist-who-died-in-syria/.

4. Tamara Cario, "IWTC Monterey Dedicates Navy Yard to Senior Chief Shannon Kent," Defense Language Institute, Foreign Language Center, August 27, 2019, https://www.dliflc.edu/iwtc-monterey-dedicates-navy-yard-to-senior-chief-shannon-kent/.

5. John W. Barry, "Shannon Kent: House Passes Bill to Name Pine Plains Post Office after Fallen Sailor," *Poughkeepsie Journal*, October 17, 2019, https://www.poughkeepsiejournal.com/story/news/2019/10/17/shannon-kent-post-office-antonio-delgado-bill-passes/4003439002/.

EPILOGUE

1. Luis Martinez, "5 ISIS Fighters Captured for Alleged Role in Syria Blast That Killed 4 Americans," ABC7 News (San Francisco), March 20, 2019, https://abc7news.com/5-isis-fighters-captured-for-alleged-role-in-syria-blast-that-killed-4-americans/5205329/.

ABOUT THE AUTHORS

Marty Skovlund Jr. is the editor in chief of *Task & Purpose,* a military news and culture publication. He is a former Army Ranger and an experienced conflict reporter who has reported on assignment from Afghanistan, Iraq, and Ukraine in addition to embedding with the US military around the world.

Joe Kent is Shannon Kent's husband and the father of their two children. Over the course of his twenty-year military career, he served as an Army Ranger and a Green Beret as well as in other classified special operations units.